HAMLET'S DRESSER

A MEMOIR

Bob Smith

SCRIBNER

NEW YORK LONDON TORONTO SYDNEY SINGAPORE

SCRIBNER
1230 Avenue of the Americas
New York, NY 10020

SCRIBNER and design are trademarks of
Macmillan Library Reference USA, Inc., used under license
by Simon & Schuster, the publisher of this work.

For information about special discounts for bulk purchases,
please contact Simon & Schuster Special Sales:
1-800-456-6798 or business@simonandschuster.com

DESIGNED BY KYOKO WATANABE
Text set in Sabon

Manufactured in the United States of America

1   3   5   7   9   10   8   6   4   2

Library of Congress Cataloging-in-Publication Data is available.

ISBN 0-684-85269-1

For Carolyn Wells Smith

HAMLET'S DRESSER

What should we speak of
When we are old as you? When we shall hear
The rain and wind beat dark December? How
In this our pinching cave shall we discourse
The freezing hours away?

— CYMBELINE, 3.3

ZOE DIED. There'll be a service someplace in Jersey, but not until late April. Zoe was in the original group of old people who came to me for Shakespeare. She couldn't bear *Cymbeline.* She turned her nose up at all the late plays.

"I'm eighty-one," she'd scowl. "Time to say what's on my mind." What was on her mind was that, at forty-six, William Shakespeare'd run out of genius.

"What about *The Tempest,*" I'd plead, "or *Winter's Tale?*"

"Robert, dear. . . ." She'd twist her face into a mock sourpuss. "You are grotesquely sentimental." She was wrong about Shakespeare but probably dead right about me.

Zoe was no worshiper, except for dance. She adored the ballet. Her dreary one-bedroom apartment in the Penn South middle-income housing project was a grotto shrine of dusky ballet slippers swaying on shimmering ribbons. Whose? I always wondered. Zoe had never been a dancer. She was short and stout. By the time I knew her she had close-cropped snow-white hair and always wore a particular black dress. It was her uniform, and was usually a repulsive collage of food stains and dandruff. The dress was a mess but Zoe wasn't. She'd worked as some kind of math genius. Retired, she devoted her time to culture.

One day I made the mistake of telling her that I was on my way to see the movie *Babe*. She acted betrayed. "Talking pigs?" she winced. "Don't expect George Orwell." Zoe disdained the intellectually puny with an exaggerated roll of her eyes and an agitated pinch of her small wrinkled mouth. But despite the protest, an hour later there she was at the multiplex, propped up in an aisle seat in her awful dress and a worse shawl, waiting sour-faced to prove herself right. God, how I love old people.

For ten years I've been reading Shakespeare with seniors. I'm no scholar. I've got no formal education past high school. But in run-down centers and sleek over-air-conditioned Manhattan auditoriums, I pore over the texts with hundreds of unsentimental octogenarians.

Zoe was ringleader for a group of women who'd grown up on the Lower East Side. Seventy years later they still traveled as a gang. Navigating the crisscross grid of New York City bus routes, they transferred to movies, ballet, and Shakespeare. Eventually they found me and immediately started acting like a fan club. They'd show up wherever I was speaking. For a while, in restaurants, they'd huddle together a few tables away, mooning over me like bobby-soxers. The old ladies would have the waiter bring me a glass of red wine. They'd gesture a toast.

"We don't mean to bother you," they'd coo. "We're just so excited about the Shakespeare that we couldn't wait till next week."

It's almost impossible to say how much it meant to have those tart old women on my side. Love in the romantic sense has mostly skipped past me. I have no children, no witness who's been with me the whole way. My childhood was consecrated to a sick sibling and

I never completely emerged from that darkness. Those geriatric cheerleaders gave something I hadn't had since my grandparents.

For a while Zoe acted like a smitten seventh grader. She'd shove bunched-up notes into my fist. They weren't personal in the ordinary way. They were about Shakespeare.

"Merchant?" was scrawled on an envelope she dropped into my bag. Inside, she'd neatly written an appeal.

> *Dearest Professor* (Zoe got a kick out of ennobling my status),
>
> *What would you think of us reading the* Merchant of Venice *next? Many in the group are Jewish. Is the play anti-Semitic? Please consider this a respectful request.*
>
> > *Your admiring student,*
> > *Zoe*

The morning we started *Merchant* there were eighty people jammed into the back room of the senior center.

Ten minutes into the play, Zoe's hand shot up, her patience already worn thin. "He's of his time," she pronounced. "William Shakespeare's no philosopher. He's not a deity. Shakespeare's *depicting* the world, not fixing it."

Eventually we landed on the scene where Shylock's daughter elopes. Knowing she'll break her father's Old Testament heart, Jessica steals his money, some cherished jewels, and at night, disguised as a page, runs off with a Christian boy.

> JESSICA   Here, catch this casket, it is worth the pains.
> I am glad 'tis night—you do not look on me,—
> For I am much asham'd of my exchange:
> But love is blind, and lovers cannot see
> The pretty follies that themselves commit,
> For if they could, Cupid himself would blush
> To see me thus transformed to a boy.

LORENZO   Descend, for you must be my torch-bearer.

JESSICA   What, must I hold a candle to my shames?—

> They, in themselves (goodsooth) are too too light.
>
> Why, 'tis an office of discovery (love),
>
> And I should be obscur'd.

LORENZO   So are you (sweet)

> Even in the lovely garnish of a boy.
>
> But come at once,
>
> For the close night doth play the runaway,
>
> And we are stay'd for at Bassanio's feast.

JESSICA   I will make fast the doors and gild myself

> With some moe ducats, and be with you straight.

—*The Merchant of Venice*, 2.6

When I paused, a woman at the back stood up as stiffly as a kid in parochial school and in a thick New York accent she said, "Salvatore Massuchi."

At first it sounded like a single word: "salvamusuchi." Italian? Maybe Latin? The room was packed with retired teachers. Was it some obsolete syndrome in rhetoric? My usual pang of undereducation pricked.

"He was a boy on Mulberry Street." The old woman smiled. "He lived right across the air shaft. My mother warned me never to look at him. We were Orthodox Jews. My father was strict. My little brothers wore payess."

The woman watched all of us watching her. "Salvatore Massuchi had beautiful eyes and shiny hair like chocolate. He was so handsome in his Saint Francis Xavier Grammar School uniform. We never spoke to each other, not even in July standing together in line at the ice wagon. Then one day my mother said that the Italians on four had moved to New Rochelle or Rye, some exotic-sounding place north of the city."

"What about Salvatore Massuchi?" I asked.

"My daughter married an Italian. I think I encouraged her

because in 1919 I wasn't even allowed to look. My husband's been dead for ten years. I've never thought of another man, but while you were reading I kept picturing Salvatore Massuchi. I don't know anything about literature, but I think maybe Shakespeare's not mad at Jessica."

In the front row Sara raised her hand. I don't think I'd ever heard her voice. Zoe usually did the talking. "That's exactly how it was, just like she said, religious parents new to America, but trying to stay faithful to the past. Now that I'm old it's easy to see what a difficult balancing act it was."

She looked at me for a minute. "I'm on Jessica's side, too. Venice for a Jewish kid must have been a little like Mott Street." The old maid got angry. "Damn it, Jessica's got a right to her own happiness."

Everyone laughed, and for a few minutes some very old women said the names of little boys who hadn't quite faded into the abyss of memory, Salvatore Massuchi, Mike O'Rourke, Frankie somebody, Billy . . .

> My heart, sweet boy, shall be thy sepulchre,
> For from my heart thine image ne'er shall go.
> —*King Henry VI, Part III*, 2.5

It's eight years later and I'm starting to read *Hamlet* with a huge group of old people at the Ninety-second Street Y.

> *Enter Barnardo and Francisco, two sentinels.*
> BARNARDO   Who's there?
> FRANCISCO   Nay, answer me. Stand and unfold yourself.
> —*Hamlet*, 1.1

When I talk about the plays I unfold myself to myself, and sometimes hidden in the folds are forgotten events that can, for a moment, make the standing a little harder. Some days, discussing four-hundred-year-old words with the elderly, it's about ghosts. Zoe's dead, so's Sara, maybe even the woman who'd loved Salvatore Massuchi, and that's an important part of it, too. The impermanence of life is all around me. What's left is memory. It's such a huge part of Shakespeare, so many specters and resurrections, so much haunting from the past.

In its own way, my life is a resurrection and I am most certainly haunted by a delicate and undismissible ghost.

Right after I started reading Shakespeare with old people, I decided to move back to where I was born. I rented a tiny dilapidated house that was built before the American Revolution, 1770. I live near a river, a mile or so above where it meets Long Island Sound. I've come back hoping to find something I dropped in my first desperate need to leave. At twenty-one I had run from an unhappy childhood and, too young to know better, I thought I could hide from memory.

For almost forty years, it was as if I'd hidden something deep in the breast pocket of a coat that I no longer wear. Every so often, I'd put the coat on and tentatively reach into the pocket half believing my buried thing wouldn't be there anymore, expecting it to have crumbled with age and neglect or to have simply disappeared. It never has. It never will, because it's not a thing, it's a person.

When I was twenty-one and my retarded sister was almost eighteen, my parents decided that we could no longer care for her. The decision was made to find a place for Carolyn to spend the rest of her life. A "school" was selected that met with what my family could afford. It's a state institution.

The day she left, my father asked if she wanted to do her favorite thing—take a ride. She bounced toward the car with her bizarre, palsied gait, her hands—her beautiful long thin pale hands—twisted grotesquely around each other and held high just under her chin. She always shook with excitement at the idea of a ride. She's fifty-seven now and I'm told that she still shakes wildly when there's a ride and ice cream. I haven't seen her do it since that day so long ago, when she left our house and my life forever. It's like one of those late, melancholy, Shakespeare plays that mathematical Zoe never understood.

Six weeks after Carolyn went away to the Southbury Training School I was allowed to visit her. Until then she had to be acclimated to the place. It was a world she could not have known existed, and as the only world she did know, we couldn't interfere. The waiting passed painfully. The worst of my own terrors of abandonment haunted me. I couldn't stop the pictures in my mind of how afraid and lonely she must feel.

Finally the day came to see her. I was terrified. I felt sick all the way on the long drive. How could I just walk out after a visit? How could I see her often? Was it more hurtful to come and not take her home? It tore at me. I was young.

When we reached the Southbury Training School we drove up the hill to a tall, mock Georgian brick building. It was a cliché of the 1930s institution. I asked my parents if I could go in alone to get her. I needed my first reaction for just me and her. It was hard to see her again, here, to know that I would just stay awhile and then go back to New York and leave behind this person who in many ways I knew much better than I knew myself.

Inside I asked a friendly nurse for directions. As I went up the iron stairs and down the long white hall I could hear my sister. She was saying my name over and over. She knew very few words—car, go to bed, Bobby. Even now in my old red house by the river all these years later I can hear her voice, her young lost voice, singsong—"Bobby . . . Bobby . . . Bobby."

I took her carefully down the stairs and out into the October sunlight. We walked hand in hand to my parents' car and got into the backseat. We went for a ride in the beautiful Connecticut countryside, and at a certain point my father pulled the car off the road. I think it was somewhere on the school's property. There was a hill and a cornfield. I helped my sister out of the car. I took Carolyn's beautiful hand and together we carefully climbed the hill. The

October air was wonderful. There was a warm wind. I remember thinking that my parents, in the distance below, seemed little and old and lost, standing by our car. I took Carolyn through the rows of corn. There was a stone wall to sit on with a view of the beautiful Connecticut valley with all its autumn color. I was overcome by sadness. I didn't drive. I couldn't get back on my own. I said out loud to no one, "Why did they give you a brute's haircut? I've always loved your hair. I've always loved you. I've always taken care of you. Please let me go!"

> There is a willow grows askant the brook
> That shows his hoary leaves in the glassy stream.
> Therewith fantastic garlands did she make
> Of crow-flowers, nettles, daisies, and long purples,
> That liberal shepherds give a grosser name,
> But our cold maids do dead men's fingers call them.
> There on the pendant boughs her crownet weeds
> Clamb'ring to hang, an envious sliver broke,
> When down her weedy trophies and herself
> Fell in the weeping brook. Her clothes spread wide,
> And mermaid-like awhile they bore her up,
> Which time she chanted snatches of old lauds,
> As one incapable of her own distress,
> Or like a creature native and indued
> Unto that element. But long it could not be
> Till that her garments, heavy with their drink,
> Pull'd the poor wretch from her melodious lay
> To muddy death.

—*Hamlet*, 4.7

CHAPTER 1

On Thursday, the tenth of July 1941, just after three A.M., my mother's kid brother pressed his face to the plate glass.

"Look at him," he yelled. "Ten pounds nine ounces! Ya gotta call him Bob. He's built for football and Bob Smith's a sure thing for 'All-American.'"

My fire captain grandfather agreed. The big boy baby was Harold and Margaret McKeon's first grandchild. They'd come from potato famine immigrants, and in that war-shadowed summer "Bob Smith, All-American" sounded just right.

As it is with maternity ward prophecy, I never quite made it to the gridiron, and for six decades kidders have had a great time giving me grief about my plain name.

For the first few years, almost anywhere I went, I went sitting alone on the backseat of my grandparents' big black car. The interior was a somber gray, thick-piled fabric. The elegant old Buick was like a room or, even more, like a coffin, all metal and shine outside, all tufted and claustrophobic within.

One wet March morning in 1944, my grandfather backed his huge sedan out of the cinder-block garage to make a second trip to the gloomy Bridgeport Hospital. I was three when we drove up the icy Boston Avenue hill to fetch my fragile mother and brand-new, luckless baby sister. Through sideways sleet I watched my skinny father balance a gigantic umbrella over the nurse who wheeled my mother to the curb—the infant was hidden, wrapped in petals of pink wool blanket. My young mother's face was gaunt and expressionless. When my grim grandmother opened the massive car door, she gently placed the baby next to me on the puffy, iron-colored seat. "S-h-h," she whispered, "it's your baby sister, Carolyn Wells Smith."

Six weeks later I sat in a big church with my mother. It was the first of May, but Saint Charles Borromeo was chilly. The warm sunny outside air hadn't yet reached inside the enormous brick and marble sanctuary. This was the old church where, "outside the rail," my parents had married. "Outside the rail" referred to a limitation placed on couples when one of the partners wasn't Catholic. Such couples were allowed to marry in the church but only outside of the communion rail that surrounded the altar. It was, in the 1940s, a compromise to "mixed" marriages. In sixty years I've never heard my father say a single word about God, sin, heaven, or hell, nothing about the bits and pieces that "outside the rail" he promised to let my mother teach me. She's Irish and devout.

When my mother was nine or ten, her artist aunt, Mary, gave her a children's book. It was called *Marjorie's Maytime*. My mother fell in love with the book. The story took her away from her average child's life into a much better world where she spent time with a princess in a little girl's fantasy. Marjorie's life wasn't at all like my mother's, not the Irish-American working-class world where she was "drudge" to her strict, religious mother. Marjorie filled her with hopes for a life far more romantic. In a sacred child's oath my mother pledged to name her own child, her own little girl, after the author of *Marjorie's Maytime*. I remember the name written in worn gold leaf on the side of the dry bleached blue book, Carolyn Wells. This little old book held a place of honor in our house for years as a symbol of childish hopes perversely come to reality and dashed. My father's name is Raymond *Wells* Smith. Did my mother marry my father for his middle name?

At Saint Charles Church that May Day in 1944, my mother was frail and nervous. She had very red rouged cheeks and wore a shiny green and white dress that was cold to touch. She was crying quietly into a white handkerchief. My mother was sad and I felt helpless.

A procession of self-conscious, stiff little girls walked like bride dolls down the long center aisle of the church. They wore lace dresses and had white hair ribbons falling behind their heads, shiny black Mary Jane shoes with white socks uniformly rolled over tiny ankles. Step—pause—step. The very serious little girls were part of a ritual dedicated to innocence. The day is set aside to honor purity and virginity. It is the Virgin's special day. "Holy Mary Mother of God . . ." One chosen girl will climb a flower-laden ladder and place a garland of white roses on the head of a life-sized painted plaster statue of Mary.

Of course my mother was crying about Carolyn. Something was very wrong. Everyone who dared say it said she was "not right." As a child, my mother, Mildred Mary Elizabeth McKeon, had taken part in the May march down the church aisle, but in a thousand thousand years her own little girl, Carolyn Wells Smith, would not be able to join this ceremony. She was at home with my grandparents and "not right."

As my sister's problems grew and my parents became more thwarted by them, my mother's mother seemed to be the only one to recognize *my* plight. "Robert, howza bout a stroll down East Main? Could ya fancy a bit of ice cream or maybe a B.L.T.?"

But when I was five, I was doing something my grandmother thought needed correction, and she and my mother's sister, Claire, took me aside. We stood in the doorway to my grandmother's pantry as she perched on a painted white kitchen chair. Reaching up to the topmost pantry shelf she brought down an old Howlands Dry Goods Store bag. From the bag she took an object that was bundled in yellowing tissue. As Claire helped her down, my grandmother unwrapped a large and grotesquely distorted votive candle.

We stood in a shaft of sun-flecked, somersaulting dust specks. Thumbtacked to the pantry door was a wildly overcolored *Marriage at Canna* by Paolo Veronese courtesy of George Pistey's Funeral Home. I loved those calendars with their vulgar colors and overwrought biblical scenes.

My grandmother thrust the big, used candle at me. "Look at this very carefully," she said gently. All the while my "old maid" aunt was broadening and narrowing her eyes as she always did to convey the seriousness of a talk.

"I lit this," my grandmother whispered, "and it stayed lit for all the time that you were being born. It took two days and two nights! Your mother was in violent pain and you *wouldn't* be born. You were too big. You weighed too much. Your mother was in pain and you wouldn't be born. You hurt her. When it came time for Carolyn to be born she couldn't because you spoiled your mother *down there*."

My five-year-old's mind tried to wrap itself around the idea. "I wouldn't be born," didn't want to, I guess. "I don't want to be born, not born, not now!" So, *down there* is spoiled! My grandfather said, "Don't give him more cake, you'll spoil him." *Spoil him!* Spoil me? Down there? *Down where?* "Carolyn couldn't be born because I'm spoiled!" I am not spoiled! I never do anything bad. I help all the time. I'm good in church, except for playing with the kneelers. I'm not allowed to pee until the Mass is over. I have to "hold it" till it hurts *down there*! I cry with my mother when she cries about Carolyn and because my father is in the army. She said he didn't have to go but he hated all the crying.

Of course I thought that my grandmother's accusation was true, that I had somehow, willfully, selfishly wanted not to be born, and I'd ruined my baby sister. For many years I heard confusing stories of what had happened to Carolyn.

My Irish grandfather said playfully to me, "We'll give you back to the Indians!" The Indians! I stood on a stool and got tall enough to reach the radio on top of the refrigerator to hear "The Lone Ranger." Tonto spoke "Indian" words like my sister's gibberish. Was she an Indian? Should we give her back to them? Would she stop crying? Would my mother stop crying? Would people stop telling me to be a perfect little boy, especially now that I had to be "a little boy *and* a little *girl*"? Would my father come home?

When I was four, my father joined the army—"to be a man," my mother said. She thought he'd abandoned her, and for a while he probably did. He went away because everybody cried all the time.

"He didn't have to go!" she'd say tearfully. "He wasn't drafted! You and Carolyn's sickness would have kept him out!"

Right before he got into the car to drive away, he smiled at me. "Kid," he said, "don't eat anything ya don't like!"

A week after he left, my mother shook and cried and got on a train with me and Carolyn and that pink blanket. We followed him all the way to Florida where he was "learning to be in the army." It was hot there. We stayed with my grandmother's mean sister and her fat husband who picked oranges and teased everyone until they were hurt and mad at him.

"Oh, Joe, leave the boy alone. You know he has a sadness, the girl's 'not right.'"

Sometimes my father and mother went out. Carolyn and I stayed with the mean woman and the fat man who scared me.

One night when we were in our hot room with the door closed so they couldn't hear Carolyn cry, and the window closed so the neighbors couldn't hear Carolyn cry, Carolyn looked up at me. I was by her crib making faces. Suddenly she stopped crying and just looked at me for a long, long time. I was amazed and a little afraid. I never saw her look at *anyone*, she never did! She was looking at me. And *not* crying! Then it happened, the thing that was better than George Pistey's Funeral Home religious calendar. My sister *smiled* at me. She stopped crying and right there in that small, hot room with everything closed out, the world not able to hear, and the Florida sunset burning through the cracks at the sides of the old window shade, no mother or army father, no grandmother or aunt with narrowing eyes, no little girls lined up for the Virgin Mary, no soldiers that held me on the train, no cabdriver who looked pathetically at my mother, no fat people, no teasers, no mean people—just me and my baby sister. I took her hand and the pact was made, *forever*, no matter if everyone went away or if I got big first, *never, never*, to *never* go away!

The mean lady threw us out and her husband gave us some oranges in a bag. He couldn't take the crying. A few days before he'd asked my mother when would she be taking the "baboon" out of his house? Over a lifetime she's repeated the cruel words a thousand times and always as if they'd been said only last week.

My father went to Italy and we went home. On the way back, watching my young mother stare into her own tearful reflection in the train window, it was obvious that she was quietly descending into a breakdown.

CHAPTER 2

WHEN I WAS thirty someone gave me a brown
leather bag. A relic of the sixties, it had long hippie fringe and a
wide shoulder strap. For years I took it everywhere, filled with
Shakespeare books. At some point I cut the fringe off, and by then
the ripped strap had shortened into a knot of awkward handle. For
twenty years I had a crescent of oxblood leather stain arching
across my right palm.

> HAMLET   How long will a man lie i' th'earth ere he rot?
> GRAVEDIGGER   Faith, if a be not rotten before a die—as
> we have many pocky corses nowadays that will
> scarce hold the laying in—a will last you some eight
> year or nine year. A tanner will last you nine year.
> HAMLET   Why he more than another?
> GRAVEDIGGER   Why, sir, his hide is so tanned with his
> trade that a will keep out water a great while, and your
> water is a sore decayer of your whoreson dead body.
> —*Hamlet*, 5.1

I loved the way the weight of the heavy bag was tanning my hide. Finally torn beyond use, it's crammed into an upstairs closet. With an assortment of crowns and daggers it reappears from time to time as a worn peddler's bag in one of my Shakespeare projects.

I've always found comfort in old things and old people. When I was a little boy my grandparents provided what affection I got. Every so often I'd take those trips in that big Buick with my old-fashioned grandparents elegantly propped up in the distant front seat.

"Robert, will ya look at the color of those trees! There's nothin' on God's earth like the Mohawk Trail in October. Glory be ta God, just cast your eyes on those clouds!"

In the passenger seat my grandmother was almost teary under a comical hat. With her gloved hand she'd point a shaky finger at a fiery sugar maple. "I'd like to die in the fall," she'd say, "so everything could die with me."

"Aw, Peg, don't talk nonsense." My grandfather's teeth made a clacking sound on his pipe stem. "You and me, we were built for a long race."

Growing up, adoring them, I felt as if I'd just missed the very best of everything, that it had all slipped silently away a minute before I was born. And what was left were these fragile witnesses and their stories of the long ago and far away, when the world had plenty of time to venerate the October color of a Massachusetts maple.

All the worse times when my mother was sick and my father was gone to the war, I looked for him in the faces of soldiers' pictures in the newspaper. I dreamed that he'd come home and make life okay, that we'd laugh again, maybe have a good time. I wanted to go to the beach with my father.

My mother started to have adult conversations with me. In her awful need she rarely noticed how old I was or how old I wasn't. Her own isolation elbowed out appropriateness.

She started to clean. Endlessly, pathologically, she scoured every object in the house, sometimes several times a day. She felt that she'd done something that destroyed my sister's brain and body and sent my father away. My mother thought she was to blame. I thought I was. We spent a lot of time feeling guilty and we washed things. To maintain the illusion of control, she cleaned all day and into the night. As a child she'd been the one who'd scrubbed, washed, and ironed. A victim of her own childhood slavery, she didn't think twice about chaining me to these neurotic tasks.

I worshiped her. I would have done anything to relieve her crying and the depth of her sadness, so we scrubbed and hosed things down. We got in and out of the bathtub several times a day. We washed and rewashed our floors, our bedclothes, even the beds themselves, and our fingernails, especially our fingernails. We "aired" everything. When it was fifteen degrees outside, all the windows were open! We used bleach until our eyes burned and the air was stinging to breathe. Everything metal had to reflect us, everything cloth had to smell like mountain air.

My mother's worst fear was odor. As if they had voices, smells could tell on us. They could say how imperfect Carolyn was, how imperfect and sinful *we* were.

GLOUCESTER   O, let me kiss that hand!
LEAR   Let me wipe it first, it smells of mortality.
—*King Lear*, 4.6

Our mortality was making us uncomfortable. It embarrassed us and left us feeling inadequate. We would do anything to hide the grossness of our mortal smells, of my baby sister's sickness, of our sickness.

After one of the middle-of-the-night baths, with all the windows open, I stood wet and naked in front of my maple kid's dresser. Staring into a supply of astonishingly white little boy's underpants I played a sort of game. In a way it was the first game that Carolyn and I played. She was in her crib at the end of my bed. Our house was small, only two bedrooms. A year later, in a house with many rooms, she was still in a crib at the end of my bed, and again in the house after that.

From my underwear drawer I grabbed a super white elastic-banded pair of shorts. Freezing, naked, wet, I wanted to jump up on my little maple bed. Definitely not allowed! My mother constantly inspected the chenille spread for any wrinkle or pucker. If found out, it was the back of a large tortoiseshell hairbrush. She'd hit and cry until she wore herself out. "I'll shoot you!" she'd shriek, "I'll shoot you!" or sometimes, slowly, to engender terror, "I . . . could . . . shoot . . . you." Kneeling next to my grandmother in a dark corner at the back of Saint Charles Church, as she lit the red candles that flickered in front of Michelangelo's huge statue of the dead Christ being held awkwardly in his young mother's lap, I used to wonder, "Did she shoot him?"

Wet, naked, underpants in hand, and Carolyn in her crib, I decided the chance was worth it. I jumped up into the pristine grooves of the impeccably stretched bedspread. I felt the gushy ridges and valleys of the blue chenille, caterpillars between my kid toes. Carolyn focused on the movement. I looked at her, past her at myself reflected in the mirror that matched my bed that matched my dresser. And over my bed behind me, I could see a large mahogany cross with a twisted ivory figure of Christ's body hanging tormented from a couple of savagely pounded nails. The torn flesh was fanatically depicted. The grotesque intersected feet economically took one long spike to pin him ferociously to the cross. There was blood everywhere. Thorns pierced his forehead. On the pale ivory, the terra-cotta blood wandered the length of his body. A wound on the right side was explicit, almost vaginal, sexual. Like Saint Thomas, I wanted to get my fingers in there.

I shoved my underpants between my legs and pinned one foot

over the other, only half balanced on the bouncy mattress, perilously messing up the lined ridges of chenille. In the mirror, past my baby sister's crib, I looked from the five-year-old to the reflected thirty-three-year-old Christ hanging naked, agonized, *glamorized*, over my bed. I thrust my skinny white arms out in imitation, crucified!

Catholicism and my family were teaching me that everything represented something else. The blood of Christ was wine, the bread was his body, and by some ritual sleight of hand at the Mass, it really was his body. The statues, the beautifully colored windows, were filled with images of the pain of how we lived. Before long I would repeat long passages of the Latin Mass, which I'd learned by rote. The implied eloquence of un-understandable Latin wasn't for working-class us, it wasn't for *here,* it wasn't for *now.* It was all about a long time from now, *after* the valley of tears, *after* we'd washed a million diapers and cleaned the cellar a thousand times. *Then* we'd all sit around in big robes on marble benches in front of Palladian palaces. *We'd* be the aquiline beauties in saturated colors posing for George Pistey's Funeral Home religious calendars. Taking her cue, my adoring Irish grandmother started to fill my little boy's head with the privilege of the priesthood. One ill, misshaped child could be justified, counterbalanced, by a little blond kid who could, at five, repeat, phonetically, most of the Latin Mass.

Surrounded by lonely, pained women who were directing all their frustration toward my vocation, and with no Yankee father around to cut them off at the pass, I was on my way. My mother, my grandmother, and my aunt Claire began to drive gold nails into the coffin of my masculine self-image. I was being taught to act perfect *no matter what.*

CHAPTER 3

THERE'S A racket going on in my red house by the river. Just over my shoulder through a wavy little window, the wind's whipping what's left of Christmas decorations. They sound metallic, like tiny bells, as they slap the old glass. *Ping . . . ping . . . bang . . . scrape . . . ping!* It's a noisy five A.M., January 1, and it feels like snow any minute.

My old blue Peugeot ten-speed bike is leaning against the wall of a small barn behind the house. Every morning for a couple of years now I've taken it down to the river. When the weather's raw I pile on some baggy sweaters and a frayed striped muffler that was my favorite Christmas present twenty years ago. Last month the two little kids next door borrowed it for their first snowman. Across the frozen milk-white yards the excited little boy pointed and yelled, echoing himself, "Bob, Bob! Look, look!" It had a nose, a hat, and a pipe. Ryan's exactly how old I was when we got back from that awful trip to Florida fifty-six years ago. His baby sister Hannah is just the age Carolyn was; it's sometimes hard to watch them.

These days in the cold mornings before the sun comes up I ride along the old dirt road that follows the river. Walkman earphones keep my ears from freezing, and under my yellow parka hood a CD blasts rock and roll or lately Mendelssohn's "Scottish" Suite, to which I am for a while addicted. Buried deep in warm clothes and feeling wild with the music, pedaling faster, breathing harder, it's easy to forget how old I am. Just as the cold air stings me awake I can pick out a sliver of dirty amber horizon on the water east toward Milford. For an hour speeding along the bumpy dirt road past rows of ghostly winter-wrapped boats and feeling finally at peace with my life, I get to be the happy kid I never was.

As it reaches the water, the narrow road gets narrower. It passes a few weather-beaten nineteenth-century houses. Winter-dried weeds and windblown thorny rosebushes whip an old wall. The land on the right climbs and levels off into a bluff that overlooks the river. In hot weather it's covered with honeysuckle and Queen Anne's lace. In early July hundreds of common orange daylilies spike up through the undergrowth. All summer the bees go nuts. Under the tangled weeds is a rotted stairway. It once took people from the river up to the field above.

All of a sudden I feel very cold. In the cardboard dawn it's starting to spit snow.

I stop by the old stairs to twist my scarf up around my face. When I pull off the earphones the silence, after the blare of the music, is shocking. Now I can hear my frantic, old man's icy breath, and the whistle of the wind behind me as it blows in off the river.

In the flying fat dots of wet snow, the odd old building at the top of the stairs could break your heart. It's a theater. It was the American Shakespeare Festival Theater and Academy in Stratford, Connecticut. For decades it attracted crowds to the big field on the bluff. Then financial trouble, artistic trouble, and the regretful world mostly turned its back and left it to fall apart. In the sharp wind and feathery snow, it looks sadly like Miss Havisham's bride cake, a bizarre crumbling icon to a long-ago dream. It's up there in the field, forgotten for so long now that everyone's stopped looking. I ride here in the dawn before my day starts. Before I take the 8:03 into the city, I stop to be a witness. Little boys used to keep their kid treasures in cigar boxes or tobacco tins—"Prince Albert in a can." This old decaying building, fuzzy in the snow, was once my tin, my box, my kid's treasure place. It's a long time ago now, forty-two years this New Year's Day. I never needed anything so much as what I needed then, and never has so much been given to me as in that incredibly hot summer more than four decades ago.

It's an odd thing about memory, how a smell or sound can ambush you emotionally, leave you mystified.

Forty-two hot humid Connecticut summers ago, up there across the field, past the old building, in one of the huge cement parking lots, the night guard sat smoking in his creepy little car. Hooked over the rearview mirror was one of those suffocating little deodorizing pine trees. It twisted in the acrid wheeze as he exhaled. Every night, except Mondays, he sat there until eight A.M. Once an hour he drove around the big building to turn his flashlight on the doors and windows. He circled while he was sober, but usually by two o'clock he was limp and snoring, drooling on the steering wheel. There was always a ribbon of smoke braiding up from a pile of brownish butts in the car ashtray.

In the intense heat of the August night, he'd be locked in, windows up. I'd bang on the greasy windshield. Startled awake, like an angry animal he'd show a flash of discolored teeth, then recognition. Bleary, glad to see me, he'd wave a tepid beer.

Through the thick glass and radio noise, he sounded submerged. "Jesus, kid, ya scared me! Get in!"

In slow motion he'd reach across to unlock the passenger door. I was sixteen. He was much more than double that, but boyish the way some wounded, failed men get. In the long lonely hot summer night, he was bored and desperate for company.

The night guard was the porter from *Macbeth,* all gross and sexual, trying to get a rise out of me or any of the other kids who stopped by his car for free cigarettes and booze. He was the gate-keeper. Attached to his skinny, cheap, western-style belt was a set of keys. *They* could open the odd building that he was supposed to be guarding.

In the summer of 1958, I was a lonely, screwed-up kid, but the circus had come to town. It had put up this strange tent, and I was being seduced to run away with it, which of course I did.

The theater audience had left the big dark parking lot hours before. At almost three A.M., listening bored to the night guard's drunk talk, I smoked a chain of cigarettes and took breaks outside to pee beer into the hot, wet dark. For almost three hours I sat with him in the boiling pine forest car.

Suddenly in the middle of a drainingly familiar story he startled me. "Ya wanna 'nother beer? Ya wanna go in now?"

I smiled relieved, grateful to him. Shy, I whispered, "I think I'll go in now."

For a couple of months I'd been sleeping on the beach or under the big elms nearby. I slept on porches, lots of porches. Sweet old ladies, now decades dead, used to leave pillows and bedclothes on aluminum gliders and porch swings for me. I was excited and getting worn out. I'd found my mountain, and I was mostly exhausted from starting to climb it.

Some nice regular person might ask, "Where are the parents?" Somebody might say, "It's 1958, Eisenhower is the president! The kid's a junior in high school, in Connecticut, not some ghetto somewhere! Who's watching?" The truth is no one was. My parents seemed overwhelmed and otherwise engaged and paradoxically hopeful that I'd find a way to escape from them, and from Carolyn.

*   *   *

It was just before three A.M. when the night guard turned the key and I heard the firm click of the big Yale lock.

"No lights!" We had a deal, no lights. I had to do what I had to do in the light of a few scattered red exit signs that glowed over doors in the otherwise black backstage.

I walked past him into darker darkness and watched him close the door behind me. As the spill from the flashlight caught his face, he looked weary, bone tired, and lost. He'd forget me until the next midnight when I'd pound on his car window begging to be let in, and, for some company and drunk talk, he'd unlock the big theater and leave me alone inside to sleep safe in the second dressing room from the end.

By August of 1958 I'd been working at the theater for almost four months. I was Hamlet's dresser, paid $18 a week. Through May and part of June, I'd cut out of school early on Wednesdays for the matinee or any other time I was needed for a rehearsal. Slipping out after algebra and before U.S. history, I felt like Romeo scaling the Capulets' orchard walls. Rushing down Main Street past the churches and the railroad station through the center of town past the big white funeral homes and Lovell's Hardware, I was literally running past my painful kid's life on the way to the theater.

In the dark backstage those late nights, there were lots of theater smells, and despite my mother's fears, smells were okay, even wonderful. There was spirit gum to glue on beards and acetone to take them off. The hairspray on wigs was sweet and heavy in the air. The wigs sat in the dark of the wardrobe room methodically, elegantly lined up, pinned to beige wig blocks. In the blood-red light of the exit signs they looked like faceless victims of the guillotine! I could smell baby powder. When I was six, after my father came back from the war, that strong fragile smell meant "Mommy's going out! She won't come back, she hates us!" And in the hot wet backstage air was leftover Tareyton cigarette smoke. Everyone that summer seemed addicted to them. Mixed in was the wild combination of cheap drugstore perfumes that the actors used to camouflage the nasty smell of sweat.

I could smell myself. Exhausted, dripping from the heat, and a little drunk from warm beer, I needed to get clean. At the end of the long dark cement hall was the actors' shower room. Large, gray, depressing, it had sinks and toilets along one wall, and on the opposite side were six or eight metal shower stalls.

I'd stand in the hot, dark rush of noisy water breathing in the invisible steam as the thundery stream smashed off the metal shower walls, reverberating in the pitch black. Everyone knows that theaters have ghosts. The masses of people, the four-hundred-year-old words, all the emotions, left something, like the smells, hovering in the late night dark.

One torrid night after the long *Hamlet* performance, a group of us piled into an actor's rented car, eight or maybe ten of us. Jammed in, we sped the couple of miles to the Sound. Minutes later, in full moonlight, we ran through tall grass and down wide wooden steps onto a beautiful rock-covered beach. All of us, shy or not, took off our clothes and fled into the silvery black midnight water. Imagine splashing around with Ophelia, kidding about drowning? That summer when I turned seventeen I didn't always know the difference between the characters and the people who played them. And sometimes there was no difference.

On the big rocks in the moonlight the actors talked about acting and I listened, watching myself watch them. By then I had been Hamlet's dresser for a couple of months. With a costume over my shoulder and a sword through my belt I stood in the vast darkness just inches from the blasting stage lights, and listened to the most famous of the self-watchers. Night after night I heard him take his own pulse, crippling action with examination. It fit my life, this list making, this terror of retribution. Guilty almost from the start I had looked at myself in a distorted mirror and therefore seen the world disproportionately. Hamlet was giving me company in my guilt.

> Your chang'd complexions are to me a mirror
> Which shows mine chang'd too; for I must be
> A party in this alteration, finding
> Myself thus alter'd with't.
>
> —*The Winter's Tale,* 1.2

The Shakespeare Festival presented three plays in four months. The first two, *Hamlet* and *A Midsummer Night's Dream,* were running in repertory. Late in the season a third, lesser-known play was added. It would have fewer performances, but if the critics and audiences liked it, it could be brought back the following spring for the student season: with the costumes and sets done, it would be relatively easy to revive. The selected play for the third slot late that summer was the dark comedy *The Winter's Tale.*

The Festival rehearsed in a big empty storeroom up over Lovell's Hardware. The early sunlight dazzled through a row of large east-facing windows and the place was packed with people. There was an exuberant, dreamy summer theater atmosphere. Actors with combed hair still wet from morning showers sat around mumbling lines to themselves. Scripts, rehearsal props, books, bicycles, and paper coffee cups were scattered in the musty doughnut- and Tareyton-smelling room.

By July, I'd sat on that floor and watched the bits and pieces added up. People tried, failed, and tried again. Rehearsal was a chance to mess up, and in the mess could be a kernel of something important that, without the messing up, wouldn't have been found.

The actress playing the queen in *The Winter's Tale* had extraordinary speeches about honor, which is more important to her than life. It was my first time with Shakespeare's preoccupation with reputation.

At the rehearsal the actors and the famous director went back over the work again and again. Adjustments were made, ideas explored, used, or discarded. As the people in the room inched their way through the text, the story of the play started to unfold and I found myself literally holding my breath.

Mesmerized, I watched the actors explore a scene in which a powerful woman brings to a mad, sexually jealous king his new-born baby girl. It is clearly *his* child, but he thinks that his best friend, not himself, is the father. Paulina tries to get him to see that the child is his and that the accusation against his chaste wife is crazy. It's a defense of innocence, which is an important part of what the play is about—childhood innocence, broken, ripped apart, and lost forever.

> We were as twinn'd lambs that did frisk i'th' sun,
> And bleat the one at th'other: what we chang'd
> Was innocence for innocence: we knew not
> The doctrine of ill-doing, nor dream'd
> That any did.
>
> —*The Winter's Tale,* 1.2

That July day over the hardware store I watched my life in the rehearsal, my helpless sister, my angry father, my wounded mother folding under the pressure. And there's a brother. The little lost baby girl has a brother. When the play starts he's waiting for his sister to be born, like I did in the back of the big old Buick.

He dies. Consumed with worry for his mother his heart just stops. Shakespeare kills off a lot of heartbroken people—Falstaff, Romeo's mother, Desdemona's father, and that longing sister he keeps talking about in *Twelfth Night* and *Loves Labours Lost.* His own son had died at eleven.

Oh Lord! my boy . . . my fair son!
My life, my joy, my food, my all the world!
                                                    —*King John*, 3.3

I wasn't watching "art," I was going to school those days and nights in the theater. I was being taught that poetry and beauty are not simply antidotes to horror, sometimes they are the horror. I was learning that art can be a brutal thing, not just some decoration placed over the truth, but like Picasso's *Guernica* or Shakespeare's *Winter's Tale*, it is the truth itself.

When Paulina is so clear, when Shakespeare is so clear, about what should be the privilege of innocence, I loved him for loving it and, because of my poor sister, for seeing its value.

And so on those hot nights, that summer when I was mostly lonely and afraid, the night guard would let me in to take the long shower in the dark and make my way along the unlit hallway to the second dressing room from the end to lift a huge heavy cape from its big hangers. It was green, a dark bluish jade green, nubby, woolly, and voluminous, with a hood and splits at the sides for arms to come through. Paulina carried the baby hidden under it when she brought the infant to prove to the father that it was his. Believing that the minute he sees the child he'll see his error and relent, she takes the risk, and in the cold unwelcoming world she kept the baby safe and warm under the big green cape. Alone in the dressing room those nights, I would put it on the cool, washed cement floor and, still wet from the shower, sleep naked inside it.

In the sixteen years of my boy's life it was the first place that I'd ever felt safe, inside Paulina's cape in the black backstage at four A.M.

Twenty years later I was directing a production of *Othello*. Riffling through a mile-long pipe of hanging capes in a costume rental shop in New York, the second my fingers touched it my whole body knew. There it was, like an old childhood friend, worn out by

time and abuse, but an object of incredible love. All those years
before it had given me—

> The sweetest sleep and fairest-boding dreams
> That ever enter'd in a drowsy head.
>
> —*King Richard III, 5.3*

CHAPTER 4

W<small>HAT HAPPENS</small> to the babies?" I'd wondered
hiding under my grandparents' large hall table. Newspaper pictures and radio voices had started to sift into my small child's
life. I'd begun to know that the war was happening. I knew it
mostly from two picturesque postcards sent by my father from
Trieste and Switzerland. The little photographs were tinted in
saccharin Easter-egg colors. Runny orchid skies shone over a
peach-colored fountain and a silly pink Matterhorn. The postcards were a soft pretty lie about what the soldiers were actually finding.

In the swirling, sweet smoke of Granger pipe tobacco, my
grandfather leaned into his cathedral-shaped radio as a phony-
sounding voice said frightening things. Under the table I stared at
my face in the meticulously polished floor. Through the gurgle of
my grandfather sucking his pipe, the voice said that somewhere
children were being frightened and hurt! In the paschal postcards
from my father, laughing Italian children chased each other around

the peachy fountain. Could they be afraid? Could they be hurt? "I could shoot you!"

Last year I gave a series of talks about *The Merchant of Venice* in a splendid old convent on Washington Square. While I was speaking I looked down at a bony woman in the front row. She was wearing a foolish-looking wig, though it wasn't so much the wig as how it was plopped on her head. In the afternoon winter light she had a beautiful, worried face. Struck by her, I looked more closely. My eyes stopped at a tattooed number on her wrist. It was scrawled, like a casual note to herself. Living in New York I'd seen such a thing before, but that day, for a reason to do with her beautiful face and *The Merchant of Venice,* I remembered the little postcards. While I talked, I imagined the old lady to be one of the little girls darting around the fountain in the pale picture sent by my father so long ago.

Later she asked if she could bring two photographs to the rest of the lectures. With a gentle European accent, she said, "They died together in the war. They died in front of me." She wanted them to be a part of this talk about hatred; this dangerous talk in the safety of the lovely old room perched above the north side of the snowy square.

She'd sit on the aisle; second row to the right, with the two, large, crumbling pictures of her parents propped up in her lap, like disintegrating biblical tablets. Maybe the beautiful old woman *had* been the laughing girl about to disappear behind the fountain.

What happens to the babies is that, sooner than anyone can ever realize, they become old.

> Though now this grained face of mine be hid
> In sap-consuming winter's drizzled snow,
> And all the conduits of my blood froze up,
> Yet hath my night of life some memory;
> My wasting lamps some fading glimmer left;

My dull deaf ears a little use to hear—
All these old witnesses . . .

—*The Comedy of Errors*, 5.1

"My niece lives someplace out on Long Island," the old man said. "I don't have a phone. She calls my neighbors to check up on me. She's after my money and in the end she'll get it."

Joe was in the first group of seniors I worked with over on Ninth Avenue. He'd grown up eighty years earlier in a tenement with a bunch of older siblings. By the end of the century he was the only one left. Joe loved me from the start. He'd bring me apples or an orange. He'd shove broken cookies and bus transfers into my jacket pocket.

"I saw Maurice Evans as Richard the Second," he said. "It must be fifty years or more. Did Richard deserve the bad things that happen?"

Joe wanted the world to be a finer place than he'd ever found it. Despite no formal education past grammar school, he spent most of his time rewriting the great thinkers. He'd reconstructed Dante and Rousseau. Every week when I gave him the play copy, he'd hand me a stained beat-up notebook or a frayed twenty-five-year-old vanity press paperback.

"Tell me what you think, Professor?"

The rewrites were all pretty much the same. He'd fastidiously refocus facts to take out pain. Extracting the stinger from Goldsmith or Voltaire, what he kept was a dull, no-fault world where everyone gets home before dark. Joe was a tender guy. When we'd get to the inevitable viciousness in the Shakespeare he'd excuse himself to hide in the bathroom; when we got to the sadness he'd weep so pitifully that anyone near would be compelled to put his arm around him.

One Thursday when I handed out the play copies he grabbed the text with a colorless "Thanks," his usual luster gone flat.

"What's up, Joe? You mad at me?"

"Nah, Professor. How could I ever be mad at *you*?" But the melancholy went on for weeks, no gift apples or pudding-stained Heinrich Heine.

One day after everyone left he shuffled back. He'd decided to tell me. "It's my leg. I've got this sore on my leg. It's giving me trouble. It's been there a couple of months and it's not getting any smaller. I thought my niece would call. Since my brother died she always gets in touch around the holidays, but I didn't hear anything."

We'd talked about Shakespeare and art and religion and growing up Italian or Jewish or Irish on Mulberry Street, but I didn't know where any of the old people lived or how they lived.

"You have anyone else, Joe, I mean besides your niece?"

He looked feisty, then tears. "Don't be mad at me, Professor. I'm just scared. I gotta keep coming to the Shakespeare. I gotta be able to just walk around and think. I don't wanna end up staring at a wall in some veterans hospital upstate."

By now I've heard it a thousand times, the terror of losing. So many of the old don't have anyone to help them keep safe. The ones who are alone hold on, trying not to let anyone know how solitary and fragile that safety is.

"I don't have a phone. My niece calls my neighbor. I was sure she'd call and I'd pay her to go with me to the V.A. Sometimes if I give her a 'little something' she'll help out."

"Where's the V.A., Joe?"

"Twenty-third, near the river."

"Why not me? You wouldn't have to pay me. I'd just tag along so you wouldn't be alone."

"You don't wanna do that, Professor. They make you wait for hours. They insist that you make an appointment and after you spend the whole day scared to death somebody says, 'Come back tomorrow!' It's tough to be old. Besides, a guy like you has better things to do."

"I've read what you write, Joe. I know you wish the world was

a softer place, so do I. Whattaya say? Make an appointment with
the V.A. and call me. Here's my number."

I wasn't sure he would, but at dinnertime the phone rang.

"Six o'clock!" he yelled. "That's what time they want me there,
six A.M.! It's too early for you, Professor, and besides, you
shouldn't waste your time with an old fart like me."

He was at the pay phone at Fifteenth and Eighth. I could hear
voices and traffic. He hollered into the receiver, "I gotta tell you
how grateful I am for the Shakespeare. It's a beautiful thing you do
when you come in and take us through. You're putting magic back
into a lot of old people's lives."

Some car was stuck at the light, honking. Through the clamor
Joe sounded just like my mother, convinced that nobody loved her.
In Joe's case I'm not so sure that anyone ever had.

I yelled back through the street noise, "You asked me about
King Richard, Joe. You said you felt sorry for him. Maurice Evans?
Fifty years ago? How about it? I'll bring two copies and meet you
in front of the V.A.? We'll get a couple of gallons of coffee and
while we wait we can see if we feel sorry for Richard? Whattaya
say?"

> In winter's tedious nights sit by the fire
> With good old folks, and let them tell thee tales
> Of woeful ages long ago betid;
> And ere thou bid good night, to quite their griefs
> Tell thou the lamentable tale of me,
> And send the hearers weeping to their beds . . .
> —*King Richard II*, 5.1

"See ya in front of the V.A., Joe, five-thirty, dress warm!"

It was a toe-curling dawn hovering on the edge of snow as I
watched lethargic people hanging sleepily to a bus shed. Waiting

numb for the number twenty-three crosstown they look like boats in the river facing the tide. Joe's late. Through the haze and sleet I'm trying to make out his bobbing figure in the blur of umbrellas moving in my direction from First Avenue. Behind me the main entrance to the veterans hospital is dark. It's not open.

Dripping wet and concerned that I'd got the time wrong, I thought about how I'd ended up here. Not since Carolyn had I felt the kind of devotion I had for these old people, and there wasn't much doubt that what I felt for them they felt for me.

It started in a deceptively casual way. I owed a nice woman a favor and on a February morning she called. Susanna was connected to a senior center and she needed "something special" for March.

"It's Women in History Month," she said. "I thought of you and Shakespeare and calling in my favor." She was kind and gentle. "Nothing too prepared, off-the-cuff would be fine. These are wonderful bright old people. I know they'll be grateful for anything you have to say."

It's always seemed to me that most people who love Shakespeare love talking, but I didn't. In shyness or maybe shame I'd turned down extra pay to lecture on campuses for years and said no to anyone who thought I should make a speech. Actors were the exception; I could always talk with actors. "What about actors? If I brought actors they could illustrate the text."

Susanna paused at the actor idea. "We couldn't pay anyone. We *feed* people. For some it's the only food of the day. We could offer lunch. I know it's nothing, but would they do it for a good hot lunch?"

Actors knew I'd never make them rich. At best I was a very small tributary far from the mainstream. Working with me wasn't about money. A little Shakespeare in a run-down senior center where people had come mostly for the food was right up my alley and they'd understand that. I called eight actors and without a pause eight actors said yes.

At the time I lived in Brooklyn in what had once been a music room in an opulent 1850s rectory. The ceiling was almost twenty feet high, but what was more remarkable was that the room had been built in the exact shape of a violin. If you lay stretched out flat on the floor and looked up, the ceiling was a perfect Stradivarius. To maintain the instrumental configuration, all of the doors and windows were rounded. The place was decorated like a pastry with Robert Adam carving and a huge white marble fireplace dead center on one serpentine wall. It was about the most romantic space in which anyone could imagine reading Shakespeare.

The actors sat in a circle in front of the fire and I handed out scenes and speeches. By then I'd put together scores of Shakespeare compendiums. The year before I'd won an award from the New York City District Attorney's Office for a compilation of the voices of Shakespeare's abused women. The benefit raised money so that no rape victim would leave any of four major New York hospitals without someone to see them safely home.

For years I'd rehearsed in church basements, back rooms, and industrial lofts. I once staged *Richard the Third* in an obsolete operating room at Mount Sinai Hospital. For weeks doctors and nurses ate lunch with their feet propped up watching devious Richard operate on anyone who stood between him and the English crown.

For Susanna's "Women in History" we'd need a rehearsal space less congested than my furniture-filled "violin" room.

"Use the senior center after hours" was Susanna's solution.

The Fulton Senior Center was on the ground floor of a typical redbrick low-income housing project.

The room in which the actors would perform was an enormous reverberating lemon-yellow cinder-block cube with a noisy automated room divider set on a metal track in the middle. On one side was a cafeteria with gleaming steam tables and noisy vending machines. Just opposite, across the huge space, was a small stage that sat four or five feet off the floor like a box chipped into the wall.

For a couple of weeks we practiced while fascinated Jamaican women scrubbed aluminum pans and tried to figure out what we were up to way on the other side of the big yellow room. Every day a couple of exhausted maintenance men sucked secret smokes as they watched us go over and over our work.

"This is pretty good," a janitor said to me. "I like when the kid kisses the foreign girl."

He meant Henry the Fifth proposing to the French king's daughter, making his case for long love lasting beyond youth to flourish in old age.

> What, a speaker is but a
> prater, a rhyme is but a ballad. A good leg will fall, a
> straight back will stoop, a black beard will turn white,
> a curled pate will grow bald, a fair face will wither, a
> full eye will wax hollow; but a good heart, Kate, is the
> sun and the moon, or rather the sun and not the moon,
> for it shines bright and never changes, but keeps his
> course truly.
>
> —*King Henry V,* 5.2

Henry the hero didn't make it to the stoop and the bald head. He died a year later, leaving an infant king and Kate, who grieved and then remarried, literally setting seed for the Tudor monarchy.

In the middle of the big cinder-block room "Women in History" snuck a look at Shakespeare's vicious view of Joan of Arc. Railing pregnancy and wedded to the devil, through pope-hating Tudor eyes she's hardly a candidate for canonization. Later, dead Henry's child king grows up with a moroseness honed in Hamlet. Henry the Sixth married Margaret of Anjou by proxy and, sorely disappointed with her king in the flesh, she prefers the jock who'd stood in at the substitute wedding. After years of secrecy, the affair is discovered and Margaret's lover is banished. I love the good-byes in Shakespeare. They meant something much different before telephones and frequent-flyer miles. They often meant . . . good-bye.

"It's you who should do the talking, Bob," Sarah insisted. We'd known each other a long time. We'd done a lot of Shakespeare together. She's a wonderful actress. In "Women in History" she was reading Lady Macbeth. "You've spent your life inside these plays. No one can share it like you. We should play the characters, be the actors. *You* should guide the old people through the story." She'd seen me struggle with this before.

"I wish I could, but I see a crowd and I'm sweaty and tongue-tied."

"Can't you pretend that the old people are in the play, that they're actors, too?"

The morning of the presentation we arrived early. It was a warm day for March. In the tacky little garden behind the center, actors were clustered running lines. Going over bits of direction they looked beautiful in the budded slum garden. As I walked through I heard snippets of the characters who'd been in my life longer than almost any actual person: King Henry, Katherine, Margaret, La Pucelle, Suffolk, the Macbeths whispering in a corner—

MACBETH   My dearest love,
     Duncan comes here to-night.
LADY MACBETH   And when goes hence?
MACBETH   To-morrow, as he purposes.
LADY MACBETH   O! never
     Shall sun that morrow see!

                                   —*Macbeth*, 1.5

The big yellow room was filling up. It was an hour until the "talk" but already it was mobbed.

Instead of the little built-in stage, I'd decided to use the floor, with the closed divider as a backdrop. A round tabletop I'd hung two-thirds of the way up the brown divider served as a moon. Old and worn, it looked like the sicklied orb of a mysterious autumn night. I filled the original stage with chairs to make a balcony. "It's like The Globe," I whispered to Susanna. "They can look down on the action just like in 1600." I spread a borrowed oriental carpet on the linoleum and unscrewed all the lights except what was over the actors and took what few stage lights existed and refocused them out onto the playing area. With the windows masked and lots more seats in a circle around the huge rug, it suddenly looked like a beautiful theater.

On her way to makeup Sarah said, "Look at all those old people. Look how beautiful they are, how excited. If you can't talk, we're ready. But if you can we'll help, we're right behind you." Sarah's known pain. Sarah ministers.

There was taped music playing over a primitive speaker system, Samuel Barber and Ralph Vaughan Williams, classical but not altogether from a world before cafeterias.

As the music faded and actors took their places, I decided to try an introduction.

"Hi, my name is Bob, Bob Smith." As I looked around at a couple hundred old people with coats in their laps or angled in wheelchairs, in the semi-darkness of the audience I saw my grandparents. There they were, my sweet old long-dead grandparents just as I remembered them so many years before. Old men in ties and ladies in nice-looking dresses, something familiar, safe.

"I want to tell you about some things that are important to me. . . . I want to tell you about my relationship to Shakespeare."

They applauded! The whole group smiled and clapped their hands in encouragement. "You can do it. We know you can. Tell us what's in your heart. We won't laugh at you or think you're foolish. Tell us! That's what we want! Tell us all about what matters to you."

"When I was a kid . . ."

The actors were grinning their approval and just then I remembered the most important thing. I'd not been able to remember it because it was so painful, but here, now, in front of all these loving old faces, with Henry about to woo Kate, I remembered once again

that it was March and my baby sister's birthday. As I introduced the
scenes I suddenly felt thrilled to be the storyteller, to be taking the
old people through the Shakespeare journey I'd mapped out at my
dining table. There was so much love in the room, so much permis-
sion for me to be myself.

Joe didn't show up at the V.A. till almost nine. "What happened,
Joe? I thought we had to be here by six?"

"Oh, did *I* say that? Oh no. I don't think so. I don't think it
opens till eight-thirty. Have you been standing here all this time?"

"Yes, Joe. I didn't know what to do since you don't have a
phone and I don't know exactly where you live. And you know
something weird, I don't know your last name. You know something weirder . . . I knew you'd be here because I *trust you.*"

He reached into his pocket. "I brought you a postcard of Anne
Hathaway's cottage," he said. "It's old and a little ripped. I don't
know where I ever got it. It's been on my bureau for years."

Every week someone presents me with a fragment of his past,
tattered programs from forgotten productions, an antique book-
mark purchased seventy years ago at a visit to the Shakespeare
Memorial Theater. I have shelves of battered volumes happened
onto in basements and attics. "I was throwing some stuff away
and found this torn old Shakespeare. Would you have any use
for it?"

A man named Arthur once dragged in a box of scratchy LPs,
stilted monologues huffed and puffed by Edwardian luminaries of
the British stage. I resisted. "These just might be valuable."

"All the better." He smiled. "What you give to us doesn't have
a price on it."

I refused, but just before he died he brought them in again.
"Take them," he whispered. "Where I'm headed I won't have any
use for them and you'd get a kick out of how it used to be."
Ghosts.

The torn postcard from Joe with the washed-out ink of fifty years reminded me of the two little stamp-covered cards that I used to bury deep in the soft white cotton underwear in my kid's maple dresser. In 1945 they were the only proof that my father still existed.

CHAPTER 5

Before my father came back from the war, my mother would sometimes take Carolyn and me on two different green and yellow C. R. & L. buses to visit my father's parents in Stratford.

At that time the Smith house over on East Broadway had only old people living in it. My father's four brothers were grown and, like him, had gone to the war. A star-shaped sticker on the window of the large front door honored my grandparents' contribution. The big brown house, surrounded by dark, prickly hedges, was built by my great-grandfather. When I was a little boy and he was a very old man, people liked to shove us together to take our picture. Before Carolyn came I was the youngest and, at 102, he was the oldest person in our family.

Jesse Wells sat in a deep brown leather chair staring through a window in one of the two front parlors. Every day, including the day he died, he wore a dark, striped, vested suit and a celluloid collar with a tie. Like most successful men of his age, he wore a long gold chain ending in an opulent Victorian watch. Not far from any place he sat would be a hat, bowler in winter, straw skimmer in the hot months between Decoration and Labor Days. He was a proper Edwardian, outliving his generation.

In some photographs of family outings at the beach or in a forest, my young father and his four brothers are half dressed, drunk I think, with girlfriends. In the midst of silly theatrics staged for the camera, my great-grandfather sits, ignoring the world. Like an anachronism dropped in from a Manet or a Degas, he is fully, formally dressed. Scornful under his skimmer, staring down the photographer, he's the conscience of the group.

My great-grandfather had a full white beard and a mustache. When I was plopped into his scratchy lap, he was by then mostly out of words and would grumble and fart while I whispered unheard into his deafness for a bike or sled. Of course, at five, I thought he was Santa Claus.

He liked *very* burnt toast. It had to be completely black and always seedless rye. Sitting at the kitchen table in his tie and vest by 5:00 in the morning, he'd turn the heavily buttered graphite-colored slice upside down. "To get the butter first," my grandmother animated behind his back.

It was thought just short of a miracle when, a decade later, my sister picked up a piece of toast and, before her shaking hand put it clumsily into her mouth, she flipped it over "to get the butter first!" My mother smiled. Like toes or eye color, more sure than DNA, everyone rejoiced and winced at heritage! Then and whenever after that Carolyn upsided her toast, nothing could have said more to my parents. She, and just maybe what was wrong with her, was my father's, too.

Unlike my own mother, my father's mother wasn't consumed by hygiene. Ethel Smith had a deep love of animals. She kept an owl as a pet, and for years a good-sized alligator that she'd brought back on the train from Florida resided in a galvanized tub. Even a praying mantis sits contented on her finger in an old photograph.

As a young woman my grandma Smith had been raven-haired and trim with amazingly dark eyes and perfect teeth. By the time I was born she was no longer the graceful object of everyone's praise. She'd had a tough married life, mostly poor, with five little boys. She'd lost a couple of full-term babies and had uncounted miscarriages. By the mid-1940s she'd grown to be a very large somewhat timid old woman.

Jesse Wells hadn't wanted his only surviving child to marry Earl Smith. And when she did, her parents stopped speaking to her. For years my grandparents were disinherited until, late in his very long life, Ethel's lonely father built that big brown house over on East Broadway, and called her home to care for him. She tended him through his eighties and all of his nineties until his death from an accidental fall down the front steps on the day he turned 103.

At the back of that house, down past the barn and rhubarb, past the wildflowers and the raspberry and blackberry bushes, just where the property ends, is a marsh. When I was five or six my father's kid brother called it the swamp.

The *swamp*! In my child's mind I used to wonder if crocodiles and boa constrictors lived there. Did native women wash brightly colored clothes or their children in the muddy water? Were there sometimes drums and exotic birds? Was there quicksand and even maybe, or especially, Tarzan? Could I, with luck, catch a view of any of this on a hot July afternoon?

On a rise at the very edge of that place were three ancient apple trees. They grew exquisitely deformed in the way that old, long-neglected apple trees do. Encrusted with deeply grooved bark and decades of scars, they wore their history on their skins. Even then there was no use for the apples that grew, dangling and inedible, in bizarre shapes like German Christmas ornaments. When I was five those trees seemed to send a witch's gnarled finger crooking invitation for me to climb and be high up over the "swamp." The old trees made for easy climbing with lots of perches for a child's sitting.

With the young men gone to the war the place was solitary. Those long afternoons when my father was away and my mother sat at the kitchen table playing Parcheesi with my grandmother, and my sister slept on the sofa walled in with pillows, I'd sit high up in an October breeze, listening to the trees groan as the wind shoved the big, old, apple-filled branches around. Bobbing in and out of sunlight, cold one minute and warm the next, as the swaying branches exposed my face or legs to the sun.

I think it must have been there, sitting by myself in those old trees, that I first realized that I felt close and safe with old things, old ideas, old people.

> That time of year thou mayst in me behold,
> When yellow leaves, or none, or few do hang
> Upon those boughs which shake against the cold,
> Bare ruined choirs where late the sweet birds sang;
> In me thou seest the twilight of such day
> As after sunset fadeth in the west,
> Which by and by black night doth take away,
> Death's second self, that seals up all in rest;
> In me thou seest the glowing of such fire
> That on the ashes of his youth doth lie,
> As the deathbed, whereon it must expire,
> Consumed with that which it was nourished by;
>   This thou perceiv'st, which makes thy love more
>   strong,
>   To love that well, which thou must leave ere long.
>   —Sonnet 73

With my father's brothers in the army and my mother's brother in the paratroopers, most of the men in my life were old and came from a generation where adult men mostly ignored young children.

In my world boys were girls until they could throw a ball. When I'd visit my mother's parents on Stillman Street, my grandfather would take me to the firehouse where he was "captain." I remember lined-up rubber boots paired like licorice soldiers waiting at attention, and how the men plunged down the incredibly polished brass pole. My grandfather put his enormous fire hat on my head, his voice would go high, and he'd call me "Bucko" or "Me Bucko." He'd pat the leather fire engine seat. "Jump into the front, Me Bucko!"

He could take *anything* completely apart and put it back together in an afternoon. He loved cars. In his seventies, retired from the fire department, he took a job in an auto repair shop and cowed young grease monkeys and tow-truck drivers with his skill. On a garage floor surrounded by oily car parts, he was in paradise. My mother's father was a man's man. His sinewy forearms were patterned with exotic tattoos from his Merchant Marine days. He liked tough language. My punctilious grandmother made pious proclamations against profanity. She'd "lay down the law" about what shouldn't get said in *her* house at *her* table. His concession was to replace words with initials. Blistering at page one of the *Bridgeport Post,* he'd look over at Nana. "That G.D. mayor is gonna bankrupt this town, the S. of a B.!"

Hard-boiled as he acted, I think my mother's father was the person in our family who was the most wounded by my sister. He'd stare at her for the longest time, his voice would go Irish tenor high, and the brogue rubbed into him by his County Cork parents would come back. His voice would shiver almost soprano! "Peg, ya got any ice cream for our little girl? Get 'her nibs' a cookie."

When I was five and convinced that I'd hurt Carolyn, I was sensitive around teasing and criticism and could easily get teary. With a sour face but meaning well, my gristly grandfather would warn me about the unfathomable dangers of being a "pansy." I was a little kid and understood less what he meant than what his disapproval felt like.

I look exactly like him—it's almost eerie. Some woman, Irish and loud, maybe a relative, once grabbed my cheek hard and twisted. "Harold McKeon will never be dead as long as Robert's alive!" Over the years the words were repeated a thousand times. When he was dying of colon cancer in Bridgeport Hospital and I was shaving his version of our face, a nurse stuck her head into the room. "You couldn't be anything but a grandfather and grandson!" He was the first of my four grandparents to die.

At Pistey's my mother's sister Claire was tacky and tearful. Tanked up, she was taking grotesque snapshots of my grandfather's emaciated corpse! Puffed and ravaged by alcohol it was sometimes hard to remember that my mother's only sister had been beautiful. When Claire was just two a photographer stopped my grandmother on the street to inquire if she might want the "gorgeous infant" to be a Gerber baby? Most likely it was a clever ploy by an enterprising photographer, but it marked Claire for envy.

In the forty years my aunt lived on Stillman Street, she grew into a cliché of those frustrated women stuck at home with aging parents. Piling up ugly bridesmaids dresses, every year she got more nervous.

She started to dye her hair a bright strawberry color. She smoked and wore huge garish earrings. My aunt Claire was a cartoon with bowed red lips and scarlet cheeks. She was always perched perilously on high backless toeless shoes and she wore an ugly, rust-colored fur jacket. She nervously chewed gum making a continuous muted popping sound. She got a job in the office of the United Illuminating Company, probably payroll. She knew all the men and all about all the men. As I got older I could see that she wasn't the kind of girl you brought home to your folks.

In the dim, working-class, east-end neighborhood, she drew too much attention. On the way to Mass in one of her "getups," reeking from "enough perfume to choke a horse," she looked like a movie star. She broke all of my grandfather's rules and his old-world Irish heart. Watching her wiggle down the communion aisle at Saint Charles Church, he'd lean into me and whisper, "Get a load of that one, Bucko. She's a G.D. fool."

The day of his funeral, time came to close the coffin lid. Already a six-pack into the morning, my tipsy aunt stumbled to the front of the room. "Dad, Dad, oh Dad," she wailed as she planted a gross iridescent 1970s hot pink lipstick print smack on his dead, hollow, looking like me, cheek! It covered half his face. As she careened back to her seat, the funeral director was calling people to their cars. It was over. My very serious blue-collar grandfather went to his eternal rest with a bright pink theatrical canoodle on his sullen face.

These days Claire sits in a wheelchair, mostly out of it. Staring from a convalescent home window, she surveys the blighted neighborhood where she spent most of her life. Her gum snap and ass wiggle have been devoured by time. When she sees me she cries. Older now, I look like a ghost of her father.

When I was a kid she lived lonely in the back bedroom of my grandparents' incredibly clean apartment. Like me she had a maple dresser. Kids had maple, adults mahogany. Her dresser had drawers filled with silk flowers. They were cloyingly scented and arranged by color, row after row of gaudy, kaleidoscopic blossoms that she'd wear in her hair or on the lapel of that vulgar mink.

Smacking her vermilion lips into a tissue my glamorous aunt would coo, "Come on, Robert, pick one, *you* pick one, pick a flower and I'll wear it on my date!" Pleased by what she saw in her kid's maple dresser mirror, she'd concoct a silly expression, pop her gum, and laugh that nervous frightened giggle.

CHAPTER 6

Even for a young child there was an intoxication in the months just after the war. The winter my father came home, good had conquered evil, right had pulverized wrong, and that Christmas our little house on Tulley Circle was finally a wonderful place to be. Like spring melts the cold of February, real warmth returned to our lives and we were a family again. As little boys do, I saw the world through my father's eyes, and what I saw was how much he loved my mother, my sister, and me. In the national delirium he talked to me more than he ever would again.

He had to go downtown on some business to do with his army discharge. "Howz about goin' with me? School won't matter for a day!" He wanted to take me on the bus, just him and me! He wore his army uniform, and like his beautiful mother, he was good-looking, like her he had black hair and very dark eyes. When I was young I felt disappointed to be pale and blond, to look so much like my mother and her family. I wanted to be dark and handsome. I wanted to be a man in exactly the way I thought my father was.

It seemed like the whole world knew him. We stood in long lines, and friendly, excited people shook his hand and patted my head. For once I felt as if I belonged to him and that he was very glad that I did.

On the yellow and green C. R. & L. bus home, we sat close in the front seat right behind the driver. I remember our legs touching and how we talked and talked. Ecstatic, slapping the heels of my Buster Browns against the shiny steel legs of the bus seat and flirting like kids do, I was the happiest I'd ever been. "Jabber, jabber, slap, slap, jabber." Nobody laughs like my father or tells jokes like him, or smokes like him! My father forgets and leaves the Frigidaire door open, he "wastes electricity" and doesn't care! My father even forgets to flush! "Oh Mil . . . ," he'd say, pretending impatience and winking at me to make fun of some trivial thing that my mother was nervous about.

Those first months after the war we stayed up late. I wouldn't leave the room, even when I had to pee so bad my teeth felt tingly. I didn't want to miss a minute. We ate gallons of chocolate ice cream from a place called Paradise Green. We didn't even use dishes, we ate with little flat wooden spoons scraping the dark delicious frozen cubes until they melted, and we could dig in for a big mouthful. We dripped it on our clothes and got it on our faces. Black hair, black eyes, chocolate ice cream mustaches, dark is for men. *And* for little boys with their fathers. My mother would only eat strawberry, from a *dish*. Pink is for girls. Strawberry, eck.

Carolyn had the ice cream, too. My father fed her with the tiny, flat wood spoon. He held her and made her laugh, and I was so grateful he wasn't mad at her. He was happy to be the father and that made it seem as if nothing was wrong.

That winter of 1946 the four of us would sit, after church on Sunday morning, on the cheap, coarse, oriental rug on the living room floor and talk. My mother was beautiful and, for a while, she wasn't so jumpy. She laughed and said that it was really stupid for us to be on the floor when Mr. Nothnagle had charged so much money for the two chairs and the big hard green sofa. With sheets of Sunday newspaper pages flying around, and the radio always too loud for my mother ("Watta ya, deaf? I could shoot you!"), we heard the New York mayor read the funny papers. I can still hear the radio static and see my father's young finger trace the words for me. He laughed at Dagwood and Blondie or the Katzenjammer Kids.

And in the late nights I felt small and a part of things. Deep inside my Navajo blanket bathrobe while my mother and father talked quietly, it was easier to fall asleep than it has ever been since.

In the months after the war my father bought a blue car and we went to see people and people came to see us. We ate big meals at crowded tables. There were plans to get up extra early with special places to go. There was falling asleep in a chair late in smoky rooms with young laughing uncles and pretty girls. And the air smelled more like coffee or beer or cigarettes or perfume than bleach. I couldn't know that the happiness would evaporate as suddenly as my father's return had created it. As surely as if he'd died or gone away again, he would quietly, without an explaining word, close the door on me, never to let me into that warm safe childhood place again.

He still stands silent behind the heavy door he closed so long ago. Uncomfortable, he waits for me to give up and go away. How it lacerates, and still I go on knocking!

He never ran away from Carolyn. He still hasn't. In my mother's lifelong need to tell on him, to sneakily squeal on the good and the bad, she tells me a heartbreaking almost unlistenable story of him strapping a harness around my sister so that she couldn't get away from his feeble old man's grasp on the way, *last week,* to the inevitable ice cream. He's been loyal for the 39 years of the 1800 Sunday institution visits and quivering trips to the little broken-down ice cream stand.

Thou shalt not sigh, nor hold thy stumps to heaven,
Nor wink, nor nod, nor kneel, nor make a sign,
But I of these will wrest an alphabet
And by still practice learn to know thy meaning.
                                        —*Titus Andronicus*, 3.2

There's a newspaper photograph from that happy family time in 1946. It's of me and Carolyn sitting on that scratchy rug in front of a scrawny tree. The picture shows that there's no art in the decoration of the tree. It looks worn and cheerless for a Christmas tree. We're surrounded by toys, and I'm wearing a heavy flannel bathrobe and looking intently at my sister. The caption comments on my expression of adoration and brotherly care.

Neatly upright in her little pink robe, Carolyn stares, like her great-grandfather used to, without expression, directly at the camera. If you look more closely than a stranger might, you can see that her expression is vague. There is no thought behind it, though it's hard to see through the sweetness of the picture exactly how vacant that stare really is. Her legs are folded symmetrically under her, looking as if they could have gotten there by themselves. Beneath the quilted robe you can't see how twisted and powerless those little legs actually are. In 1946 it would be a while still before my sister would, against all odds and medical opinions, stand on those weak limbs to take her first step.

We're a couple of china dolls, my sister and me, props for the postwar Christmas newspaper spread. Blond and blue-eyed, Betty Crocker pure, we sit under our dour tree, the sweet survivors of the deaths of so many other innocents. Who would guess that the pretty little girl doll is so broken or that the devoted boy doll has already started to break up inside? My parents still keep a copy of the picture on their TV. When I look at it I feel uncomfortable, like a witness to a horrible accident that won't leave my memory.

CHAPTER 7

FIFTY YEARS later I sat on a rug at the Veterans Hospital on Twenty-third Street. Joe was right, we did wait all day and it *is* tough to be old. At first we sat on a sofa in a small windowless waiting room on the fourth floor. We'd been sent there by a woman at the main desk, but there wasn't anyone on the fourth floor.

I left Joe with *Richard the Second* and took the elevator back to the lobby. "No one's up there," I said. "There doesn't seem to be anyone on the whole floor."

"Just wait," the receptionist said. "It's early, doctors are operating. They don't see patients till the afternoon. Someone will show up!"

Back on four Joe was buried in *Richard.* As I flopped down next to him he sounded like a bright kid. "The language, that's what it is, it's always the language. Just look at the first line. I've been staring at it all the time you were gone." He'd forgotten about doctors and lousy legs. He shoved the paperback at me. "Just look at the first seven words."

"I know them, Joe, I know the first seven words of *Richard the Second:* 'Old John of Gaunt, time-honored Lancaster' . . ."

" 'Time-honored.' " Joe looked uneasy. "Has time honored me? I'm a scared old man worried about a hole in my leg. I don't feel so 'time-honored.' " He looked ten years old, he pointed to the book. "Was that a better world? Were old people time-honored? Has it all gone to shit?"

It was a good question. I was getting used to good questions. "No, Joe, look at King Lear. See how Gaunt ends up, and Gloucester."

There's a mythology about gracious, painless old age. People are so scared about it that they pretend it's not going to happen. As a result, we see the old as if they're "not right," as if they've done something wrong. We want them invisible. We want Grandma "over the river and through the woods," not next door and certainly not dying in the next room.

It's all in the second scene in *Richard*. Gaunt visits his widowed sister-in-law and Shakespeare doesn't pull many punches about loneliness and geriatric isolation.

Despite the centuries and enormous class distinctions the Duchess of Gloucester sounds just like Nana the year before she died. Alone in her house she would serve stale Ritz crackers with Tetley tea and slightly rancid milk. She'd hold me captive while she searched her mind for lost threads of unraveled memories. "Oh you can't leave yet, you just got here. Stay awhile. Want soup? Don't go yet, please not yet." Mother Teresa said the world's dying of loneliness. Shakespeare agrees.

DUCHESS   Yet one word more—

She stalls. She doesn't want him to go. She knows she'll never see him again. It's the end of their generation and the memories of good times long ago. She starts to say good-bye but can't.

Lo, this is all—nay, yet depart not so,
Though this be all, do not so quickly go . . .

She promises to pull herself together.

I shall remember more.

Finally she gives in.

> Desolate, desolate, will I hence and die:
> The last leave of thee takes my weeping eye.
> —*King Richard II,* 1.2

A cleaning woman pushed a screeching metal bucket into the hospital waiting room.

"Is anybody around?" I asked. "We've been sitting here for a couple of hours."

"There'll be a nurse at the desk down the hall. She's always there by the time I finish."

Joe looked resigned. "Read to me like you do in class. You make it all so clear."

The day after the Women in History presentation I stopped by the senior center.

"The phone's been ringing off the hook." Chris the program director was glowing. "Could you ever see yourself doing it again? They got so much out of it. They want more."

"Truth is, *I* got so much out of it." The love in the room had been palpable.

I'd been startled by how alive everyone was. I felt stupid to have thought that old people somehow get smaller and tighter. A lifetime of lessons had been wasted on me. Who should have known better that things aren't only what they look like?

I suggested a small study group. "Not more than ten or twelve people? We could meet for a month or six weeks. I wouldn't bring actors, there'd be no performing, just me, the text, and ten old minds?"

Chris jumped at it. "Yes." The expected caveat followed. "We don't have money. We could cover expenses, provide the room, nothing more. Oh, Bob, let's try. They're so thrilled."

"We'll need copies of whatever text we'll look at. They should be able to follow and make notes. And no matter what, let the copies be free. It's got to be about what's *inside* the people. It shouldn't have anything to do with money."

Chris showed me to a little back room they optimistically called the library. It was another cinder-block space with a few books and mostly empty shelves. In the middle was a rectangular worktable surrounded by the ubiquitous metal chairs. "It's fine," I said.

It was April, and almost Shakespeare's birthday, by the time we settled on Thursday mornings and came up with some money for the copies. "How about the sonnets?" It seemed like a good idea to sit around that table and take fourteen self-contained lines at a time, no plot, no bigger issues.

We started with three married couples who'd known each other since they'd been kids on Avenue A, Joe, a sweet gay man from the Bronx named Mike, and Zoe and her friends from the housing project on West Twenty-third. Mike is the only one still living. Every Thursday morning we pecked our way through the sonnets—all 154.

At the time I was also directing a project for the Musical Theater Works. The students were from NYU and I was developing a Shakespeare theater piece with them. They were a mixed bag of performers, mostly singers. I loved the kids and how remarkably talented they were, but I found myself looking forward to the hour of brilliant old people and sonnets more than anything in my week.

> Let me not to the marriage of true minds
> Admit impediments; love is not love
> Which alters when it alteration finds,
> Or bends with the remover to remove.

O no, it is an ever-fixed mark,
That looks on tempests and is never shaken;
It is the star to every wand'ring bark,
Whose worth's unknown, although his height be taken.
Love's not Time's fool, though rosy lips and cheeks
Within his bending sickle's compass come;
Love alters not with his brief hours and weeks,
But bears it out even to the edge of doom.
   If this be error and upon me proved,
   I never writ, nor no man ever loved.

—Sonnet 116

CHAPTER 8

Soon after the war my father took a job three hundred miles away in Syracuse, New York. A week before we moved my family drove up to Hartford. The GI Bill was enabling us to look for someone to help my sister. My father's parents waited in the car while the four of us went into a gigantic hospital. I'm not exactly sure why I was there. I was six, and sometimes it felt as if I was shoved into rooms first to make everybody comfortable before my sister was hauled in.

Three doctors asked some questions and instructed my young, nervous parents to put Carolyn on the floor. Someone pulled a couple of chairs off a rug. My father put Carolyn down. They asked him to step away and leave my sister alone. The men slowly walked around her. They clapped their hands and made sudden noises. They bent close to her and spoke to each other as if we weren't there.

"You have an 'imbecile'! Put her away! Put her away *now*! An institution's best, best for you, best for the boy. Put her away!"

Put her away? Does it mean "shoot" her? "I could shoot you!" "Put her away!" "Give her back to the Indians?" "Did I hurt my mother down there?" Put her away? Suddenly my mother was crying harder than when my father went to Italy to the army to be a man! My father stared at the floor. My skinny, timid, shy father didn't look dark and big, he looked pale and little and sick. "Doctors hurt you!" My mother had told me that doctors smash babies' heads.

I screamed, "No!" I picked Carolyn up. "No! Put her away? No! We whispered in that hot room in Florida! We whisper at night at the end of my bed! This is a hospital. The doctors are hurting my mother! Away? No! No away! No! Not now, not ever!"

"Put her away." For almost twenty years those words were carelessly repeated by well-meaning observers who thought they'd earned the right. Good times and bad, the world sent us messengers who'd repeat, as if they'd been there, what was said in that heartless room in Hartford.

On the ride back from the brief, devastating examination, I understood why my grandparents had come along. They were there, in their kindness, to soften what I think everyone but me knew would get said. People who have alligators in galvanized tubs and watch the sun come through jack-in-the-pulpits, people who keep owls as pets, might think that a little girl who would never walk or focus might just be another way for life to be. Like a twisted leaf, my grandparents knew that my little sister might have her own rights to life.

In Syracuse my mother had to cope in strange surroundings without her family. Alone in upstate New York her depression deepened and her behavior grew more strange.

To calm her, over the next few years we went back and forth between Stratford and Syracuse many times. In the warm months, the roadside was strewn with overheated cars. Stopped on the gooey tar with hoods raised, spewing steam, an exasperated father would be hunched over the engine while screaming children, glad for the break, chased each other into a pasture or woods. Under any available roadside shade, an elm or in a field under an umbrella, sat the grandparents, old folks, formal, patient, and probably thinking, "Get a horse!"

On one of the summertime rides my father's obese mother came along, taking up an embarrassing amount of the backseat, leaving me and my little sister to divvy the rest. But the sacrifice was well worth the thrill of having my favorite person join us for the dull trip. By then my parents had started a lifelong cycle of petty, escalating arguments that resulted in days of weighed silences. On the long car trips the eight-and-a-half-hour aphonia was interrupted by the odor we didn't want the world to know about and Carolyn's tantrum as we changed her again. In the backseat the job was mostly mine. My father was driving, my mother tight-lipped, staring out the window, nauseous with a headache.

On the August trip with my father's mother our car overheated and we had to stop, like all the others, in the swelter of the steamy road heat. My grandmother said, "Bobby, let's take a walk!" Making our way up the gentle slope of a Catskill foothill, we climbed through a battalion of black-eyed Susans. Breathless, she stopped to pick a big bunch of the brilliant yellow flowers. In imitation I picked more. She laughed and grabbed a bigger armful. By the time we got back, we could hardly carry all the flowers, hundreds of them. We filled the whole inside of the car and made the rest of the long trip in a bobbing bower of friendly black-eyed Susans. My lilac-smelling grandmother produced easy magic for me and my sister.

My mother said that in the sixty-one years of their marriage, my father cried only twice, the day his mother died and when he left my sister at the Southbury Training School.

*   *   *

Lots of things happened in Syracuse, but first above every other memory is snow. I've never seen it so deep and constant as the years we spent there. Our house on Hubble Avenue, just around the corner from Onondaga Park, was make-believe Tudor with rust-stained stucco and heavily carved porches hanging all over it. My mother hated the big dark house. She still goes wild when she sees a stucco building. Of course, it's connected to those times and to how afraid she was. Now she and my father live in a tiny house with a small ordinary backyard. She feels safer, able to see everything at once, no hidden corners where the bad things lurk.

When we got to Syracuse I registered myself at the Most Holy Rosary Catholic Grammar School. It was part of a complex of buildings surrounding a large yellow-brick church. The elementary grades were taught in a gray Victorian house that was attached to a second building where the nuns lived. The smell from the convent was always of furniture polish and boiling cabbage, even at 9:00 A.M.

At Holy Rosary no student could cross the path of a nun without a full and respectful bow. If you even stepped into her line of vision, you had to bend deep from the waist; the little girls curtsied. In the depth of the bow you had to say, "Excuse me, Sister!" The nuns taught this as if it were essential to salvation. In the mornings or just after school, the little slapdash hall that spanned the school and convent was mobbed with children bowing and shrieking childish choruses of "Please excuse me, Sister!" "Please excuse me, Sister!" And we could walk only on the right, never on the left side of the old wooden stairs or in the hallways, or even on the street. "If everyone, everywhere, always walked on the right no one would ever bump into anyone. And we'd all get where we're going a lot faster and a lot safer!" I'm sixty and I've been walking on the right for fifty-four years. I catch myself feeling bitter on a crowded New York street when it's completely obvious that everyone else is ignoring what the nun told them in the first grade!

Sister Elizabeth Joseph sat us at our little oak desks according to

our scholastic abilities. The little innocent "dumb" kids sat farthest
from the distracting windows. Their row was called cherubs. There
were cherubim rows and seraphim rows. The one nearest the windows was kept for the best students, and we, at seven, were
archangels. You always knew where you stood by where you sat at
Holy Rosary.

When I was new to the first grade, I couldn't get the hang of
closing the metal clips that fastened my galoshes. Those defeating
metal fasteners on the front of my rubber boots were the only
awful thing about the enchantment of all the snow. Because I
couldn't close them, I wore the boots unsnapped. No one noticed
except a mean old nun. "A nun of Winter's sisterhood" . . . "The
very ice of chastity."

"Don't forget your galoshes!" my mother would call from some
place deep in the big old house.

The muted sounds of a blanketed world lay just on the other
side of our heavy front door; a chorus of early-morning shovels
pushed along buried neighborhood sidewalks, the tap-tap of melt-
ing porch icicles, loose chains on car wheels like troika bells—
cha-chink, cha-chink, cha-chink—and best, the screams of the
boys across the street threatening each other with snowballs! A
pure white adventure lay over my six-year-old's world for the five-
block walk in my falling-off, unbuckled galoshes. Nothing, except
Shakespeare, is to me as good as snow—still.

At the end of the school day, the old nun spotted me with my
rubbery boots flapping wide open. As I jumped off the porch into
the shoveled yard, she called out, "You! The blond boy! Yes, you!
Come here! What's your name?" She took me up the stairs into a
classroom and instructed me to "work on the snaps." She sat at her
desk leaving me to figure out what I didn't know how to do.

For a long time we sat in silence. The only sounds were the
shuffle of her correcting papers, the raucous bang of pipes as
the heat in the venerable building went off for the day, and the little click of the fasteners as I tried to close them. As the afternoon

darkened, I heard the ping of snow against the west-facing windows, and finally, when I wasn't able to see past my tears, the nun took pity and liberated me.

People who liked me when I was six called me Bobby. "Robert," she said, "I've got all day. I live here. I'm not going anywhere, but I'm sure you'll want your dinner." She never looked up, never helped me. She finally waved me away with affected disdain; I flopped my way down the stairs and out into the snow and understood for the first time the terrible feeling of being "not right."

I'm nervous around the machines of the world. I still don't drive. Thank God for the old blue ten-speed and the 8:03. When I need to, I hire drivers or get rides with friends. Speeding along the crest of Mulholland Drive in a convertible, a pretty redheaded actress at the wheel laughed at me. "It's unbelievable that you've never been alone in a moving car!" I hadn't thought about it before.

When I was a serious little kid filled with worry about my sister and increasingly about my mother, our teacher told us that we each had a soul. The young nun said that our souls were just like the bottles of pure fresh milk on our doorsteps, where they sat with all the rich cream gathered up at the top. Sister got a sickened expression and explained that sin was like black spots that taint pure milk. She said that every time we did anything bad a drop of soot fell into the pure milk of our perfect souls. She told us that evil souls were more soot than cream, and reassured us that we were still pristine. She warned that at almost seven, we'd begin to find it harder and harder to stay pure. It's amazing how much anxiety was handed over to children, how guilt was expected to drive faith, and it did!

Sister was a big movie fan. She lived in the theology of religious Hollywood, Father Flanagan, and the Bells of St. Mary's, but she went much further. She told us that God had a camera and it was

trained on our little-kid lives. She made us nervous when she said
that we were never, *never,* alone. God's camera was always there.
She warned that after we died we'd sit with God and look at the
movie of our life and be very ashamed of our secret bad behavior
when we watched it with God! To Sister Elizabeth Joseph, God the
Father was cranky Louis B. Mayer.

Because of all the grief about my sister's toilet issues, I was
myself a bit edgy in the bathroom. Nervous and with "stomach
troubles," I had a hard time in there. The young nun said that on
one side I had a good and pure guardian angel and just over the
other six-year-old shoulder a bad angel was looking for a chance to
tempt me into an "impure" act! Now there was also a camera
making a movie of me on the toilet!

Shortly after we moved to Syracuse, my mother seemed more lost
than usual. I was helping her put some clothes through the wringer
on the top of our fat, round washing machine. *Ga-swish, ga-swish,
ga-swish.* We were in the cool stone cellar toward the back of the
house. Some light was making its way through a cracked glass
panel in the green cellar door. *Ga-swish.*

"It's a blood clot!" she said. "That's what it is! When she got
smashed on the head, that's what happened."

Later upstairs she was holding Carolyn. "Touch it, Bobby! It's
right there in the center! Touch the soft place. There it is, in
there!" Then she said the most dangerous words I'd ever heard
spoken.

"It could melt, you know! Some night when we're all asleep it
could just dissolve. And our baby would be okay!" *Our* baby?

It was about faith, she said. If we prayed and our goodness was
acceptable to God then just maybe, early on some snowy morning,
I'd look down at the end of my bed and Carolyn would be sitting
up in her crib waiting to go out and play.

Meanwhile, during lunch at school, the young nun read to us

from the pain-filled and miraculous *The Lives of the Saints*. While we ate peanut butter, the dead came back, cancer was instantly cured, blind men regained their sight, and twisted children got to walk and run for the first time, and all through faith and sacrifice! Sometimes in the magical tales the goodness of one person helped another! Why not me? Why not Carolyn? Why not the stupid blot clot just under that gushy place on my sister's skull? I thought that it was called a blot clot!

I asked my mother if I could build a chapel under the porch at the back of our house. Our steep driveway dropped down into a backyard much lower than the front of the house. This added an extra level to the rear of the foundation. Under the porch was a damp area enclosed on three sides by rotted trellis where I could make a place to pray for Carolyn's blot clot to melt! I looked through the dank garages. I found broken chairs and a kitchen table for an altar, to make the chapel.

With my mother not well, my Catholic grandmother came to stay. Happy that I was preparing to practice my priesthood, she took me to a large religious store. "For the chapel," she said. Nana bought plaster statues and a real, but tiny, white marble and gold-leaf altar. She bought pictures of my favorite saints and a big crucifix.

My mother's mother was religious in the Irish way. A gigantic safety pin attached to her rigidly boned, ivory-colored girdle held an enormous collection of holy medals and small tin crosses. You could hear them rattle when she walked.

Nana was disappointed when I told her that the little, under-porch chapel was called Saint Lilac after my other, atheist, grand-mother's favorite smell.

As I knelt in the cold, wet place, I could hear the boys across the street yelling and running, chasing each other. And I longed to be with them. I still do.

"In the name of the Father and of the Son and of the Holy Ghost—

"Please, God, my sister is sick. She can't play with me. She doesn't even go outside. I love her so much. I talk to her all the time, and I think it would be easy for you to fix her. She can't walk or talk. She pees and poops on everything. She has a blot clot on her head. Mommy's mad at her. Please, God, I'll be so good. I'll do anything! Anything! Did I say please? And could I have a black-and-white puppy?"

We did get a dog but he didn't last long. Pal was a small black-and-white terrier, and like Carolyn he pooped everywhere. Sometimes I wrapped his little hard stools in newspaper and hid them. My mother said that she would "shoot him"! And I didn't want her to.

He got distemper. I watched him tear around and around the backyard. He threw himself at the garage doors and tried to run up the side of the house. He foamed at the mouth and it was the most horrible thing I'd ever seen.

When Pal died I got awful stomach trouble. It was hard to breathe and I couldn't walk. I cried and my mother let me stay home from school. I almost never cried because my father would say mean things about me not being a real boy. It hurt to be hurt for being hurt already.

When my stomach ached and my eyes were teary, my mother got impatient. "Stop it!" she said. "It can't hurt that bad. Help me make the bed." When we shook the blanket, I made a noise. She came around to the side of the bed and started to tickle me. I was very ticklish. My mother put her fingers under my arms and along my sides. The pain was so bad I thought I'd explode.

"Smile!" she said. "Show me how happy you are! You are not sick. There's nothing wrong with you. I have one sick child! I will not have two. Laugh, damn it!"

I got away and crawled under her bed. There was blood in my mouth and I was terrified. She crawled under to drag me out. She was laughing like a crazy person and tickling me.

"Laugh, damn it, laugh! See, it's not so bad. Drink some milk. Laugh! Laugh! Laugh!"

I started to go on imaginary trips in my sleep. I'd will myself to places where life was fun.

In my dreams Pal was alive and Carolyn could walk. At night I'd take them to Switzerland or Italy, or to visit our grandparents far away in a place that one of our neighbors called Con-eck-tea-cup.

On a Saturday night when the snow came down harder than ever, I asked my sister where she wanted to go and I was sure that she whispered "Santa." What a good idea! Me and Carolyn and Pal on one of our trips. This time to heaven, this time to see Santa. Everybody knew that Santa lives at the North Pole and the North Pole's just next to heaven.

I knew from *The Lives of the Saints* that Santa Claus was really Saint Nicholas and that he was the patron saint of a big old place called Russia where there was snow all year even on my birthday, July 10, so we should take the big wood skis my father brought from Switzerland. After my bath I piled blankets and a pillow at the bottom of my bed near Carolyn. We were right next to each other with just the crib bars between us. As I started to get sleepy I could hear my sister making sounds. I heard the wind and the wet snow hitting our window. Hanging just over her head in the crib was a tiny bell, and as I fell asleep, I heard the fragile sound as the draft caught it. *Tinga-linga-linga-ling.*

We took an old-fashioned train in the snow, not at all like the one we'd taken with my mother to Florida. It was a small, fat train that chugged up a huge mountain. We skied on the old wooden Swiss army skis. I held my sister and the little dog as we whooshed through incredible mountain passes and down the astonishingly postcard-pink Matterhorn. In my dreams my sister was my friend, she could walk and talk and play like other children. Only later, when I was an adult, was she more misshapen and brutally retarded in my nightmares.

It was cold and wet and thrilling in the dark. Pal barked at the reindeer. Carolyn got afraid of Santa's beard. I told her that he was really old Grandpa Wells and that they both ate their burnt toast upside down, to get the butter first! We laughed at that.

It got windier and colder. My pajamas were wet and sticking to me. My feet were so cold that they felt hot. I told Pal to lie under a big tree, and I wrapped Carolyn in my blue Navajo bathrobe. I put myself over them to keep them safe. The snow was stinging my back but I was happy to protect the little creatures that I loved most. I felt like a big boy sheltering the two sweet babies beneath me. I remember there was a light. It was a brilliant awful light. I thought that it was the train coming toward us!

When I half opened my eyes I could see the wind-driven snow filling all the painful light made by the car headlights. A voice, kind, old, sweet, worried. "Bobby, Bobby Smith, oh dear, wake up! You will get very sick, oh, oh!"

When I opened my eyes all the way I saw our neighbor, Mrs. Fleming. She was a beautiful lady with gray hair. She was wearing a black coat with a huge fox collar, and she had a little hat on. She was trying to pick me up but she couldn't. She was too old and I was too big. "You were too big, you hurt your mother, down there!" I wanted to be little.

Mrs. Fleming's car lights had caught me asleep in my pajamas under the big tree in front of our house. In my sleep I'd walked right out our front door. I was almost completely buried in the heavy snowfall. I remember that I didn't feel at all cold when she put her coat around me. Sometimes outside of Saint Lilac, I'd seen Mrs. Fleming in her yard, and I thought that she must be a wonderful mother. She would stop me on the sidewalk and ask about school and Carolyn. One time she said that I was very handsome and that I should buckle my galoshes.

It's a funny thing, but over all of the years since Mrs. Fleming found me outside asleep in the blizzard, whenever I see a coat with a big fur collar in a movie or on TV, I can see her pretty, concerned face with the car lights blasting behind her and the flying snow mixed with the wisps of white hair not caught up under her hat. She thought I'd get pneumonia and die. I just got a cold. A few days later she rang our front doorbell to bring me soup and a couple of spectacular Wonder comics.

CHAPTER 9

THE LITTLE BOY who lives next to my rented red house is holding a goofy kid's umbrella way up over his head, not that it's raining, or even cloudy. In fact, it's a perfect summer day, July, almost my birthday. For half an hour Ryan's been leaning against the other side of the fence waiting for me to come out.

"Bob! Bob! Look at my uhbwella!" He's excited. "I got it at the mall, I ate a hamburger and a pickle!" He points to my garden hoe. "Whazat?" I show him how it works and he shows me his silly umbrella and an annoyingly noisy yellow dump truck that's big enough for him to ride. We're both getting better at talking. These days I understand at least every third word. He's telling me about his swimming lessons. I'm almost positive we're talking about swimming when his mother brings his baby sister outside. Now he's showing me his tiny blue Mickey Mouse flashlight. Part of the demonstration is the demonic thumping of his sister Hannah's head! Whack! Smash! She doesn't cry, doesn't even seem to notice, she's looking benignly at me. She's adorable and knows it. At the moment I'm the object of a shameless flirt, all coyness and drool. Crack!

"Your sister was hit violently on the head. A doctor, young, stupid . . . the stupid young doctor did it! The stupid young doctor panicked. There's a blood clot. . . . It could melt, ya know! One morning in her crib she will be . . . okay! Our baby will be okay!"

My earliest glimpse of friendship appeared when I was seven, just after our first winter in Syracuse. It was spring, the snow was mostly gone. Months of a little boy's prayers had gone by, too. Before school and after homework, in front of that little white-and-gold marble altar from my grandmother, I'd offered a kid's orisons to a deaf deity. The snow had melted, the blood clot had not. With the ego of a zealot, I was sure that it was me, that something in me, or about me, was unworthy. There was no sign that my sister was any better. She'd mostly lie on her back unfocused and crying. Where did all the pain come from? What hurt? How could we make it better? And by then everyone's patience was fraying.

About that time my sister started to go to a school of her own. A physical therapist wondered if those twisted little legs and turned-in ankles, hidden in the high, stiff, never-walked-in baby shoes, might get strong. And she was right!

That spring for a couple of months, a little yellow bus picked up Carolyn just before I left for Holy Rosary. Every morning, like a sick joke by Hieronymus Bosch, the bus arrived crammed with children who all had terrifying disabilities. Behind smudged bus windows sat rows of convulsing, slobbering kids, and every morning we carried Carolyn out to the bus and strapped her into a seat.

After school I'd wait on our front porch steps for the bus to bring her home. Across the street lived a houseful of boys. "Holy terrors," my mother called them. "Ragtag, they look like they don't have a mother!"

I watched the brothers from behind the panels of thick Irish lace that shrouded our three living room windows.

"Whata ya lookin' at them for? They're wild! Look at those clothes! They look like they never even heard of a bath! Did you remember to wash the back steps?"

I watched the boys come tearing around the side of their house like a pack of wild puppies. They yelled and shrieked and pushed each other down. Worn out, they'd sit together on their front porch steps. With their shoulders hunched up, they whispered and laughed, and took instructions from the oldest one. He was an altar boy at Holy Rosary, and I think he was eleven. Through the pattern of the curtains I could see that, like my father and his brothers, there were five of them. And like my father's brothers, they were dark. Tawny, not black—that couldn't be on Hubble Avenue in 1948. But they were definitely brown, not pale and scrubbed and anemic like me, still taking at least two scalding baths a day.

I'd sit out on our front steps hoping the kids across the street would ask me to play. Of course they never even looked at me. There was no need to look outside their big family for companionship. I was invisible to them. I watched and pretended to play with them. After I went to sleep Carolyn and Pal and the boys and I played tag and ring-a-levio and hide-and-seek and you're getting warmer. We played cowboys and Indians and cops and robbers. We definitely did not play "priest," we definitely did not pray for the old "blot clot to melt." In my dreams we were silly, incredibly, astonishingly, repulsively, mother-angeringly silly!

Then, on a day after the snow was long gone and the spring rain had stopped, and the trees were just starting to be pale green, on a day when my coat was suddenly too warm and bird chirps made you look around, God showed me his full-out face. Not surprisingly his face was grimy and the hair in his eyes hadn't been washed in a while and his fingernails were incredibly dirty.

I was walking home from second grade when one of the boys

from across the street ran to catch up with me, *ran to catch up with me!*

"Hi."

"Hi." My heart was banging so loud I could hear it.

"Wanna play with us? My brother has to take piano lessons. He can't come out. Wanna play with us?"

"Do not, I repeat, do not . . ." My mother's instructions were always overacted impersonations of warnings from the twenties tommy-gunned at her by cranky nuns and my sour grandmother. "Do not get dirty! I have enough to do. Be very polite and for God's sake don't accept anything! Don't hurt anyone's feelings, always be polite, but say no! No to cake. No to candy, food of any kind, cookies, a ride in their car! People don't have things to give, even if they say that they do! Everyone," she repeated, "everyone expects well-behaved children to always say no! Say no, don't get dirty, don't sit on cold cement—you'll get piles! Don't go anywhere with them and don't make any noise. Your sister's finally asleep! Have a good time."

On the other side of Hubble Avenue, just across the street from our somber house, I did finally get dirty. I ran around making Indian war cries and falling down to skin my first time ever filthy knee. In pain, I choked back tears, happy to be like the other little boys. I was a holy terror! I was an Indian! My fingernails got encrusted with mud. Like the crucifix over my maple bed, I had dried terra-cotta blood on my scraped legs. My elbows were raw from sliding, my hair got matted in a late spring mud sling! There was no hitting, these boys had codes and stuck to them. They got along in their wildness like a pack. And they smelled awful. I ached to stink! No sniffing at things with the Geese boys—that was their odd name, Geese. They were the Geeses sent by Jesus to save my childhood! I was in second grade and I was in love with them. The mother—yes, there was a mother—with dark curly hair and a lightheartedness that was hard for me to recognize as mother, made a pile of bologna sandwiches and we ate them on the front steps listening to the eleven-year-old pound out piano notes as sour as his awful smell and all of a sudden I felt like a boy. It lasted about a month.

"We're moving," my father said. "You'll like it. It's a farm." The school near the university had pinned a note to my sister's sweater; they just couldn't keep her without toilet training. My parents were heartbroken, and not long after that my father told me we were leaving. In a serious little kids' talk on their front porch steps, the Geeses promised to come on a Sunday and play with me. They just couldn't say which Sunday. For a year I sat waiting on a triangle of grass near a traffic light. Once or twice I thought I saw a car full of little boys barrel through the green light. Was it them?

Our new address was only six miles north of Hubble Avenue, but to an eight-year-old it was the end of the earth. The farm wasn't much of a farm anymore, just an old house surrounded by a corn-field. A few chickens cackled in a falling-in coop and a broken pump sat rusting in the muddy backyard. A little luckier than a couple of our neighbors, we had indoor plumbing. A mile down a relentlessly straight road, generations of indigo drips dribbled across slanted desktops and, under lift-up lids, layers of not-so-secret secret carvings gouged the dry wood. The old-fashioned schoolhouse had eight grades jammed into a pair of identical rooms.

If one grade had a math or English test, all the other kids got to run around acting nuts until Mrs. Stanley waved the bell to bring us back inside. The two country teachers hadn't exchanged a civil word in years. A couple of times a week the old ladies exploded, to the delight of the students who'd get sent outside to slosh around in the muck until a truce was called.

On the walk to school the only buildings I passed were another ruined farm and a small rural gas station. Catching the early morning sun, the young attendant would lean way back in his kitchen chair. Squinting with a cigarette between his thumb and index finger, he'd wave a sleepy expressionless half circle at me. Farther down the road I picked up sticks for throwing and explored a collection of farm tools left to rust in a sandy trench that traced the tar.

> the whining school-boy with his satchel
> And shining morning face, creeping like snail
> Unwillingly to school.
>   —*As You Like It*, 2.7

I creeped but I was very willing. No matter what form it came in, school was kids and Crayola crayons. It was that icy milk carton smell at 9:45 and dreaming of places to take my sister on the huge canvas pull-down maps. Late some afternoons, when the regular lessons were over, Mrs. Stanley would hand me her teacher's pointer and roll down one of the shiny, oilcloth-smelling maps. From the back of the room she'd fire out, "Sweden . . . ? Peru . . . ? India . . . ?" I'd point to the lime or ocher or raspberry shapes. "Excellent," she'd say. "Name the capitals."

When the November snow came I sledded on our neighbor's hill. I got a kick out of skidding across an icy hollow while eighty-nine-year-old Mr. Richardson sat bundled up watching me. When winter came full force I'd drag my sled through the furrows of his stubby corn. In the flat fields the wind was fierce. At night the sound of it beating the rafters over my room was thrilling. Even the icy gloss on the forsaken iron swings whining in front of school was a desolate alchemy of winter on the secluded farm.

> When all aloud the wind doth blow,
> And coughing drowns the parson's saw,

And birds sit brooding in the snow,
  And Marian's nose looks red and raw,
When roasted crabs hiss in the bowl,
Then nightly sings the staring owl . . .

—Loves Labours Lost, 5.2

In the spring, under the brownish gray barn behind the chicken coop, Mrs. Hull's cat had four kittens. After school I'd lay flat in the dirt and peer into a crevice in the stone foundation. I took Carolyn there and we'd sit on the wet ground. I offered food, but food had no meaning. The kittens were too young and waited for their mother to sneak down to feed them.

Eventually they ventured out, first a paw chasing a bug, or I'd catch sight of a beautiful amber eye. And there on the ground behind that big barn, my sister started for the first time to listen.

"What's in there? Is that a kitty? Did you see the kitty? Did Carolyn see the baby kitty? Oh . . . here it comes again." On the wet grass she tried to understand me. Over the weeks the little cats got to trust us. Somewhere inside, they as much as me, as much as Carolyn, wanted a connection and for a while we found companionship. The kittens jumped into our laps and at any noise they'd scurry back into the wall. Carolyn would shake and laugh. It was there that she first started snaking her hands around each other. Inches from her face, she'd wrap and unwrap her lovely hands, in her excitement winding and rewinding her long graceful fingers.

My father worked at the enormous General Electric plant in Liverpool, and a nice man who worked with him asked if we'd join him and his son for a night at the colossal New York State Fair. It wasn't far from where we lived. The boy was a little older than I, maybe eleven. I remember that he was a friendly, outgoing kid. In the early evening we strolled around looking at farm implements and animals. We ended up on the big gaudy midway. The nice man's nice son wanted to go on the bumper cars. He'd ridden them before and was wild to do it again. The round little hot rods had a pedal, a steering wheel, and at the back a pole that curved up to a metal ceiling where it hissed and flashed sparks. They made a horrific grinding sound as they slammed into each other and that was the fun of it. It's an auto crash you walk away from, having had a good time.

When the chaos started my little car didn't move. The pedal was stuck, no sparks flamed from the pole, it was a dud. Everyone started bumping my car. Laughing people hurled themselves at me. Everyone was having a great time. The other kid kept calling my name and smashing into me. I felt frustrated not to be able to smash back.

My father and the boy's father were leaning against a fence that wrapped around the ride. It was the first time I saw that expression on my father's face. He was ashamed of me. Trapped in the broken bumper car, being knocked all over the place, I wasn't like a real boy. I remember thinking, "My father thinks I'm a sissy, and he's right. I walk in my sleep, and get terrible stomachaches. My father's right, and it makes me sick to hurt my father."

The kid's father thought I should get to take the ride again. "It's not fair," he said. "Bobby's car didn't work. It's wrong not to have had the ride."

"Forget it," my father said, "it's late."

CHAPTER 10

In the sixty-plus class at the Ninety-second Street "Y," Rose is ninety-nine. Her sister died last year and Rose feels guilty. Her sister was only ninety-six. "I'll be one hundred on July 1. It should have been me. I'm the oldest."

"How are you today, Rose?"

"I'm just marvelous." She means that she's not supposed to be anything else. "I'm almost one hundred and everyone says how good I look," and she does. Rose resents her caregiver. So many of the old people do. "It's my freedom," she says. "I can't move without being observed and it drives me mad. I miss even the semblance of independence. I know I'm old, but I still want not to have to answer to anyone. You think that's stupid, Bob?" She crooks a beautifully manicured index finger toward me. "Come a little closer, I want to tell you something."

I kneel to get right in front of her mouth. Her lips are close enough to tickle my ear. "I'm leaking," she whispers. "I can't stop peeing. I look *fine*." She draws the word into a long painful sound.

"I *am* fine, but everything I've got is a century old. The plumbing is leaking, drip, drip, drip. Oh Bob, it's such a bore." She smiles. "But whatta ya gonna do? It's wonderful to be here. What's a little drip when there's Shakespeare? When you read some important line and look over at me, it's worth it. In a lifetime, what's a little pee?"

Carolyn never understood about the toilet. For all the years I lived with my sister we engaged in futile plots and odd rituals calculated to get her to go just once on the toilet. I did thousands of impromptu little plays for my sister. The bathtub shower curtain was the proscenium. I'd stand in the tub behind the pink plastic ready to pull it aside—"I'm going to fool you. . . . I'm going to be a bunny and hop, hop, hop. . . . I've got a really stupid hat on (I'd make hats from bath towels). . . . You're going to laugh your head off when you see this stupid hat."

I'd act nuts because Carolyn loved it. She'd laugh until her twisted feet rose from the floor. She'd laugh until she shook and her hands started to twirl and wind, until tears rolled down her beautiful face. But she never once made the connection, not ever, not one single drop. Of course, a minute after she got up, she'd wet everything like all along we'd known she would.

One day on the farm our neighbor Mrs. Hull was visiting. When I came in from school, my mother decided that it was time for Carolyn to go into the bathroom. She disassembled all my sister's paraphernalia and placed her on the toilet. Carolyn didn't want to stay. By that time if she had any idea that she was being restrained, she'd panic. In 1949, though, this had just begun and my mother wasn't used to it. As she tried to reason with my sister, she was complaining, "This will drive me right out of my mind. How long can I keep this up?" Little did she know that she and my sister were just starting a dance they'd be locked into for almost fifteen years.

Maxine Hull was an old farm woman with large coarse hands and a plainspoken heartlessness. She was getting annoyed at the grotesque routine. My sister would throw her arms upward, leaving nothing to grab, and she'd slide to the floor trying to escape, leaving my mother to repeatedly lift her back onto the toilet. I saw the bizarre pas de deux over and over and all of it always for nothing, everyone in tears and for nothing.

Mrs. Hull snarled that there was "only one way to handle a child who won't do exactly what you want her to." Completely ignoring my sister's complex set of disabilities, not the least of which was cerebral palsy, Maxine Hull hauled off and smashed her. Carolyn wailed. Maxine grabbed her and continued to slap her head and arms. My mother was horrified. Finally Carolyn crawled into a corner under the dining room table. My intimidated mother acted like it was okay. "I'll try again later."

Maxine Hull also killed the kittens—plain country people handling things in a plain country way. There were enough cats.

My parents kept a friendship with Maxine and her husband, John. The last time I saw Mrs. Hull she was feeble and alone but I never lost the picture of what she did to Carolyn. It's like what Hamlet's father says.

> Leave her to heaven,
> And to those thorns that in her bosom lodge
> To prick and sting her.
>
> —*Hamlet*, 1.5

On Friday afternoons after the Caring Community, I meet more seniors at the Stein Center on the second floor of the International Center for the Disabled. It's a glass-and-steel complex that couldn't be more different from the little convent on Washington Square, and gets a much larger crowd. We used to meet in a run-down Boys Club on Twenty-ninth Street. For years we worked our way through

Shakespeare while kids dribbled and shot hoops in a gym on the floor above us. "Listen to the meter," I'd say, "the kids beating out iambic pentameter."

Just now we're working on *Troilus and Cressida*.

"Bob, listen, I gotta tell ya something." Bernie is edging me into a corner. He's been coming to the Shakespeare for years. He has an uncanny ability to retain what he's read. Like a computer he can fire out matching sentences written centuries apart. Bernie's main concern, though, is sex. Anything erotic in the text and he's right there bright-eyed with six ribald examples from the Greeks.

At the moment he's got that look on his face and he's lasciviously talking from the side of his mouth. "Viagra," he half whispers, "the doctor gave me Viagra." He makes a sour face. "You're still young, you don't know what it's like when no one's home down there." Half a century after my grandmother, people are still mumbling to me about "down there."

Bernie leans in. Behind his big glasses he's pulling me into focus. "I'm seventy-eight," he hollers, "and I can't get hard!" His pride's on the line. "A guy's gotta think he's still *ready* if ya know what I mean."

"So . . . how's it going?"

He coughs up a raucous hoarse laugh. "It's a disaster, absolutely nada." His look switches to worry. "The doctor says it could shoot my blood pressure through the roof. Too strong a dose and I could have a stroke or a heart attack." He suddenly rubs his hands together in a show of wicked anticipation, and in a booming stage whisper he bellows, "Ya know it just might be worth it. Everybody's gotta go sometime."

Like aging Olympians, the old push back against nature. Mostly death's not the terror it is for younger people. Philosophy's found a practical place.

> If it be now, 'tis not
> to come; if it be not to come, it will be now; if it be not
> now, yet it will come. The readiness is all.
>
> —*Hamlet*, 5.2

It's what Shakespeare is all about—life, community, and the "readiness."

An old lady at Stein is falling apart. Her world's collapsing one death at a time. She's been shifting to adjust, but a few weeks ago she took a spill and it looked as if she'd used up what was left of her jiggle room.

Blanche is a big woman who colors her sparse hair carrot. She meticulously styles what's left into a lacquered helmet with rivulets of bright pink scalp flashing through. She dabs her face white and red like the aged Elizabeth the First. She's got a bundle of geriatric ills, a voice like a Bronx truck driver, and I adore her.

At first glance I figured she wouldn't be much interested in Shakespeare. Fooled again. Week after week she sat way at the back of the room. Every few minutes she'd walk around to get her "circulation" going. Resting against a wall, with her phosphorescent hair and crimson cheeks, she looked like the Virgin Queen when she refused to sit or sleep, thinking to con death into passing her by.

A few years ago Blanche took over the attendance sheet. Hunched like a garden ornament, she ferociously guards the door. "Did you sign? If you want the Shakespeare, sign the sheet." She's the bulldog. Everyone else is the mailman. "Leave him alone," she barks. "Can't you people see he's got better things to do?" Anyone annoying becomes "you people." "Will you people sit down and stop disturbing everyone?"

When she took the fall she was on the street. Someone rushing past knocked her flat. Falls are a terror. Break something major and there goes the outside world. Despite her protests E.M.S. carted her off to the nearest hospital. The admitting doctor suspected depression and assigned her to the psychiatric ward for a "look-see."

Nancy called me. She's the director of the Stein Center. She's a wonderful person who's exactly right for her job. "Blanche has had a fall. She's in the hospital. What would you think of taking a walk after class tomorrow? It would do her a world of good to see you."

Blanche seemed so dainty without her facade, not ugly, not broken or weak, just fragile. The three of us sat in the hospital hallway. Blanche sat in the middle and talked about all the teenagers in the ward. "Drugs," she said, "they do such good and such harm. . . . I've been feeling down for a few months," she whispered. "Being here will help." She paused and smiled. "But I missed the Shakespeare. Today at one-thirty, when I knew that you were starting, I felt lost."

We talked about class. We kidded about sexy *Troilus and Cressida*. She acted pleased. Just like Nancy said, the visit did her good.

As we were leaving, Blanche said, "Maybe I'll be able to come next Friday." I remember thinking that the few blocks to the Stein Senior Center seemed like such a long way, but when I hugged her she was the happiest I'd seen her in years.

She made it to *Troilus and Cressida*. The very next Friday there she was stooped in her chair taking attendance. I know how it goes. She won't always come, but for now I love to see her all dolled up and protecting me as she lays down the law to new people. "Sign this sheet, here's a copy of the play, don't bother him with stupid stuff." On the piano next to where I stand she always leaves two small cartons of fruit juice and sometimes a banana. "Take a minute, have a sip, these people can wait." With no one left to take care of her, she looks out for me. Old ladies are very special in my life, they always have been.

That summer on the farm my father's mother came to visit, and she was so good-natured that she made us much happier, too. With all of us crowded into the small farmhouse, my grandmother slept with me in my single maple bed. In the lilac-smelling dark, she'd answer my long list of kid questions. Did she really have a brother Willy who died when he was nine? Did she think Carolyn would die? Had she ever heard of a blood clot, and did she know where on the big canvas pull-down maps her family came from?

"England," she said, "mostly. Yankees." Some on the *Mayflower*. Did I know what the *Mayflower* was? I did, Plymouth Rock, 1620.

"Who came on the *Mayflower*?" Was it her grandfather? She laughed at me. "Land O'Goshen, no!" It was her mother's great-great-great-great-great-grandfather. "His name was Jones." That was her mother's name, Johanna Jones. "Oh, and French," she said, "we are a very little bit French."

"France, a whole country just the size of Texas," Mrs. Stanley said to the third grade, "the capital is Paris." It was green on the roll-down map, just like the U.S.

With the plaid moon coming through my little boy's blue Bates curtains, my grandmother fibbed. "I speak French," she said. Did I want her to speak French to me?

"Oh yes, please!"

She rolled away, almost taking the whole sloppy mattress with her. "You tickle my back," she said. "I love having my back tickled. You tickle my back and I'll talk French."

Every night that August, after I asked a million questions, she'd click out the lamp and let me tickle the white mountain of lilac-smelling flesh above the curve of thin lace on her slippery cotton nightgown. Suspended just before sleep, she'd mumble words that to my nine-year-old ears sounded like the magic of French.

"La lu mon pu cheri bon bon la pu."

"What did you just say, Grandma?"

"Huh?" Nodding from my worshipful tickle, she'd invent, "Oh . . . I said that heliotropes are purple and that stars are gas."

Like a gigantic John Falstaff in the midsummer moonlight, she beguiled me and I'd gladly have done anything she'd lead me to.

Marry then sweet wag, when thou art king let
    not us that are squires of the night's body be called
    thieves of the day's beauty: let us be Diana's foresters,
    gentlemen of the shade, minions of the moon; and let

men say we be men of good government, being
governed as the sea is, by our noble and chaste
mistress the moon, under whose countenance we steal.
                                    —*King Henry IV, Part I*, 1.2

The new Stein Senior Center where Blanche saves me her juice
from lunch is just around the corner from the Veterans Hospital
where I started to lose Joe. Now every Friday on my dash from
Caring to Stein, I look down the block and remember that raw day
we read *Richard the Second* up on the fourth floor.

Let's talk of graves, of worms, and epitaphs,
Make dust our paper, and with rainy eyes
Write sorrow on the bosom of the earth.
                                    —*King Richard II*, 3.2

We'd been in the waiting room for a couple of hours when a
family from Staten Island bounced in. The pale old dad sat in a
corner while his kids joked around and devoured pounds of
McDonald's fries. They smiled at me and Joe with our matching
paperbacks. "Poor old guy," they probably thought. "The son
must be an English teacher. Bastard! Making the old man read
Shakespeare."

"I can't stand this," Joe whispered. "They're so noisy it's making me nuts. Let's go someplace else."

A nurse finally appeared. "Excuse me, my friend has an
appointment."

"Be patient." She sounded Jamaican. "We'll get to you."

We found a dead-end hall with a west-facing window and we
sat on the hospital rug.

"You tired, Joe?"

"Not at all. It's keeping my mind off things."

We didn't finish the play that day. We finished it six weeks later at the upstate V.A. when Joe was in a wheelchair and he looked like cardboard. I really didn't know him, just through the Shakespeare. He didn't have a phone and he was determined that I never see where he lived.

One day before he landed upstate, he surprised me. At the Sirovich Senior Center on East Twelfth Street, I always sat on top of a kitchen table. A retired Sicilian barber cut hair in a back corner. The rolling blackboard in the lobby always had Elizabethan spelling, "1:30 kitchen Shakspar Bob."

We were working our way through *Antony and Cleopatra* when Joe showed up. I'd never seen him at Sirovich. By then some people followed me from place to place, but I'd only seen Joe on Thursdays at Fulton—and he'd been absent from there for a while. At the V.A. they'd found signs of a recurring cancer. He looked awful, smelled sour, and hadn't shaved or changed clothes in a while.

"I have a book for you," he said. "It's Dante and Beatrice on the Ponte Vecchio." He looked around at the gang of mostly Jewish seniors. "Hitler gave orders not to bomb that bridge." The crowd looked startled. "I walked all the way over here." He was limping badly. He smiled. "Who knows what's comin'. I wanted you to have this."

"Today it's *Antony and Cleopatra,* Joe, the Battle at Actium. Stay, we'll talk later."

"No time. Be back on Thursdays the minute I feel better." He kissed me. Nobody got impatient, they know there's a contract. It's mostly unspoken but it's in blood and the kisses are a part of it. Everyone loves the kisses. I love the kisses.

The last time I saw Joe was the Sunday I took the Orange Line bus upstate. He'd called. "I'm scared, Professor. I'm pissing my pants. This is it."

He wanted to finish the play but he kept falling asleep. He was dying. I'm used to it now, but that was the first time, and I wasn't sure what to do.

The following Thursday there was a message at Fulton. The program director handed me a little pink While You Were Out note. It was from Joe's niece. "Joe died. He wanted you to know how much he missed the Shakespeare."

His life was gentle, and the elements
So mix'd in him, that Nature might stand up
And say to all the world, 'This was a man!'
—*Julius Caesar*, 5.5

CHAPTER 11

AFTER THE summer of talking French we drove my father's mother the eight hours to the big brown house over on East Broadway, and when we got back to Liverpool my father said, "We're moving back to Stratford. We're going to live down the street from your grandmother. You'll like it." And we left the bleak house on the monotonous road as suddenly as we'd moved there the year before.

My mother was grateful to desert the lonely farm. During the few years we spent in upstate New York she had developed more headaches and spent more time in bed. Somewhere along the way she started to watch her own sadness. Like a Shakespearean heroine, she'd begun observing herself.

For about a month after we'd left the farm my mother was unrecognizable. Being near her family again let her be more like a mother. She even went with me to register in the principal's office down in the basement of Center School. I was ecstatic. She got dressed up in gloves and a little hat.

In layers of lipstick and vermilion rouge, it was easy to see that she and Claire were sisters. "Are my seams straight? Any lipstick on my teeth?" She'd lick her palm to flatten my cowlick. "Why won't it lie down?" Sitting with her legs crossed in the principal's office, she looked like a movie mother. Mr. Westly was handsome with grayish hair and a pencil-thin mustache. He was soft and polite as my nervous mother puffed away and continually pinched little bits of tobacco from the tip of her tongue, hiding her terror in smoke and rapid-fire chat.

I was assigned to Mrs. Burke's fourth grade. When I arrived in late October, she was finishing a month's reading of *Little Lord Fauntleroy*. Pretty Mrs. Burke leaned against her desk crossing one ankle over the other, holding the book just at chest level. She was spellbinding and I had a crush right away. She spoke to me as if I were the most important nine-year-old she'd ever had the privilege of teaching.

Just down the block from the school we'd moved into the ground floor of a massive Victorian house. The owners, Mrs. McGill and her sister, Jenny, lived above us in dead quiet with the penetrating ticks of opposing clocks. Their brother had worked for the New York, New Haven & Hartford train line, and he'd left his eccentric sisters the gargantuan set of railroad clocks.

Not accustomed to tenants and nervous about the water bill, the old ladies wouldn't let us have a washing machine. Because of Carolyn that was a terrible hardship. In a deep sink my mother smashed and mashed and squeezed and rinsed only to have to start all over again an hour later. For the two years we lived at 840 East Broadway, the apartment was a maze of dripping bedclothes, but just outside, the little town was perfect for a kid looking to belong. It still is.

It's where I live now, less than a five-minute walk from my old school. Unlike fancier places closer to New York, Stratford is mostly working class and an unashamed architectural muddle. On the six-minute walk to the 8:03 a score of stoic colonials stand squeezed by perky sixties ranches and a handful of nineteenth-century homesteads, hanging on as seedy boardinghouses. Around the corner on Main Street a couple of seventies additions shame the beautiful churches they're tacked to. At my corner the cement and brick rectangle of the Knights of Columbus sits like an over-scaled garage between turreted Edwardian homes long since converted into mostly unrented office space.

When I was in high school much of what was beautiful got ripped down for the superhighway that slashes through what was the oldest part of town. But when I was ten at Center School, Stratford was still far more connected to the nineteenth century than to the edge of the twenty-first. It was more the world of my grandparents' childhood.

While we'd been away living on that long straight country road in Liverpool, my mother's mother had missed me, and when we came back to Stratford, Nana decided to be my best friend. Nervous about not knowing anyone again, I was happy to accept her offer. I'd take the C. R. & L. after school to meet her in downtown Bridgeport. I'd get off the bus just across from the tiny Mr. Peanut peanut shop where she'd greet me with a little greasy bag of hot cashews, "Hello, Robert, fix your tie."

Fifty years ago we must have looked like a *Saturday Evening Post* cover, me in the tie and short pants and my grandmother in a silly hat. She'd grown up with fifteen brothers and sisters. By the time she was my grandmother only two brothers and that sister we'd stayed with in Florida were left. Like a lot of poor immigrant girls, Nana spent her childhood working. That's how she met my grandfather. Just back from the Merchant Marine, he was the handsome curly-haired chauffeur at a great house in Southport. Margaret Hennessy was a sixteen-year-old undermaid.

Burnishing Beaux Arts peacockery in a mansion on Long Island Sound, she developed a lifelong romance with "things." Over lunch in department store cafeterias she'd muse about exquisite draperies and extraordinary polishes on hall tables.

Nana McKeon was pious and artificially proper. In old pictures it's obvious that she's vain. On an automobile running board in a raccoon coat or straight-backed in a photo studio rowboat, her propriety looks acted. In picture after picture she affects misery at a circus or on a farm with sheep. Even with her own children there's detachment. My mother was cripplingly timid, her sister, Claire, knocked down by alcohol, and their brother Bob seems to have fled my grandparents the minute he left high school. But I was different. Nana was completely at ease because we were so alike.

When I was nine and back from the cornfields, she decided to share her passion for beautiful objects. Her classroom was the china department of any dry-goods store, and Bridgeport had two. In the fall of 1950, Howlands and D. M. Read's were shrines for old Irish women. At soda fountains or in the ladies lounges, my grandmother recited endless catechisms on the trivia of other people's lives.

"And dear Mrs. Eckwall, how's the cat? And your granddaughter, Mrs. O'Boyle? Have the doctors in New York found what's tormenting the wee thing? Mrs. Kiley, is it the priesthood that young Maurice would be after? My own grandson here, Robert, has an eye for the cloth and don't ya just think he'd be a handsome fella in a collar? Robert, sit up straight, ya wouldn't want to end up stoop-shouldered on the altar now, would ya?"

The department stores seemed glad to have us. To encourage staying they set luxurious benches in make-believe gardens. D. M. Read's constructed a gorgeous atrium with tufted settees to urge conversation. Everything was painted apricot or dusty rose, gentle old-lady colors. In their youth my grandparents glimpsed great wealth from the chauffeur's apartment up over a row of garages. All these years later in temples of commerce, my elderly grandmother could have lunch, leave a "decent" tip, and after she

reapplied her lipstick and patted each side of her nose with a tiny
powderless puffless powder puff, move on to buy a dish or hat.

"Jesus H. Christ! You are not gonna wear that thing! Not with
me you're not. No wife of mine will make a jackass out of me.
Take it back." Then my grandfather would look over at me. "And
what were *you* thinking?" Overwrought, he'd go soprano. "You
should stop her. She's a fool and you encourage her. She looks like
a tart. Maggie, you can make an ass of yourself, but ya won't make
one of me."

To my grandfather a red hat was the courtesan's code. Harold
McKeon thought that a wife should have very good shoes and an
excellent watch. She should otherwise be smart enough to handle
the money, the house, the food, and the education of the children
all without drawing the least attention to herself. Nana fit the bill
on all his requirements except that she liked being fashionable, too
fashionable. And she loved red hats. On our sojourns to downtown, she bought dozens of red hats and swore to him she'd take
them back.

When I was fourteen, on one of the last nights I slept up in my
grandparents' wood-smelling attic, Nana showed me an old pine
cupboard tucked away under an eave and covered in a carefully
ironed strip of yellow muslin. Behind two pierced tin doors was a
lifetime's collection of squirreled-away red hats.

I only saw her wear one once. We'd just come back from downtown when my grandmother received a phone call from a man
who'd worked on the Sturges's estate with my young grandparents.
Apparently he'd been in love with my grandmother all those years
ago, and before he retired to join his children in California, he
needed one last peep at the "little blonde." At the time Nana was
miffed at my grandfather about something, and in a showy over-
polite way, she invited the old butler to stop by for a piece of cake
and a drink.

When the strident doorbell rang, as usual my grandfather had
his head buried in the cathedral radio. From the other side of her

closed bedroom door Nana called out, "Robert, will you get that? *His highness* is too *thick* to be polite." I went down the phenomenally polished front stairs to open the door for the bashful little man. Like a serf he held his hat just in front of his mouth. "Is Margaret Hennessy here?" He used her maiden name.

I showed him up the stairs and past my grandfather's chilly greeting and out she came, new dress, new shoes, gloves, and a ludicrous feathery red hat. My grandfather turned off the radio and joined them in the living room. They had a couple of hours of Irish whiskey and memories. No one mentioned the hat.

Nana taught me about beauty in the china departments in Read's and Howlands, where table settings hung, defying gravity, on impeccable beige walls.

"Which one?" Nana would ask. She'd have us stand back on the rounded steps just far enough to see all the dishes at once. "Which pattern is the best?" I always picked Moss Rose. Botanical and too organic to be pretty or feminine, I liked it best. "Why?" she'd ask, "why always that one?"

"I like it, Nana. I like the colors. I think it's beautiful. I'd be proud to own it."

"What a sweet little boy, what a smart good-looking little boy!" the saleslady would purr as Nana unwittingly continued driving gold spikes into the coffin of my maleness. Those afternoons when I was ten and all dressed up being a very good boy and having a wonderful time, those afternoons when other boys were playing baseball, I felt something else, too, something that made me ashamed.

"What table would go with those dishes? Or chairs? Let's walk over to Mr. Nothnagle's and pick a table to go with the Moss Rose dish. You're absolutely sure it's the Moss Rose?" We'd take the elevator down and the little boy in short pants and the old white-haired lady (who was younger than I am today) walked out of

D. M. Read's and through the arcade to Nothnagle's Furniture Store to find a perfect table to complement the moss rose pattern.

"Mr. Nothnagle, could you get someone to put that big table *and* the eight chairs over here? We like it where it is but my grandson thinks it looks more cherry than mahogany. We'd want to see it in the sunlight, and thank you very much." It was a kind of madness. We did it over and over again, at least twice a week for a couple of years.

We were friends, Nana and me. She asked me about my thoughts, not afraid like my parents of what the answers might be.

I was forty when I rented a summer house, desolate and beautiful on the coast of Maine. Noisy seals barked on the rocks just outside the windows, I painted and stared astonished at inky night skies with uncountable stars. On my way back to New York I stopped in a food market in Brunswick. In the next aisle just over the canned goods, I saw her. I was stunned. "Nana, what are you doing all the way up here?" As she turned, familiarity melted to embarrassment. Of course it wasn't her.

An hour outside of New York I stopped at my parents', no one home. I felt for the extra key on the rusty nail, near the clothesline. Inside there were folding chairs folded in stacks everywhere and flowers. Had I missed some birthday? Then I saw the book. On the hutch in the hall between the kitchen and dining room was a register from Dennis and D'Arcy Funeral Home, Margaret Elizabeth McKeon. My crazy parents hadn't bothered to call me. My mother was out of her mind with grief and my father had never once talked to me on the telephone. My grandmother had had a fall and in a week she was dead. When I read Shakespeare to beautiful ladies in their eighties I miss her.

* * *

"I had a son, his name was Ike, he died. Tell me where it's from, that piece you read about the dead child? Please, what play is it in?" Since AIDS, it happens over and over again. "Tell me about Shakespeare's dead son. Do you think he died of a plague, too?" as they try to make sense of it. A picture in a wallet. "Look," old people say, "this is my beautiful child, he died a year ago . . . three years . . . last month. Read it again, that part about grief. Would you write down where it's from and please would you read it again."

> Grief fills the room of my absent child,
> Lies in his bed, walks up and down with me,
> Puts on his pretty looks, repeats his words,
> Remembers me of all his gracious parts,
> Stuffs out his vacant garments with his form;
> Then have I reason to be fond of grief?
>
> —*King John*, 3.3

Shakespeare says it exactly as they feel, only better, much much better.

A month after I began at Center School, the landlady started to worry about me. Carolyn had broken her collarbone and the toilet battles continued. My parents isolated me at the front of the apartment, but it was impossible to escape my sister's wailing. My mother didn't like Mrs. McGill or her sister, Jenny, because of the washing. Their manner was gruff and I think she was afraid of them, but they were always nice to me. I was, after all, a polite kid who knew how to turn down a piece of cake or a quarter.

"Robert can't possibly study with that racket going on. How on earth do you expect him to get anything done? Let him come to us after school. We'll make tea and see that he finishes his homework away from all that dreadful noise."

My mother thought it was a good idea but I was nervous about studying in front of the landlady and her smoky sister. Jenny was cadaverous and dyed her hair the same oxblood color I slapped on my Buster Browns. She powdered her face until it beaded into the deep crevices around her eyes and mouth. She had a stevedore's cough from cartons of Camels. Jenny's rasping breath was the only other sound in the ticking silence of the sisters' somber parlor.

But right after Thanksgiving I started to sit at their big oak table with late-afternoon sun dribbling across the lace tablecloth, my books and pencils, a ruler, a pencil sharpener, tea, and two Arnold lemon cookies in front of me. The two women sat there, too—Jenny smoking and coughing and Mrs. McGill reading a newspaper. Both childless old ladies focused on my every move. If I looked up they'd cry out in unison, "Anything wrong? Do you need something? Is there something we can get for you? Do you want more tea?" They'd whisper like it was a mortal sin, "Do you need to use the bathroom?"

Every day they made sickening Lapsang souchong tea and set out the two cookies. Every day, except the days I went downtown to look at dishes with Nana, we'd sit across from each other, the dueling railroad clocks challenging the silence with not quite syncopated ticks. *Tick, ta tick, ta tick, tick, tick, ta tick, ta tick, tick.* It wooed me to sleep, but if my head dropped a quarter of an inch there they'd be. "Do you need something?" Shrouded behind thick winter curtains with the ceiling light ceremoniously snapped on at 3:30, then in springtime with sheers blowing across the table, I sat with the two caring old women who knew less than nothing about being with a kid, though maybe not less than I did.

It's early September. Autumn is barely beginning to thread through the warm breeze. Today I pruned back a ravening rambler that has spent the summer devouring the east wall of my kitchen. For a couple of years now this broken house has been my sanctuary. I've filled it with model sailboats and wooden oars I've found lost near the river. Weather-beaten birdhouses swing on the crooked porch and a family of cardinals frolic in a venerable mountain laurel that presses against the bubbled front windows. Scorching days and snowy, the little red birds flash through the enameled leaves.

People have an emotional response to the place, even the delivery guy from Jerry's Shakespeare Pizza. Anyone can see that there's an intended innocence here, a sense that harm isn't let in. Like up in those old trees by the swamp behind my grandfather's barn, there's a palpable atmosphere of safety.

In the September Sunday morning quiet I can hear the kids next door. They're noisy running around behind carved railings on their big yellow and white porch. Last week Hannah helped me to paint my side steps, of course she painted mostly herself. She likes it when I lift her over the fence to drop down for an adventure on this side, in my world. All summer in her high chair at an open window, she called, "Hi Bob! Hi Bob! Hi Bob!" Like a tropical bird almost invisible behind a lace curtain she screeched my ordinary name over and over.

Her brother stopped me at the fence last week for a talk about teeth.

"What about teeth?" I asked.

"Pointy teeth," he was convulsed with giggles, "and gooey stuff that stretches over everything."

As usual it took me a minute to put it together—Halloween! He's delighted telling me about Dracula and stringy fake cobwebs. He's getting ready to scare everyone, and maybe mostly himself.

The little family seems so neat, no rough spots showing, nothing much scarier than the purchased Halloween horrors.

It's what a gardener once told me about a tulip bulb, if you slice it right down the middle everything's already inside. The miniature stem, leaves, flower, are all compressed and ready to burst out. You can see exactly what it's all going to be.

That's what it's like next door. The sweet children will become the nice simple parents and they'll teach their own baby boy to play baseball and train his adored sister to answer to "Who's the prettiest girl?"

"I am!" Hannah shrieks before the question's even finished.

The mother stays home to be with the kids and happy, bored, gets chunky from snacks. The dad comes home for lunch. *Beep! Beep!*, short almost inaudible bursts of Volvo car horn coming up the drive. *Beep! Beep!*, like recognizable lowing and the little calves tumble out to greet him.

It's so old-fashioned and anachronistic. It's what my parents pretended to be, dreamed of being, couldn't be. And sometimes it makes me, the odd other-side-of-the-fence observer, feel . . . intergalactic.

CHAPTER 12

Iₙ ᴛʜᴇ ᴋɪᴛᴄʜᴇɴ at the Sirovich Senior Center on East Twelfth Street two women are arguing. Dora and Rosemary have been friends for seventy years. They're wildly loyal to what they call "The Shakespeare."

Like Blanche, the woman at Stein, Dora takes attendance. "Sign your name," she hollers. "If you don't we lose funding and you can kiss Mr. Shakespeare good-bye. Wanna say bye-bye to Shakespeare? . . . I didn't think so."

At the moment I walked in, Dora was making a point by shoving her finger at Rosemary's chest. "He's a bum. No two ways about it. He's a drunk and a bum and I don't care how handsome he is. I wouldn't stay with him for five minutes."

"She's no saint," Rosemary snapped. "Just look at how she plays with him. He's married. She should leave him alone."

One of the men looked over at me. "Listen to the two of them," he said. "They sound like they'll kill each other. They must be fighting over some geriatric maniac in the bridge club."

"He's a bum."

"She's the bum."

"He is."

"She is."

"Shut up."

"You shut up."

"Ladies, what's going on?"

"What else?" Dora smiled. "We've been at this all week. . . .
Antony and Cleopatra, he's a bum."

"She is."

"He is."

It's not just the poetry that engages everyone.

People ask all the time: "Did Shakespeare's audience understand all these words? What about ordinary people? Were they swamped by metaphor and classical allusions?" Of course the plays weren't meant to be taken apart and analyzed. Any scrutiny of the details proves frustrating. Geography's fanciful. There are seacoasts in landlocked kingdoms. Ships travel west to go east. History's worse. People occupy the stage together who lived generations apart. None of this matters in the least. If you're watching the time line or how old Hotspur actually was at Shrewsbury, you've missed the point far beyond Shakespeare's miscalculated miles.

It's the language that's everyone's domain. It doesn't belong only to the educated or the clever. Shakespeare argues constantly that words can be dangerous in their seduction, they just might not signify the intent of the speaker: "These fellows of infinite tongue who can rhyme themselves into a lady's favor can always reason themselves out again, a speaker's but a prater a rhyme's but a ballad. . . ."

Geography aside, Shakespeare's language can be shockingly precise. As a kid I longed to understand the world I was in, and words mattered. When I was ten or eleven I started to do my own research.

"Go to the library. It's halfway between school and College Place. It's quiet and you can do your homework and learn the Dewey Decimal System."

Starting the first week of January, the year that I was in Miss Wilcoxson's fifth grade, I stopped sitting in Mrs. McGill's parlor and instead walked down Main Street to the little gray-stone library.

The room would be considered small by standards of important city libraries. In 1894 the architect had lined it with dark oak and in each corner he'd set a large gray pillar. Down at the east end over an elaborate fireplace, a brooding portrait of the founder, Birdseye Blakeman, glowered with Yankee reserve. When I was ten each big table had its own set of tall bronze reading lamps with parchment shades. The effect was rather grand for a little town library, more like a baronial drawing room than a place for a fifth grader to learn his sevens tables. It was a kind of stage set designed for the act of reading.

The place was completely silent. The gardenia-smelling librarian made sure it stayed that way. Miss Russell also showed me that a lot of the things people thought worthy to write down were all around me.

In the beautiful little granite library I started to look up words about my sister, words like retardation, blood clot, grand mal. And I'd found my way to "naked." I knew what it meant of course, but it started to feel very good just to look at the word, to mouth it silently to myself.

Naked—completely unclothed; bare, nude, uncovered, exposed without protection, additions, ornaments, disguises or embellishments, plain, stark.

Staring into the big *Webster's Second Edition,* copyright 1939, I said it along with my sister's words, "abnormal, impaired . . . naked."

One February day I came into the library out of a heavy downpour. There were piles of newspaper on the marble vestibule floor. From behind the carved oak counter the librarian warned, "Drip where you are, don't bring all that wet in here." Without looking up she continued, "Put your umbrella and galoshes in the coat rack."

What umbrella? What galoshes?

"No rubbers?" She squinted over her glasses. "Are your feet wet? You must be drenched! You'll catch pneumonia!" The gruff old maid acted the concerned mother. "Take off your shoes and socks. We'll put them on the radiator." She handed me a fistful of rough brownish paper towels. "Dry your hair before you get sick and drip on the papers. Don't move until you're through dripping."

Standing barefoot on the pile of pungent newsprint, I looked around. We seemed to be alone. . . . "Who's the window supposed to be?"

Opposite where I stood leaking, up on the fireplace wall, was a little round stained-glass portrait. Before then I'd never noticed it. It's the image of a bald fat man with a silly pointed beard and a cockamamy mustache that curves up goofy at the corners. When I was in the fifth grade, Mr. Truman was the president and the boys I knew got zip haircuts that left no hair. Nobody in my life had any face hair except Jesus, Santa Claus, and placid Mr. Westley, my grammar school principal. The moronic man in the rain-beaten window looked like a baker or a German butcher or Oliver Hardy. I knew all about Stan Laurel and Oliver Hardy because the little brick movie theater had started to become my nighttime hiding place. For two dimes I'd watch a couple of cartoons, a *March of Time, Selected Short Subjects,* and two different movies (one in Technicolor)—and I saw it all *twice.*

The librarian was stamping a diminishing stack of oaktag cards that towered in front of her, *cha-chink, cha-chink*. I rubbed my wet hair as hard as I could with the paper towels and rolled my thick gray corduroys up my legs.

"Can I come in now, Miss Russell, I won't mess anything?"

"Put these magazines on a chair. Sit on *them*. Your socks will be dry in fifteen minutes." *Cha-chink, cha-chink, cha-chink.*

"Nine times seven is sixty-three . . . ten times seven is seventy . . ." Eventually she tucked my shoes under the big oak table and with my warm, neatly folded yellow and green argyles, she dropped a little book at my elbow. "Eleven times seven is . . . seventy-seven."

Stamped in gold on the dark blue cover was the same pudgy face as the window. Along the side in bright gold letters, "William Shakespeare—*The Merchant of Venice*." I opened it. I could see right away that it was a play. When I was ten I hated plays. Starting as a scratchy six-year-old crepe paper carrot on Holy Rosary's health day, I'd been making my reluctant, shy way through nerve-racking Christmas plays and spring festivals.

The Merchant of Venice
William Shakespeare
Actus Primus. Scene I
Venice

Enter Antonio, Salarino, and Solanio
ANTONIO   In sooth I know not why I am so sad. . . .

In sooth I know not why I am so sad. . . .

I read it again. Ten simple monosyllabic words and of course I couldn't know what sooth meant, but it's hardly necessary. It changes nothing in the simple declarative sentence, a sentence that could not more perfectly describe the kid reading it. Suddenly the little colored window seemed much more alive in the emerging late-afternoon winter sun.

I think that the more confused you are inside, the more you

need to trust a thing outside of yourself. I was desperate to lean against something bigger than me, and it was clear that William Shakespeare understood what it's like to ache and not know why.

In our house silence was the code. Like many people, we avoided talking about what most needed talking about. Shakespeare became my secret language, an ancient remote cuneiform speech that somehow made me more visible to myself. I see it all the time now. When a phrase ignites the room with some compelling truth I watch people thrill to the confirmation. "Yes," they say, "that's it! That's exactly what I think. *When* did he write that?"

Of course my excitement about Shakespeare had nothing to do with his position at the zenith of English literature or even that he too was born in a town named Stratford. I didn't know anything about him personally and I didn't care. Shakespeare was like staring at the religious calendars or the Latin Mass. Poetry became a beautiful place to hide from my life and from my parents, a place I knew they'd never follow me to.

In New York, on her sixtieth birthday, my mother was angry at herself for putting on some weight. She'd had a bit to drink and was making too much fuss about not having even a taste of birthday cake. Everyone insisted that she was beautiful and that cake was in order. She snapped. She threw her whiskey sour across my living room.

"Stop," I said, calmer than I felt. "Don't be foolish. Have cake or don't have cake, what does it matter?"

"You," she snarled, "you're nuts!" And from nowhere, "Is Shakespeare *all* you care about?"

And truly the meanest I ever saw her get, she bent forward leering at me with slow-motion alcoholic blinks. "Nobody on this whole earth gives a damn about Shakespeare except you!" She spoke it as if exposing a deep long-buried truth that everyone but me knew. Her voice was thick with the resentment of a too long held rancor. William Shakespeare was the first name on an inventory list of superior adversaries that, terrifying, had to be hated. She had never forgiven me for joining the enemy.

Of course my first response to Shakespeare was connected to fervent Catholicism. That March I'd started a year's preparation for Confirmation. At the ceremony when the eleven-year-old is officially admitted to the "army of the faith" he gets to choose a name to add to what the parents gave at baptism. The saint who's chosen is a sponsor, an influence for life. For me it had to be the Apostle John. He was the youngest, the best-looking, and Christ's favorite. But I picked John on a far more esoteric ground. The nun at Holy Rosary once told us children that Jesus had asked John what special favor he might want. John didn't ask to be rich, or for any ordinary personal good. He wanted to see the end of the world, *the end of the world!*

Not hiding like all the others, John was right there at the crucifixion. Blood-spattered and agonized, there he was in a Caravaggio or a Piero della Francesca, on my grandmother's pantry door, Horatio to his Hamlet. "And choirs of angels sing thee to thy rest."

John wasn't afraid of what's to be afraid of—the end of the world, fire and terror, chaos and condemnation, the apocalypse— and beautiful brave young John saw it all, just like Shakespeare did in *King Lear*.

So in the spring that I was eleven, with a ceremonial slap from the bishop's chubby nail-polished fingers, I got to be Robert William John Smith. *William* and *John*. "In sooth I know not why I am so sad."

CHAPTER 13

I<small>T WAS A</small> Sunday afternoon and we were sliding on ice, making our weekly trip back from my mother's parents. For years, right after Mass, we'd eat a big formal meal at their polished mahogany dining table. White pepper was in the air. They all loved white pepper; everyone sneezing in the sunny, powdery room while Nana pleaded forgiveness. . . .

"I can't cook. I burn everything. It's that oven, I just can't get used to that damn oven." She'd owned it since my mother was twelve. Rather than cook my grandmother would have much preferred to be kneeling teary in the speckled dark at the back of Saint Charles in front of the plaster Michelangelo or, better yet, mugging, vain and self-critical, at her reflection in the big round mirror of Howlands hat department.

"Oh well, if you eat with the McKeons you're taking your life in your hands," she'd settle it by making it our responsibility.

In the late-afternoon winter light, my mother, grandmother, and aunt Claire silently washed what looked like hundreds of dishes while my father and grandfather filled the faded chintz living room with smoke. Not ever able to say much to each other, they listened half asleep to the enormous radio while I sat with Carolyn on the ebony floor, pretending to play.

"Check her, Bobby," my mother would call out from the kitchen, "check her. We'll be leaving soon. It's going to snow and we'll be slipping and sliding on the hill." My mother was terrified to be in a car when the roads were icy. My mother was terrified to be in a car. My mother was terrified.

At a quarter of five my father would drive us back over the Boston Avenue hill to Stratford for supper with his family and a night of noisy poker with his brothers. As usual about halfway over the hill my mother was sure, we all were, that Carolyn had had an "accident." That's what we called it, an "accident," as if it was a surprise and might not happen again.

"Do you smell something?" Annoyed and nervous about the icy streets, my mother would turn to me. "Check her, Bobby. She had a B.M. just before we left Grandma's. See if she has a 'load.' Do you smell something, Ray?"

If we'd run out of clothes it meant going home first. Fulfilling the only part that she still could from her *Marjorie's Maytime* dream, my mother insisted that Carolyn always look gorgeous. Over and over again all day and night, we dressed her like a beautiful doll. She wore pretty little girl's underclothes, starched dresses, those tiny rolled-down socks. If we had enough clothes with us it meant we'd arrive at my father's parents with Carolyn smelly, crying, and needing an immediate change. She was eight and no longer the adorable infant from whom you might expect and accept such things. And of course she'd be uncomfortable, which made her miserable and resistant.

On that particular snowy February twilight, we didn't make it to my father's parents. Running late and nervous on the ice, the familiar litany of accusations was dragged out.

Her: "I told you if we would just . . ."

Him: "Why didn't you . . . You never . . ."

Her: "It's not my fault, don't start blaming me."

Him: "It's not my fault, don't blame me."

This kind of exchange always accelerated until my exhausted mother got what she'd wanted in the first place.

"That's it," she'd say. And that *was* it. After "that's it," nothing could happen for days.

"I'm not going anyplace now," she'd snap, hitting all the consonants. "Let's just go home." So home we'd go. My mother would get a "sick headache" and go to bed.

Besides my name, the six words my poor sister's mind could retain were car, ick (for ice cream), an indiscernible angry two-syllable word that sounded like snot-wha, and a simple three-word sentence. She would say it clearly each time with exactly the same parrotlike inflection. She'd furrow her brow and like an angry drill sergeant she'd rata-tat-tat fire out, "*Go to bed!*"

Bobby, car, ick, snot-wha, and *go to bed* were the only words my sister ever spoke in the almost twenty years that I lived with her. Sometimes I thought she might be mocking our mother. Exasperated past coping, my mother would yell, "I'm going to bed," slamming one door or another.

"Go to bed!" Carolyn would echo. "*Go to bed.*"

The atmosphere was packed with a polluted sickness as Carolyn and I sat on the floor listening outside my parents' bedroom door.

"I need some tea for my pills," my mother would whisper or, "Can you make me some soup? I can hardly see it hurts so bad," and I knew that it did. At the foot of my parents' four-poster, with Carolyn hanging on me, I'd watch my mother hidden under blankets dazed and medicated.

MACBETH   How does your patient, Doctor?

DOCTOR   Not so sick, my Lord,
        As she is troubled with thick-coming fancies,
        That keep her from her rest.

MACBETH   Cure her of that:
   Canst thou not minister to a mind diseas'd,
   Pluck from the memory a rooted sorrow,
   Raze out the written troubles of the brain,
   And with some sweet oblivious antidote
   Cleanse the stuff'd bosom of that perilous stuff
   Which weighs upon the heart?
DOCTOR   Therein the patient
   Must minister to himself.

—Macbeth, 5.3

"You are such a good boy. I can always count on you. Do you smell something? Oh God, not again. You are such a good boy. I don't know what I'd do without you, don't forget to wipe her good."

"Don't forget to wipe her good."

The iambic line could be on my tombstone, "Don't forget to wipe her good."

On that February Sunday, skidding over the Boston Avenue hill, I pressed my face against the cold car window listening to tire chains, like the librarian stamping the frozen streets—*cha-chink, cha-chink, cha-chink*. I watched the dim neighborhoods clap past—*cha-chink, cha-chink*. It was spitting snow when we stopped at the traffic light just before Boston Avenue turns left into Barnum, in front of Holy Name Church.

At the red light my parents sniped at each other in the chilly chiaroscuro of the front seat. My face was cool against the pelted car window. "No school tomorrow," I thought.

On the street corner up over a paint store was a billboard. Through the falling snow, lit by big bare bulbs, the poster was an advertisement for candy, Valentine's candy. "Huge heart-shaped, rouge-colored, satin boxes filled with elaborate chocolate poop,"

I thought. For years everything reminded me of nauseating excrement.

The billboard was an adorable joke, a sort of good-natured commercial irony.

A boy was offering a pretty girl a couple of wilted half-dead flowers. In her precious red and white Valentine's dress, she looked sweetly disappointed. The illustrator had caught in her face a tactful letdown. In the atmosphere of anger and the dreadful odor in the backseat I felt hurt for the poster kid's shattered expectations.

The picture was a coy joke. Behind his back, the little boy balanced the biggest, reddest heart-shaped box a kid could imagine. So that after she'd been polite and accepted his stingy bouquet, the boy would laugh a kid's, jokey "gotcha" laugh and would whip the gigantic satin heart from behind his back. "Surprise!"

"I could shoot you, Ray." They were in full swing in the front seat.

There was something about the little poster girl's gentle letdown that got to me. I knew very well that it was just a way to sell boxes of chocolate, but the picture hurt me.

"Don't be so thin skinned. Stop being so sensitive." A million times in my life I've been told to care less, to just not let hurt in. My mother used to say "You'll make yourself sick." Who could know better than she?

We took Carolyn home and put all her clothes in the sink. My father was slumped in the dark smoking, watching Sunday night TV, but my mother wasn't finished. From her bed she'd yell "Turn *that thing* down!" She'd call TV "that thing." "Whatta ya, deaf?" she'd say. She still does, only now he is. "I hate TV. G.D. waste of time." Like a lonely kid begging for attention she'd call out from the dark, "How anyone can just sit in front of a television watching stupid stuff is beyond me. Whatta ya, *deaf* and *dumb*?"

The fights were skirmishes in a lifelong war about shame. My parents didn't ask too many questions about the meaning of things.

Some wild recipe of fate, nature, God, sin, retribution, and "just plain luck," my mother called it, these were the unstoppable winds blowing through everyone's existence. Bad luck was just that, bad luck. A hard life was something "you make the most of." It was rough to be part of that generation, with their feet on the slippery slope of Edwardian values and their minds bombarded with a very new world. My parents were mostly old-fashioned and that was good. And that was terrible.

The next morning the snow hadn't amounted to much. Kept home for Carolyn, I was sitting wet-eyed in my nippy front room, still hurting for the little kids in the billboard.

What got to me was that they were trapped. The little girl would never get the candy, never even know that it was there. The artist and the chocolate candy company had played a mean joke on them. If you made a kid you could trap him any way you wanted. I thought that it was cruel and it hurt nervous, fragile, sissy, pansy, trapped me.

At the library I started to memorize little bits of Shakespeare, whatever caught my attention. Mostly I didn't know what it meant. Like the Latin it sounded so good, so not from *my* world. It was probably *my Marjorie's Maytime*. I'd thumb through the *Complete Works* inspecting the claustrophobic, infinitesimally packed type. If some passage caught my attention I'd copy it in my notebook, at first just a line here or there, but eventually whole speeches. I grossly misunderstood, wildly mispronounced, but what did it matter? It wasn't for anyone but me, and I think those hours saved my life.

The Christmas that I was eleven my grandparents gave me my first bicycle. It was a fat red Schwinn and it looked like the space age, the way the space age looked in the early 1950s. It had silver and white stripes painted like lightning. Hanging from elephantine black rubber handgrips were long plastic red and yellow streamers. They simulated fire, crackling and snapping in the early spring wind, as I raced around pretending to be a hero from the Saturday afternoon serials, Captain Marvel or Sky King.

Flying down the Booth Street hill, streamers flapping wildly at my side, I'd scream out *Richard the Second*, "Down, down I come . . . ," tearing down the hill, "Like glistering Phaeton. . . ." What's "glistering," Miss Russell? What's "Phaeton"? "In the base court come down. Down court down king for night owls shriek where mounting larks should sing." Or Juliet whipping along the salt-smelling road above Russian Beach, "My bounty is as boundless as the sea, my love as deep the more I give to thee the more I have for both are infinite."

I still do it. Pedaling on the Peugeot with rock and roll blasting through the Walkman I say the Shakespeare words out loud.

It's mid-November and suddenly the old red house needs a new roof. Left rotting for years, now it has to be fixed before the weather gets colder, before snow. Monday morning, workmen are stomping on my head. I hate the noise. It sets off an alarm recorded in my nerves when I was a kid.

Dead center on my desk is a heavy iron clock. *Tick, tick, tinny tick.* The brass pendulum swings behind a small circle of incredibly shiny old glass. In a moment of blessed silence I'm watching my tiny reflection move from gold to black, gold to black, gold to black, *tick, tick, tick. Bang! Crash!*

Today I'm reading *Coriolanus* on East Twenty-ninth Street. The play's a battleground for the unalike and the unequal, a thesis on dependence and arrogance, how we grow to despise what we can't live without. And there's a spiritual poison working its way through the bowels of the writing. There are scores of cannibalistic references to eating and being eaten. It's Hamlet's graveside riff on Alexander only taken much further this time, eight years and ten plays later. By now Shakespeare's made the excruciating trip through *King Lear*, and it shows.

Over my clock is a smoky painting of Dover. Dirty sailboats and dusky gulls weave through a gunmetal gale. I bought the picture years ago because it reminded me of a scene in *Lear*. Disgusted with the world, blind old Gloucester thinks to throw himself off those chalk cliffs.

> O you mighty gods,
> This world I do renounce and in your sights
> Shake patiently my great affliction off.
> If I could bear it longer and not fall
> To quarrel with your great opposeless wills,
> My snuff and loathed part of nature should
> Burn itself out.
>
> —*King Lear*, 4.6

Failing at death, he's forced to eke out a little more tolerance for his grotesque life.

CHAPTER 14

In August of 1951 my father announced that I'd start sixth grade in another new school. My parents were building a house and it would be finished by Christmas.

I hated leaving Center School. We'd planted a tree on Arbor Day and had a great time scrunching under our desks to be as small and silent as possible hiding from the Russians. The air-raid alarm would blast and Miss Wilcoxson would get a worried look and gently say, "Children, close your books, put them away, and calmly, quietly sit under your desks."

Our new little three-bedroom ranch with attached garage wasn't like the other brand-new houses on Summer Street. They had a couple of bedrooms upstairs for kids; for us stairs weren't such a good idea. Our house had a small odd side yard. It was a rectangle of mud dropped six feet below the street grade, which made it look like an abandoned swimming pool. As neighborhood dads did, my father planted grass and built a gigantic concrete barbecue.

Inside, the house was *Ladies' Home Journal* dreamy pink. Everything in the whole place was pink, hundreds of childlike shades from powder to salmon. Even our revered TV got its mahogany cabinet sprayed a cartoon coral. The small house was an adorable reliquary built to hold the peachy innocence of 1950s middle-class America, and at last, one of my mother's little girl dreams come true.

When we finished our B.L.T.'s in Read's department store Nana acted more solemn than usual. Under the marble counter she was fidgeting with her old lady's pocketbook. "Today it's up to you," she said as she pulled up a fat wad of bills wrapped in a pristine hankie.

I hadn't known it when I got off the green and yellow C. R. & L. bus in my usual place across from the Mr. Peanut peanut shop, but it was my graduation day from the department stores.

"After your pumpkin pie we'll walk over to Mr. Nothnagle's and *buy* a dining room set. Your grandfather agrees that it should be your choice. Finish your milk and please fix that tie, it's still not straight."

We made our old lady and little boy tracks in the light snow and just down the street through the arcade Nana brought the fortune out of her bag again. "We're here to *buy* not *look*, Mr. Nothnagle, and we're interested in dining rooms. My handsome grandson wants to choose one for his new house. My daughter and her husband have built a grand place over in Stratford."

"A table," she said, "and six chairs. I think it should only be six in a room that size. And of course we'll want a china closet. And what about a buffet? Robert, is there room for a buffet?"

My grandmother was having a wonderful time. By 1951 she'd lived almost all of her adult life on the second floor of a two-family on Stillman Street. To her our new house was the next generation moving forward to own its future in America. To be a part of it she'd unzipped an old cotton purse that she kept hidden at the back of the mothball-smelling closet next to her bed. I'd seen her bring it out for a birthday or at Christmas. The little faded floral bag contained all of the squirreled bits left after the bills got paid and her three kids had shoes and Saint Charles's grammar school got its years of tuitions. It was what was left of a fireman's salary after a lifetime of red hats and little vacations in the Buick.

That December afternoon Mr. Nothnagle didn't have to hold his impatience in check the way salespeople used to when Nana asked a million questions about objects everyone knew we'd never buy. That day he was kinder and more inviting and it made the snowy afternoon seem like a party. We walked from dining room set to dining room set, from drafty floor to drafty floor in his chilly warehouse. And after a couple of hours I picked a French Provincial table, six chairs, and a matching cabinet for displaying dishes. It was light-colored with gold stippled along gently curving legs and into a couple of grooves that traced the oval of the tabletop. She really did let me choose. She kept back. She was the proud mentor and didn't interfere even though for her it was a lifetime's savings.

I was eleven when we bought the dining room set and that day started a change in my relationship with Nana. It was easy for my old-fashioned grandmother to adore me as a precocious little boy whom she supplied with pious objects. For almost a decade, medals, plaster statues of saints, religious pictures and books, had piled up in support of her conviction that I would devote my life to the priesthood. But as I became an awkward adolescent she was far less interested, that part she could live without.

It's almost unbelievable that just a few years later she crossed Washington Street to avoid me.

At thirteen, and in the throes of a mixed-up puberty, I was crazy for a girl who lived just around the corner from Stillman Street. Nana caught sight of me with my arm resting on the girl's shoulder. She raced to the phone to announce to my mother what she'd seen. She warned that before long I'd bring home a baby. She "knew" the family, she said, and she knew how the girls in that house landed their husbands. And so good night to the priesthood, farewell to the bishop's and cardinal's hats, so long to the first Irish-American thirteen-year-old to wear the three-tiered miter of the papacy.

To my mother the idea of me having sex was simply impossible. The two women sniped at each other over the phone and finally snapped "That's it" and hung up, banishing each other for almost a year.

So my fashionable grandmother crossed Washington Street to avoid me. There she went in a foolish hat, her head held haughty, her eyes fixed and steely, all love gone, or at least hidden where a nervous thirteen-year-old couldn't find it.

On New Year's Day, right after we'd moved into Summer Street, my mother's parents slid across the snowy Boston Avenue hill for our first meal at the new French provincial dining table. We always spent New Year's together. Roman Catholics go to Mass. It's a Holy Day of Obligation called the Feast of the Circumcision.

"Raymond, is there a bakery open? No one in their right mind would eat these. That damn oven!" calling to my father as she made her way up the perilously icy sidewalk. Nana was disparaging her cooking again. "They're burnt black as coal. Oh well. . . . You eat with the McKeons . . ."

We had a huge 1:30 P.M. meal, a gigantic fat ham freckled with maraschino cherries and Dole pineapple slices all cremated in a brown sugar lava. It was the kind of candy carnage we loved. After dinner everyone settled into the living room to watch the pink black-and-white TV. An opera singer was belting *Carmen*. My father sat in the corner next to the painted pink fireplace quietly checking football scores on a small pink plastic radio. Sleepy in his usual swirls of stinky pipe smoke my grandfather leaned way back in the pink Barcalounger. Aunt Claire, as always, was holed up in the coral bathroom worried about her looks. My mother and grandmother had just washed, dried, and put away a huge stack of pearly pink dishes. My sister stared through the picture window at the row of exactly matched little Cape Cod houses that lined the other side of the brand-new licorice-looking street. I lay on the floor, flat on my back, listening to hundreds of pine needles fall from our dangerously dry Christmas tree.

"What's circumcision?" I asked. Silence. No one stopped the nothing they were doing. The soprano kept singing. It was like I'd only thought the question. Just in case, I asked it again, this time much louder. *"What's circumcision?"*

For every New Year's of my life we'd gone to Mass. Even when my father was in Italy becoming a man we'd had New Year's dinner in that powdery dining room over on Stillman Street with my Catholic grandparents. The word just hadn't stuck out before. I'd never noticed it enough to wonder why the day had this odd name. Was it Latin?

When I was four or five and taking all those purifying baths I begged some little kids from across the street to take a bath with me. Acting silly, all five of us got into the tub. We were having a ball with bubbles, laughing and screaming, when my mother showed up. She was horrified. "Shame," she cried with tears stinging her incredibly red cheeks. "Shame on you. You are disgusting." On our little front porch steps for all the world to see she spanked me with a hairbrush. Bent over my mother's lap I could see all the wet little kids staring wide eyed from across the street, which is where they stayed after that day.

"Shame, shame," my wild-eyed mother shrieked with each stroke of the wide brush back, "shame." On the new pink rug listening to pine needles and *Carmen* I felt shame. The diva finished the aria and I stood up to hide in my room, to hide from a word that was tacked to our pink teapot-patterned kitchen wallpaper. Right there between the new refrigerator and stove, boldly emblazoned on our brand-new funeral home religious calendar, it was as clear as the glass in my iron clock, January 1, 1952, New Year's Day, and in old-fashioned blood-red script, *The Feast of the Circumcision.*

I sat depressed in my seashell-colored room. Just as it started to get dark outside Carolyn rubbed against my door and kicked it lightly with the side of her foot. That was always her catlike request to get let in.

After a while I heard my grandparents leaving. "Good-bye, Robert," Nana called from the safe distance of the kitchen.

"So long, Rob, Happy New Year," Claire sang flat and sad from the other end of the house.

"Is she in there? Is she wet? Time for bed," my mother said coolly from the other side of the bedroom door. "Let her out, unless she's asleep. Good night."

The next morning my mother was cheerful, starting the year in love with her pretty house and brand-new GE washing machine. She was up on a step stool putting away ornaments on a high shelf. Her head was way up in the closet. I was helping her to take down our skeletal Christmas tree. She was having a great time crabbing about her sister and how lazy Claire was. She hadn't helped to wash all of those pink dishes. My mother was telling me, for the millionth time, about her sister and men. "Man crazy," she kept saying, "just man crazy."

I chose my moment. "What's circumcision?" My mother's body stiffened and she stopped talking. I couldn't see her face. Would she say "That's it!," get a terrible headache, and go to bed for a couple of weeks? I held up another stack of weightless ornament boxes. When she reached for them she didn't look at me.

"Please, I wanna know. Tell me, what does circumcision mean?"

Humiliated she spat the childish words in my direction. "It's . . . It's a thing . . . It's a thing boys have done to their peepees." In a second she was safely invisible back up in the closet.

"Something boys have done to their . . ." In my head I couldn't finish the sentence. *What* did boys have done? Was it going to be done to *me*? When? Who would do it? Would people know? Did everyone but me know already? Did Mr. Kite, my sixth-grade teacher, know? Did my father know? "Something boys have . . ."

On the funeral home calendars, fascinated by nakedness, I'd gawked at Masaccio's fresco expulsion of Adam and Eve driven from paradise to the unprotected vulnerability of worldliness. Like Adam I wanted to cover my face and fold myself against a wall to hide my shame.

Later I threw what was left of the dried Christmas tree on a heap next to the ice-covered cinder-block barbecue. And from the pink pubescence of Summer Street I flew like Captain Marvel on the fat red Schwinn down Johnson Avenue, down the Booth Street hill to Barnum, across Barnum to King, and down the King Street hill to Main. I took a right on Main Street and pounced on the dictionary stand dictionary in the little granite library.

> circum-
> circumambient
> circumambulliatic
> *circumcise*—to cut off the prepuce of a male

Prepuce?

> prepotent
> prepuberal
> prepuberty
> *prepuce*—foreskin

Foreskin?

> foreshorten
> foreshow
> foreside
> foresight

foreskin—a fold of skin that covers the glans of the penis
   also called *prepuce*
Circumcision—(1) the act of circumcising or being
   circumcised; spec. a *Jewish* rite performed on *infants*
   as a sign of inclusion in the covenant between God
   and Abraham. (2) *cap.* A feast on January 1
   commemorating the circumcision of Jesus.

Why couldn't somebody just tell me?

After we moved to Summer Street I still did my homework in the library. I'd ride my bike down after school and at 5:00 I'd pedal back up the Booth Street hill for supper. After we ate it was my job to do the dishes. When I didn't have to take care of Carolyn I'd walk to the movies.

It was a Friday night. It had to be a Friday night because I'd already seen the feature at the Stratford movie four times, twice on Wednesday and again on Thursday night. On the walk home I was uncomfortable about prejudice. It was the 1950s and inevitably the concept was pushing in at the corners of my awareness. The movie I saw six times that week was a brand-new remake of the old film *Showboat*. In the story some people are caught between worlds. People who are part black and part white are discarded. There's a character who's kind and noble in the face of a brutal rejecting world. Her story struck something familiar.

When I turned the corner from Johnson Avenue our street was crowded with cars. Lost in nineteenth-century racism I'd forgotten that my parents were having a party. I wasn't invited. I was eleven and it was for "adults." My parents had been glad to see me pack off to the movie. My mother handed me a quarter from her little transparent kidney-shaped coin purse. It had the loudest snap sound, that little plastic purse, and you could see all the coins spooning, jammed in side by side by side.

Snap. "Here's a whole quarter," she'd say laughing sweetly. "Don't spend it all in one place." Snap.

My allowance, movie money, or the fifty cents I put in the wicker basket at Mass came from that purse.

Showboat made me worry about people getting thrown away because they're not what other people think they should be. I was ruminating about unalikeness and inequality a long time before I understood *Coriolanus*. I didn't want to just go home and sit in my room but I was nervous about Carolyn. I didn't know how she'd be at a party for grown-ups, and I was sure that everyone would just ignore her.

When I walked around the side of the garage it was sometime near eleven and it was cold. Upstairs the house was dark but there was loud music blasting from the basement and bright light was sifting through the thick cotton curtains on the oblong cellar windows. The back door was locked so I rang the little illuminated doorbell. No answer. I rang it again. I walked around to the front. Nobody answered that bell either.

Back at the back the music sounded even louder. In the din they couldn't hear me ringing. "Where's Carolyn?" I thought. "What's going on?" I sat on the cement steps. I thought about *Showboat* and being the person "outside." The red Schwinn was leaning against the house and there was a cotton bag of pink plastic clothespins whipping in the late night wind. *Rachet, rachet, rachet,* it squawked as it beat the air through the loud party noise.

Somebody laughed, giggled really. I banged on the glass of the back door and pressed my face against the cold window. The shut blind snapped open. As she turned the little brass button lock my mother said something to someone behind her. When my eyes adjusted to the moonless dark I saw women sitting, standing, leaning. The room smelled of cigarettes, perfume, and Canadian Club whiskey. The women were only partially dressed. Two were almost *naked*—"completely unclothed; bare, nude, uncovered, exposed without protection, additions, ornaments, disguises or embellishments, plain, stark." Slips, bras, stockings, and shoes were piled onto Mr. Nothnagle's pale provincial table.

Six times at the little brick Stratford movie theater I'd seen *Moulin Rouge*. It was the story of the artist Henri de Toulouse-Lautrec. Crippled, dwarfed, and cast out from society he painted night people in fin de siècle Paris. Stupefied showgirls and pie-eyed prostitutes sit dazed, drunk, or drugged. It was the first thing I thought about in the dark dining room, those lethargic Lautrec faces. Sex didn't seem like much fun, whatever it was. When I walked into the "adult" party all that I knew about sex I knew from the *Webster's Second Edition,* copyright 1939, definitions of *naked* and *circumcision.*

"Aw, hez ah-door-ah-bull." A woman's husky voice came from the dark of the living room. "Hez *k-u-t-e.*"

"Where's Carolyn?"

My mother was hiding behind the open back door. She was barefoot and wearing a white slip. "In your room," she said. "Don't be mad at me. Aw come on now, don't be that way. How was the movie? Is it still *Showboat*? I hate movies, it's so dirty in the dark. Who knows what's on those seats. Don't be mad. I'll bring you up a dish of chips. Want onion dip? Don't be a prude." This from the person who couldn't tell me what circumcision is.

My sister was sitting on the green marbleized linoleum at the end of the little hall where the three bedroom doors met. She slept wherever she fell asleep. She wouldn't stay in a bed alone. I don't always want to either.

"Cherry Pink and Apple Blossom White," that was the song that vibrated through the floor from the basement under my bed. A tawdry trumpet blasted it over and over.

Through the loud music I could hear the men whose wives were the prizes in the boozy one-way game of strip poker in the unfinished cement cellar. The houses were so close that I thought for sure someone would call the police. But nobody did.

Tipsy undressed women were roaming around outside my door

and laughing. Sex was all around but there was an implicit warning to see nothing and stay silent. On Summer Street I got to be an
old man inside a little boy, just like my ancient great-grandfather
staring at the camera in those old Brownie pictures. Now *I* was the
unwilling conscience of the group.

After a while, through the racket, I heard my mother's timid
knock. "I brought you some chips," she said. "Is she wet? Don't
give her too much soda or you'll have a job on your hands." Just
before she closed me back in the room with my sister she paused.
She didn't turn to me but I could see her face in profile. "Don't
blame me," she whispered, just audible over the music. "I do what
he wants. This is *his* idea. Don't be mad at me about this. . . . I'm
sorry." Satisfied that I'd hold my father culpable, she quietly closed
the door.

Carolyn was heaped on the floor staring at a spider on the base-
board. I watched her watch for a long, long time. After a while she
looked up.

"Wanna dance?" I asked. "Wanna dance with me?" Of course
she couldn't actually dance. Her body took only a few orders from
her broken brain. But she would try anything for me, my little "not
right" sister.

I turned out the lights except for my kid's desk lamp. It was a
copper horse with a rawhide shade. I lifted Carolyn to her feet. She
shook and started to twist her hands. I took them in mine. She
laughed crazily for a minute and then went still and distant. I put
my arms around her and started to move slowly, awkwardly,
unrhythmically. I can close my eyes now and feel us trying to dance.

In that moment when I could smell baby shampoo in my sister's
long gold hair, I couldn't have dreamed that ten years later I'd
abandon her in that high windy cornfield. I couldn't have imagined
that I'd be plagued every day for the rest of my life by the prison of
a broken promise, the oath I took by her crib the first time she'd
smiled at me in that tacky torrid room in Florida when we were
small.

*   *   *

In 1952 a kid halfway through the sixth grade might not be told anything by his parents. If he didn't have an older brother or boy cousins, if he was always the new kid everywhere and hadn't made friends, there wasn't a chance in hell that anyone would have mentioned it. We certainly didn't talk about sex in Mr. Kite's class at Nichols Elementary School. In Stratford in the 1950s there was no official school discussion of human sexuality until the second half of the junior year in high school. It would be another five years before the boys' gym teacher gave us a grotesque display of the miracle of reproduction. On a drizzly spring afternoon, muscle-bound Mr. Krump helped the physiology class dissect a stiff, flattened-down, pregnant cat corpse that stunk of formaldehyde. Hovering over us nauseous kids, he pointed to little grayish organs with the tip of his Venus pencil, while he listed the plumbing parts of human reproduction.

I was twelve the day my father caught me. He'd felt a draft under my door because I had my window open. Unlike my mother, my father never knocked. There could be no doubt about what I was doing. He didn't look at me. He just crossed the room and pulled the window down.

The reason my mother was the one to give me my allowance, from that little transparent purse, was that my father would withhold it to taunt me. I took everything so seriously and he hated that about me. With the two bucks up over his head he'd pretend to drop them. "Whoops," he'd say. "Guess I lost it, guess there's no lunch money, no more movies, guess you missed it, have to go without."

"I did the dishes, I mowed the grass, I went to the store every day after school, I washed the kitchen floor *twice,* I took care of Carolyn three afternoons and all day Sunday, I cleaned the cellar." I was desperate for the movie money. "Jeez."

He'd laugh and feign grotesque pity. "Aw, poor kid. You got it real rough. Wait till ya get inta the army!"

"Stop it, Ray," she'd yell. "Pay no attention. You're a good kid." Snap. "Here's the money." Snap.

Later I thought it must have been a thing left from his childhood poverty, some burlesque of his own kid fears about having nothing. Nobody ever gave him even the smallest thing and it made it almost impossible for him to give anything to me.

Well into his eighties he'd tease people at the dinner table. If someone asked my father to pass the butter he'd turn to my mother. "What'd the butter cost me? I'll let ya have the salt and the butter for a quarter. And to prove I'm not stingy, I'll throw in the pepper." He'd repeat the ritual every time anybody asked for anything. Five or six times at every meal.

"Ray, no one thinks you're the least bit funny and somebody could think you actually mean it." Then my mother would smile an expression that told everyone that she found him irresistible and if you gave him half a chance surely you would, too.

But the message was clear. To win my father's approval, I needed to get very good at seeming to need nothing.

The day my father walked into my room my mother wasn't home. She was visiting relatives in the dreary Wilmont Apartments over in Bridgeport. On our way to pick her up my father stopped the car just in front of Saint Michael's Cemetery. He lit a new cigarette with what was left of the old one before he tossed it out of the window. As usual he didn't look at me. "I could tell on you, ya know. I could tell your mother. Imagine what she'd think of you if I did?" Like a jealous tormenting older brother he cheerfully threatened, "I just might, maybe I will, then she wouldn't think very much of you." He finally looked over at me and smiled. He was handsome, my father, with his black hair and eyes dark like his mother's. "That's right, she won't think much of you, and you won't have a friend in the world."

I dug my nails into my hand trying not to cry, trying not to be a sissy. Of course he was right, I wouldn't have a friend in the world. Except for my sister, not having a friend in the world was what my childhood was about. By twelve I got the message that if you were always the new kid and had a sister who shook and curled her beautiful hands high in the air, if she was much too big for her little tricycle and compulsively pedaled back and forth on a fifty-foot strip singing nonwords at the top of her voice, it was a safe bet that most kids would "give you a wide berth," my mother's language again.

This year, just before Christmas, looking for those noisy little decorations in my parents' damp dreary basement, I found another thing first. In a neglected corner was a showy gold embossed box about the size of a shoe box. It had been through a couple of burst pipe basement floods and smelled of mildew. Inside was a little sandwich of Brownie snapshots. The serrated pictures were mummified, with thick, overcrossed bubble gum–colored rubber bands, twenty where one would do. They were stuck together and hard to the touch. I tried to coax them apart and one picture close to the center started to yield.

For some reason I was more gentle and patient than is my nature. After a few minutes the little picture is exhumed. It's Carolyn. She's laughing lying half on grass, half on warm summer sidewalk. Her long yellow hair covers the ground. Her smiling face in profile is exquisite. She's wearing a dress I remember, a little girl's green and red plaid with a small white collar. Just at the edge of the picture is a shadow of her three-wheeler, the one I taught her to ride.

Standing at my father's thick metal workbench under rows of aligned archaic tools, I could hear what I hadn't thought about in almost fifty years. My sister's happy. Singing nonsense sounds she pedals back and forth on the sidewalk in front of our little red

ranch house on Summer Street. For a couple of years she was a fix-
ture in shorts or summer dresses or, in spring, her child's pink coat.
Back and forth, back and forth, hour after hour she traced the fifty
feet of sidewalk, back and forth in the little housing development of
Winter, Spring, and Summer Streets. Old pictures can hurt you. We
didn't want to notice how much bigger Carolyn was getting than
her little tricycle. Some men did. They stopped to talk to her but she
could only stare fascinated. Luckily no one mentioned ice cream!

It was on Summer Street that Carolyn started to have the
seizures. She'd fall down and violently shake. Her head would roll
from side to side. Her eyes would disappear into her skull and her
muscles got as hard as stone. At first it was terrifying, but before
long we had a kind of system. We kept a wooden spoon handy to
slide into her mouth so that her grinding teeth couldn't rip into her
tongue. We shoved old plastic porch pillows and a bedspread
under her. By this time we gladly messed up the chenille to protect
my sister's frantically nodding head. After the seizure she'd pee and
go into a long deep sleep.

> CASSIO   What's the matter?
> IAGO   My lord is fallen into an epilepsy;
>   This is his second fit, he had one yesterday.
> CASSIO   Rub him about the temples.
> IAGO   No, forbear:
>   The lethargy must have his quiet course,
>   If not, he foams at mouth, and by and by
>   Breaks out to savage madness.
>
>   —*Othello*, 4.1

Years later on a drafty stage floor, memory by awful memory, I
reconstructed my sister's seizures for two actors. Othello and Julius
Caesar are both afflicted, maybe someone Shakespeare knew was?
When I was twelve I couldn't imagine that anyone might have felt
the same helplessness that I did on the Summer Street sidewalk.

I watched my sister pedal back and forth. She'd already broken her collarbone and we were nervous that she'd plunge the six feet into that little side yard or crack her head on the cement sidewalk. She was so innocent that her bewilderment at pain was unbearable. "He spends too much time alone watching her. It's going to make him sick," warned my mother's friends. As I took up deeper residency in my own head, I'm sure that in some ways they were right. Too much watching can make you passive and afraid. Ask Hamlet.

CHAPTER 15

I WENT TO Nichols School for only five months. In early spring our class packed up and moved to the new junior high. It was my sixth school in six years. Brand-new Wooster Junior High was antiseptic and institutional. Eight times a day a shrill bell ripped through the vacant white halls and hundreds of screaming kids raced like "bats out of hell." I remember actual panic as we flew up and down stairways through endless locker-lined hallways desperately trying to beat the nightmare bell to the next new desk in the next new class. Every day started and ended in our "home" room. In the seventh grade our homeroom teacher also taught us social studies, her name was Miss Hakala. She had short blond hair, big blue eyes, and even bigger white teeth. It was her first year teaching, she was young and easygoing and all the kids loved her.

One ordinary day in Miss Hakala's sunny south-facing social studies class, the part of me that did extra homework and got A's went missing. Looking down at a test paper I thought, "Does it matter if I answer all the questions or none of them?" At the end of the period, just before that awful bell, I handed back the empty sheet. The pretty teacher smiled inquisitively. I could see most of her perfect white teeth. "What's the joke?" She was sitting at her desk. I bent down. I could smell sweet spicy perfume and hairspray. I whispered past her little gold earring, "Please don't be mad at me. I'm not smart. My father says the army will straighten me out." Upset, Miss Hakala called my mother and with a couple of other concerned teachers, she made a visit to Summer Street.

How could a nice responsible kid who'd done so well in so many schools just suddenly start to fail? "Has something happened? Is anything wrong at home?"

"No." My mother was all dressed up for the teachers. She smelled like baby powder and wore white gloves and a good-looking green hat in her own pretty pink living room. "How could anything be wrong? I'm very proud of my son," she said, welling up. "He's a good boy and he's always been *very* smart. Robert was born an adult." Tears flowed, a hankie came out. "Coffee, anyone? Bobby, do you smell something?"

For the next six years I was Frankenstein. Every teacher thought they could find what I'd lost. Wonderful, caring people turned me upside down to shake out what they thought I'd hidden. In high school, of course, the pressure increased. "What about college?" My parents were silent, it didn't matter to them. "As long as you're happy," my mother would say. "Get a job" was my father's contribution, or "The army'll teach you a skill." But teachers and guidance counselors were adamant.

"Look," I said over and over, "there's nothing wrong, there isn't anything to fix." "Now is the winter of our discontent. . . . And all the clouds that lowered upon our house . . ." I was starting "in sooth" to suspect why I was so sad, and what I wanted more than anything else was to sit on the warm summer sidewalk with my sister, draw pictures, and stumble through Shakespeare.

Despite my awful grades, hopeful teachers kept me in top college-bound classes. By the time I was a senior in Mrs. Schilling's

honors English class, I'd won a national poetry award for a tiny
poem I'd scrawled. It was printed in a collection and I was mostly
embarrassed. Sometimes I carried a crazy little sign. I used to prop
it up on my desks. I made it from one of my father's gray shirt card-
boards. In black, thick, smelly, squeaky Magic Marker it begged,
"Please don't test me." Kids liked me but the word *weird* was definitely used.

When I was thirteen a teacher and some culturally minded parents
took a group of us to the Metropolitan Museum of Art on Fifth
Avenue.

We had lunch in the Roman-looking museum cafeteria. Well, it
wasn't so much Roman as "Hollywood" Roman. At the center of
the room, enclosed by huge Doric columns, was a beautiful fountain of naked boys. In the cacophony of voices, fountain splatter,
and the tinny crash of tossed silverware and slammed dishes, we
ate exotic pumpernickel sandwiches. I'd only ever eaten white
Wonder bread.

It felt great to be eating dark crustless diamond-shaped sandwiches in the big boisterous Roman room next to the spitting
fountain. I'd just seen the movie *Quo Vadis* three or four times
from the smoke-filled balcony of the cavernous Loews Poli over
on Main Street in Bridgeport. Lunch in the museum was Nero's
palace.

Later we followed our teacher through immense galleries of
Greek and Roman antiquities. We lined up in front of chipped
busts of aquiline patricians and noseless curly haired marble
matrons. Single file, like baby ducks, we chased the art teacher up
the wide staircase to the Renaissance. The rooms were packed with
familiar images from the funeral home calendars and much more.
We stopped at the Catholic baroque, El Greco and Rubens. With
the tall kids at the back, we assembled in a swaying adolescent
cluster in front of the austere Protestant Reformation, and finally

the flame in the soberness of the northern European chill, Rembrandt. If ever a place had taken me, this was it.

My introduction to the theatrics of high art had certainly started when I was five at Saint Charles as Nana knelt to pray the Stations of the Cross. Like in a museum, she'd move from one dimly lit image to another. Meditating on suffering and crucifixion, she'd murmur a collection of prayers, "Hail Mary . . ." It was theater, it was art, it was Shakespeare for the barely literate.

I made a pact with myself to come back to the museum as soon as I could, whether it meant sneaking out of school or home. On Saturdays or Sundays, sometimes both, I'd steal away. By the time I was thirteen, disappearing without explanation was a family custom. It began that time when my father snuck off to join the army right after my sister was born. By the time I was a teenager another odd departure had started.

Right after we moved to Summer Street, one day a week my father would leave at dawn and come home after midnight. Every Tuesday he was unreachable and wouldn't say where he was. No appeal from my mother exacted an explanation. My father stayed away every Tuesday for fifty years.

> For where love reigns, disturbing jealousy
> Doth call himself affection's sentinel;
> Gives false alarms, suggesteth mutiny . . .
>
> —*Venus and Adonis*

"Tuesday," my mother would say rolling her eyes heavenward. "I could be laid out at Pistey's and he wouldn't give up his Tuesday. . . . A woman." She said it a thousand times. "I know it's a woman. He's got some 'Jane'; he's just like his father, damn fool. I could be passed out on the kitchen floor but he wouldn't find me, not on a Tuesday."

Once when I was older and she'd just come home from a hospital, I confronted my father. "Ma is goin' nuts about Tuesdays. She thinks you go out with some woman. It's none of my business, but she's making herself crazy with the Tuesday thing. Can't you just tell her you play cards?"

He didn't look up from the newspaper. "Don't be stupid. When she feels better she'll forget it."

When I was thirteen, Saturday became my Tuesday. I took the Number Fourteen bus from Stratford to the big yellow brick railway station in Bridgeport. I'd catch the early New York, New Haven & Hartford train to Grand Central and walk the forty blocks up Madison and over to Fifth to reach the museum just as the doors opened. I always took two peanut butter sandwiches and a Shakespeare play and headed straight up that impressive stairway to the Renaissance. I'm a fervent watcher. I can stare at a thing for a day, weeks, years.

Soon after I stopped caring how to spell, or what six times seven is, I'd sit all day at the museum with my skinny knees slamming together. I was mesmerized by Shakespeare and Tintoretto, Shakespeare and Veronese, Shakespeare and Botticelli. I sat in the museum for years. By the time I was twenty I knew every piece of canvas, marble, or bronze in the place. Eventually I branched out to the Frick down the avenue. For years I read Shakespeare tucked on a bench under the white marble colonnade in Mr. Frick's industrialist's palace garden just on the other side of the wall from the Bronzino and Rembrandt's *Polish Rider*.

While other, cheerier kids were spending Saturday afternoon fooling around with friends, I was wandering through museum galleries convinced that I was in paradise, and I was.

In the Eisenhower fifties, museums could be incredibly quiet places. In front of great art, people acted exhausted. In the vast silence it wasn't long before I could hear the pictures. A couple of months after I started sitting alone all day I began to imagine the rumble coming from the other side of the canvases. At first it was hardly noticeable. But before long it intruded on my consciousness. More and more the phantasmic started jutting into my isolation.

The almost inaudible notes of gentle strings from Titian's *Venus and the Lute Player* blew through a foggy stand of birches in a Corot. *Yap, yap, yap, yap, yap*—a nasty little King Charles spaniel demanded attention in the big Gainsborough two galleries away. I started to invent Shakespeare voices for the people in the paintings. It was the language of my incredible loneliness.

> Such tricks hath strong imagination,
> That if it would but apprehend some joy,
> It comprehends some bringer of that joy:
> Or, in the night, imagining some fear,
> How easy is a bush suppos'd a bear!
> —*A Midsummer Night's Dream,* 5.1

Later, in high school, I started taking the train in the other direction. I took the New York, New Haven & Hartford to sneak into lectures at Yale. One of my art teacher's former students was a senior there and when he'd stopped by to see Miss Hogan he'd hinted that there was a lot a kid could learn if he had the guts to sit in the back of one of those big oak rooms up on Chapel Street. By then I knew the paintings at the Met and the Frick. Sometimes I sketched parts of them, a hand, an eye, a section of draped figure. Miss Hogan said that a kid who drew as well as I could might be an illustrator or even a painter.

The first teacher who didn't like me was Miss Shumaker. It was right after I stopped pleasing everybody. Miss Shumaker taught seventh-grade math and she acted as if my failure was a personal indictment of Pythagoras and her.

"I can fail you!" she'd threaten. "I can give you a fat F! I can make your life miserable!" At the time, except for Shakespeare and the museum, I thought my life was already miserable.

Miss Shumaker's spine was twisted in a way that made walking very difficult. Older, odd-looking, and childless, she seemed out of touch with the twelve-year-olds with whom she worked every day. One afternoon she scrawled across the blackboard in big underlined letters: NO LAVATORY PRIVILEGES. She thought too many boys requested too many trips to the toilet. Of course, the reason so many kids had to pee was simple: They were terrified.

Miss Shumaker was decapitating a twelve-year-old traitor in the front row and I wasn't thinking about math. Inside my geometry book was a little copy of *The Merchant of Venice*.

Before she'd gotten distracted by the boy in the front row, the math teacher had been talking about rose windows. Chartres Cathedral. She told us that rose windows in great churches are geometry. Then she got mad at the boy and I dove into *Merchant*.

> How sweet the moonlight sleeps upon this bank!
> Here will we sit, and let the sounds of music
> Creep in our ears—soft stillness and the night
> Become the touches of sweet harmony:
> Sit Jessica,—look how the floor of heaven
> Is thick inlaid with patens of bright gold . . .
>   —*The Merchant of Venice*, 5.1

"What's that?" Miss Shumaker shrieked. "What's that? Bring that up to me *now*. Whatever you've got in there I want to see it *now*."

No teacher had ever talked to me with dislike. I was no longer the A-student pet who deserved "in" jokes and special treatment. I carried both books up to the front of the room. She grabbed the little Shakespeare like a cobra she'd milk for venom. Miss Shumaker looked at the book for a long time. "Sit down," she whispered, showing me with her sickened face that I wasn't even worth a glance. "Sit down."

There was never a hint of what human feelings might be trapped under her geometrically patterned dresses. Her wiry gray hair was always oiled against her large skull and she wore thick glasses. To us kids Miss Shumaker was an isosceles triangle, long division, pi, r^2.

She halted around her big oak desk to toss my book into the center drawer. That was the repository for gathered evidence: intercepted jokes, captured fiendish caricatures of her, and worst of the worst, cigarettes—Camels or Lucky Strikes. As she shoved the drawer shut her glance landed back on me. Then the old teacher did this amazing thing. The heartless witch hobbled over to the row of windows and leaned, ugly as sin, into the yellow afternoon winter sunlight.

Miss Shumaker, taunting beadle of twelve-year-olds, took off her horn-rimmed glasses and for one minute and fifteen seconds she repeated Portia's famous instructions to Shylock on the properties of forgiveness.

> The quality of mercy is not strain'd,
> It droppeth as the gentle rain from heaven
> Upon the place beneath: it is twice blest,
> It blesseth him that gives, and him that takes,
> 'Tis mightiest in the mightiest, it becomes
> The throned monarch better than his crown.
> His sceptre shows the force of temporal power,
> The attribute to awe and majesty,
> Wherein doth sit the dread and fear of kings:
> But mercy is above this sceptred sway,
> It is enthroned in the hearts of kings,
> It is an attribute to God himself;
> And earthly power doth then show likest God's
> When mercy seasons justice: therefore Jew,

Though justice be thy plea, consider this,
That in the course of justice, none of us
Should see salvation: we do pray for mercy,
And that same prayer, doth teach us all to render
The deeds of mercy. I have spoke thus much
To mitigate the justice of thy plea,
Which if thou follow, this strict court of Venice
Must needs give sentence 'gainst the merchant there.

—*The Merchant of Venice*, 4.1

That was the first time I heard anyone say the words out loud. This unsympathetic woman had stored the speech in her head, not just the words but all the feelings were right there where she could get at them.

Finished, she hooked her glasses back onto her big ears and the merciless math teacher was back to grind our pubescence into a graphite point doing fractions.

It's a March morning just before Saint Patrick's Day and a strong wind is blasting a blizzard at the northeast corner of my old red house. The little kids next door are rolling the bombast into their second snowman. I can hear their squeaky voices ricochet off the barn. The storm's a surprise. Yesterday was so warm that I stopped for a beer near the train station. In the noisy bar a couple of town workers called to each other.

"Boston's gettin' a couple of feet; Providence, too. Real Nor'easter!"

"Ah, ya can't trust March, get nailed late as April. Not otta the woods yet. . . . Hey, how's your sister?"

Last week the Peugeot had a flat so I walked to Lovell's Hardware. On the Main Street sidewalk the sun was suddenly warmer. Nature's working its way back like a lover after an awful fight and it's filled me with an involuntary optimism, spring. In the face of irrefutable evidence that all things always change, where do you bury the long ago that still haunts your sleep?

"Not otta the woods yet," the old man in the smoky bar yelled to his friend, "how's your . . ."

> O rose of May!
> Dear maid—kind sister—sweet Ophelia—
> O heavens, is't possible a young maid's wits
> Should be as mortal as an old man's life?
>
> —*Hamlet*, 4.5

During the years that we lived on Summer Street I finally started to know other kids. By the time I was a freshman in high school the phone rang for me more often than my mother wanted it to. Suddenly I had things to do and boys to pack off to Friday night basketball with. Some kids called me "Shakespeare." I didn't like it; I still don't.

For a while, when I was fourteen, laughing came back. "*That* is not funny!" My mother would scowl at some adolescent joke. The closer I got to other kids' lives the gloomier mine seemed. How could I not see my sister look longingly when I'd start to put my coat on, or later, coming up the steps, I'd see her shadow as she stood holding the doorknob. She'd stand there waiting all the time I was gone. Before I had the coat off my mother never failed to describe it.

But in 1955 I did what most boys did. Sputnik or the Warsaw Pact meant nothing compared to Bill Haley and the Comets' "Rock Around the Clock." Rock and roll became the background music for every kid I knew. Elvis or Pat Boone? Every Saturday night there was a dance, or we played records in some knotty pine–paneled playroom in some kid's converted cellar.

There was the December night that a gang of us were on our way to a Christmas dance. It was snowing and four borrowed fathers' cars inched along the slippery road. All the windows were rolled down, and with the four car radios tuned to the same station, rock and roll was blasting into the silent snowfall. A song that we were wild for came on and the cars slid to a stop. Everybody jumped out to line up under a streetlight. In the driving snow twenty of us, in tuxedos and gowns, danced the stroll.

Around then I went with Billy Fogarty over to tacky Congress Street in Bridgeport where you could take a new 78 into a glass booth for a listen before you plunked down your quarter. Billy lived six houses away on the same side of Summer Street. He was younger than me and everybody said that he looked like James Dean with his pale eyes and blond hair that he greased back into a "D.A." Billy had one of those careless curls intentionally flipped onto his high handsome forehead. We wore black leather jackets and had fun on street corners acting tough smoking Luckys.

On Sundays we went to the matinee at the Hiway movie on Boston Avenue, till Billy got a girlfriend. For a while we went with two girls who were friends. I remember making out with some ninth-grader, pressed against a tombstone in the cemetery behind the little granite library, while a couple of graves away Billy was trying to give Joyce Puglice her first hickey. Eventually he got serious with a girl I didn't know. I think he married her when he was sixteen.

In high school there were clubs for everything. Kids needed to belong and for the world to know who they belonged with. Sports, science, cars, religion—any connection was a reason to have a club and to wear matching jackets or sweaters. I was popular enough, so when a club got formed at the start of sophomore year, I was in.

On a Saturday in late winter of 1957 our long-anticipated special-order dark gray and crimson club jackets arrived. My brand-new leather-smelling coat had three Greek letters appliquéd to the back and "Bobby" scrawled in stitched script over the front pocket. I was thrilled at this evidence that I was finally a part of things. That night thirty boys were going to wear the jackets for the first time.

Someone's parents had rented a hall and I planned to attend the celebration with a girl from my class. Jean was an only child with older parents. We'd developed a relationship that was, for a while, like idealized siblings. The plan was for her to pick me up after supper.

Unfortunately for me, my parents had a party of their own to go to. My father had a new job at the General Electric plant in Bridgeport and some social responsibilities had come along with it. I had to watch Carolyn, we couldn't have baby-sitters. Young girls were sickened; older women had trouble keeping up. Relatives were always a bad idea. Lots of family relationships ended over a few hours with my sister. And by that time her periods had started, once and for all making it impossible to pretend that Carolyn was only four.

"Please," I vowed years of servitude, "let me go just this once. Get someone else for tonight and I'll never ask for anything again for as long as I live."

But at seven P.M. my mother and father walked out the front door leaving the scent of Old Spice and baby powder to linger for a few moments in the pink air. I called Jean who'd waited "just in case" before she went on to the party. I took my new jacket from the dry cleaners bag and was a very proud Alpha Pi Omega while Carolyn and I played with dolls.

The next morning Jean called with a brutal message. At the party some boys were fooling around. These fifteen-year-olds didn't drink, but a group of them had apparently been out in the parking lot in some older kid's car experimenting with beer and it got rough. Someone did a mean impersonation of my sister. In tenth grade that kind of thing was normal, expected even. It was the 1950s, when any deviation was uncomfortable and scary. It wasn't intended to do more than get a laugh.

By then kids kidded me about Shakespeare and some boys knew that I went to the museum on Saturdays. There was the wacky "Please don't test me" sign and I almost never asked anybody to our house because of Carolyn's "accidents." She'd get so excited that she'd shake violently, which naturally almost always led to a mess. In seventh grade a nice kid in my class ran fleeing from our house and stumbled down the front porch steps.

At the jacket party, emboldened by a little beer, one boy announced that he had a way to tell, and that he knew beyond any doubt, that I was a queer. By nine o'clock surmise had escalated to speculation; by ten the group had decided to leave a note on my school locker suggesting that I destroy my new jacket. By noon on Monday it was finished and for the remaining two and a half years of high school, no boy I'd been friends with ever spoke to me again or even indicated that I existed. When kids had to make up class lists, I wasn't on them. When tests were passed up to the front of the row, the kid behind me handed them to the kid in front of me as if I wasn't there. Eventually younger boys started calling out punishing names and rougher kids grouped together to knock me down or terrify me into giving them money. It seemed familiar, like it had always been going on in one form or another since that time I'd screwed up on the bumper cars at the state fair when I was eight . . . "sissy." I was ashamed, and ashamed for being ashamed.

In my boy's life there was no one to talk to, and I just wasn't the kid hero who'd stand up in front of the whole world to punch the bully in the nose. The world, after all, including my own father, thought the bully was right.

Am I a coward?
Who calls me villain, breaks my pate across,
Plucks off my beard and blows it in my face,
Tweaks me by the nose, gives me the lie i'th' throat
As deep as to the lungs—who does me this?

Ha!
'Swounds, I should take it: for it cannot be
But I am pigeon-liver'd . . .

—*Hamlet*, 2.2

Last week one of the churches on Academy Hill had a fair and I walked over to check it out. As I was leaving, a friendly man stopped me on the crowded steps.

Did I know him? he asked.

I didn't.

He glowed with enthusiasm. "Surely you must remember me?"

I had no idea that I'd ever seen him before.

"Oh," he said childishly, "and *you* haven't changed a bit. I'd know *you* anyplace. You look exactly the same as you did the day we graduated from high school."

"Maybe it's your white beard," I joked. "I'm sure you didn't have a white beard then." We laughed and he introduced me to his family, as if it was 1956 and he'd never decided, with some other fifteen-year-olds, not to ever speak to me again. It was obvious that he had no recollection of abandoning our friendship and absolutely no idea of how it hurt my young life. When I shook his hand to say good-bye, I suddenly remembered him and what a really nice kid he was. For a minute I could see him all those years ago in our old high school cafeteria showing off his new red and gray club jacket with his name above the front pocket, just like the one that spent a week wrapped in newspaper hidden from my parents in our garage until Friday when the trash collectors took it and friendship away.

O, is all forgot?
All school-days' friendship, childhood innocence?

—*A Midsummer Night's Dream*, 3.2

*   *   *

When I first started working with the old people at the Stein Center on Friday afternoons there was a beautiful woman with missing
teeth. Humiliated, she'd hold her hand in front of her mouth to
apologize. "You wouldn't believe how pretty I used to be," she'd
say. "Men followed me on the street. My mother was sure I'd
accept the first one. . . . Look at me now. You'd never even be able
to tell." From behind the veil of her hand she'd lament, "I try to
look good. This is a nice dress, isn't it? Do you like it? I'm waiting
for my teeth and I'm so ashamed."

She said that I was handsome and she'd ask if I could see any
beauty still in her, was any of it left?

One Friday she told me that she had to leave early. "I don't
want to, I wait all week for the Shakespeare. But they want to see
me about my teeth. I have to leave before you finish."

Twenty minutes before the class ended she walked up to me. "I
have to go now to see about my teeth."

"It's okay, you told me. I'll see you next week." She seemed so
frail. I bent down and kissed her on the cheek. "See ya next Friday."

The old lady walked to the door but instead of leaving she circled right back to me.

"Once more," she said, "just once more. It's been so long since
anyone's kissed me. Please just one more." As I bent down her
voice was so faint that you could almost mistake it for breath. "I'm
so afraid," she whispered. "I never thought I'd be alone. My health
isn't good, but much worse is how afraid I feel."

"I think we're all afraid," I said. "Maybe it's why there're so
many people here on Friday afternoons." She looked so vulnerable
and decent, so pathetically isolated to have outlived everyone
who'd loved her.

"Why don't you come up and stand by me when you get frightened," I said. "Don't talk or interrupt, just stand with me till
you're not so afraid." For almost the whole year before she died,

every Friday she'd quietly stand right next to me for a few minutes. Suddenly she'd be there, like an altar boy with the priest when I was a kid at Holy Rosary. And I always thought about high school all those years ago and how much I needed someone who was okay to think I was okay and just let me stand next to them.

CHAPTER 16

When I was a sophomore in Miss Hogan's art class my mother started to get afraid about men in cars. My sister had become thirteen and beautiful. She certainly looked odd sitting on the little tricycle, but with her long yellow hair and her tan legs extending from faded summer shorts it was possible at first to miss the collection of disabilities. On the bike you couldn't immediately pick out the inward thrust of her feet, and with her hands tightly gripping the handlebars it was possible not to see them shake or wind around each other. Focused on singing and pedaling, she could look intent and purposeful. It was a nice neighborhood where people knew my sister by sight and, mercifully, not once in all those years did she ever pedal beyond the bounds of the sidewalk.

One early summer afternoon my mother got a desperate call from a neighbor. The woman said that she'd watched a man lean out of his car to talk to Carolyn and he'd apparently been there long enough to know that my sister couldn't respond. Carolyn was probably staring at the car. "Car," she'd say, or sometimes she'd frown. "Go car," she'd bellow. "Go car."

Not long after the neighbor gave the warning there was a second time, not the same man, not the same car, and it was around then that the seizures started. And my parents made the decision to move to the eighth house since I was born.

In the autumn of 1957 they bought a sprawling and surprisingly glamorous split level in north Stratford, miles from the center of town. It was one of a couple of good-looking houses that local builder Arthur Dritenbasse had put up on a hill behind the old stone house he lived in with his wife. They seemed nice enough until Martha Dritenbasse said a thing that would haunt our family for years. Handing my mother a tall glass of tea with an aromatic sprig of mint poking up through the ice she smiled. "I don't understand something, Mildred. You're still such a young woman and it's clearly a hardship and it's so bad for the boy. Why wouldn't you just put her away?" Not since that long-ago day in Hartford had anybody put those scary words together.

Mrs. Dritenbasse's idea struck terror in me, but my mother had always been rigid on the subject. Vague and melancholy as she could be, my mother always had the strength to assert her promise that my sister would never, never go away. And not once in all the years did my parents turn their frustration against my sister. Despite her lack of reason, she was always reasoned with. Occasionally she was forced reluctantly into the tub after an awful mess, but mostly she was patiently persuaded. It was our unstated code.

Very soon after we moved into the new house Carolyn developed a bizarre compulsive act. She was fourteen and one day while making her way past our big new refrigerator she just stopped, just stood there. She started to spend her time, all of her time, night and day, leaning against it. For three years, all day and all night, the refrigerator became the only place she could be. At first she stood leaning just a bit on her right side. Nothing we said or did, nothing we offered, none of our usually persuasive tricks, worked. She could not leave it. Every other place had become a terror to her.

For the first week she just stood, but before long she started to kick it rhythmically with the side of her foot. She always stood sideways with one twisted, turned-in foot on the floor and the other one, the left one, raised to about six inches. She lifted it just high enough to miss the recess at the bottom and make contact with the lower part of the door—*kick, kick, kick, kick, kick.*

After a month she added a new piece. She would hold the refrigerator handle lightly, passively, in her right hand and gently pull it toward her. Just before the mechanism would engage to open the door she would release it back—*chunk!* She did this more or less rhythmically, not completely or always consistently, but mostly the same—*kick-chunk, kick-chunk, kick-chunk*—for three years! She had to be fed standing there. Any attempt to move her, coax her, not feed her, failed. She would, if touched, fall to the floor flailing with enormous strength. She'd scream as if her world was being taken away, and for her it was. She would of course pee and have bowel movements standing there. To clean her while she thought that we were trying to pull her away made the job even more grotesque. I can remember wiping her, the floor, the refrigerator while she wailed in complete terror. But never, even at her most anguished, did she ever lash out at us. All of her violence was against herself or manifested itself as resistance. Years later, when political movements caused young zealots to lie in front of rolling tanks or otherwise put their power to limpness, I thought of Carolyn on the kitchen floor screaming and sobbing, not to hurt anyone, just to be left alone, to be allowed to do whatever her injured mind told her. We, all of us, were victims, but at least in our way we understood.

Sometimes very late at night with my parents asleep, in just the dark shadows made by the night-light, I would take her lovely hand and gently try to coax her weary body away. In those moments she didn't know why she was standing there any more than I did. And just for a few seconds, suspended in her trust and love for me, she would let go of the handle. Like a novice tightrope walker, longingly staring into my eyes, her body would move almost imperceptibly toward me, the odd foot would fall to the floor.

"Come on, sweetheart, come with me. We'll talk and play. We can sit on the floor on a rug in another room. Just move a little bit . . ."

It was like piling things on an unsound base, the higher you get the riskier. Then suddenly I could see the panic grow in her eyes and she would lurch away from me and lose contact, be prey again to the terrible demon that tied her, like Prometheus, to our General Electric refrigerator. *Kick-chunk, kick-chunk, kick-chunk*—how I hated that sound.

From the time I came in from school at 3:30, through supper, all through doing the dishes, the six o'clock news, "Studio One," "Playhouse 90," the eleven o'clock news, Jack Paar, and finally lights out: *kick-chunk*. A couple of times a week my father would decide that she had to sleep in a bed, her own bed. It was obvious that he didn't know what to do and that her standing there all night was an audible symbol of our failure to free her from what-ever kept her there. Twice a week he would drag her up to her brand-new frilly pink little girl's room and on to her pink and lace little girl's bed. This was a room for some child who never came to our house. This was a bed for some little girl who played with dolls, sang little songs, and smelled sweet, not for our little girl.

Once he had forced her onto the bed she continued to groan and scream. She would try anything to get away. He would slam his whole body weight down on her. I cannot forget the sound as she resisted and he, by then in his late forties, grunted and scared her. This went on until he fell asleep on top of her, with Carolyn, pinioned under him, fighting all night.

Sometimes after he fell asleep she'd get out from under him. I could hear her making her way along the hall in the dark. I'd get out of bed and switch on a light so she could go safely down the stairs and back to the only world she knew. I'd make tea and sit in the half darkness at the kitchen table, smoke a cigarette, and try to reassure us both.

During the long afternoons of the junior year in Miss Hogan's art class, I became friends with a beautiful girl named Frederika Canfield, and the relationship changed my life. "Ricky" was handsome and classical-looking with deep cerulean eyes and high shiny cheeks. She was a senior and on her way to Boston University. Like me she didn't quite fit, like me she was smart and not much interested in what other kids cared most about. Much later, in one of the more bizarre acts of our friendship, we posed as Hamlet and Ophelia for an opulent four-page spread in *Seventeen* magazine. Across the pages of stunning photography, Ricky is far more exquisite than the perky models who mug to peddle plaid all around us.

I don't know if Ricky had other friends. I'm sure she must have, but wild to be in her company I've obliterated the competition to such a degree as to not remember any. She had a wonderful car. It was an old-fashioned Ford Woody with a rattling heater hanging from the enormous dashboard. The plaque on the heater read "Little South Wind." That's what Ricky called the huge station wagon. "Let's go for a spin in Little South Wind," she'd say.

One afternoon in Miss Hogan's art class I was gluing together boxes, trying to understand Braque. (Miss Hogan was mad for cubism.)

"Do you have a suit?" Ricky whispered from a worktable across the room.

"What?"

"Do you own a suit and a tie? There's a concert Saturday night. My family's going. Wanna come?"

When Ricky picked me up in the Little South Wind, she looked completely beautiful in the ugliest dress I'd ever seen. The emerald green satin gown was the gift of some dead DAR aunt, and looked it. Slumped over the wheel with a cigarette fixed to her very red lower lip she shifted gears with the voluminous skirt hiked over her knees. To my unsophisticated kid's eye, there was a peculiar glamour in everything that Ricky or her family did.

She had two younger sisters and her grandmother lived in part of the upstairs. Her father could have been Cary Grant's brother. He was patrician and charming. Arthur liked things to stay light and good-natured. When his three very dramatic daughters got out of hand he'd beg, "Will you please take *all that* out behind the barn."

Mrs. Canfield spoke in a stentorian voice as if she'd spent a lifetime with people who couldn't hear or immediately understand her. She collected English and American antiques. The house was packed floor to ceiling with piles of astonishing objects and every afternoon there was tea from irreplaceable sets of dishes accumulated for the girls to cart off to future marriages. I'm not sure any of the teenaged daughters cared much about two-hundred-year-old canary luster cups. They played games or did homework in the shadowy furniture-filled rooms. Bent over the long Sheraton dining table the three beautiful sisters looked like a Sargent portrait. Amid the dusky antiquities and elegant rituals, there was a bungling aristocratic helplessness that sat squarely on centuries of WASP social structure, no Irish immigrants, no banging refrigerators, no tipsy naked ladies wandering outside anyone's door, and best, no adoration of the heavy heart. "Take it out behind the barn."

The night Ricky wore the ugly green dress started the biggest change in my life. In 1955 the American Shakespeare Festival opened for a brief first season. Stratford, England, and Stratford, Canada, had Shakespeare Festivals and it was the dream of a lot of scholars and aficionados that there be a third Festival in the United States. In 1950, producer Laurence Langner put it into words.

The theatre that will be built to house Shakespeare's plays will be patterned after the old Globe Theatre in London, and will have approximately 1,600 seats. It will, however, include every appropriate improvement that has been developed since, making it possible to adapt to any kind of production Elizabethan or modern.

As we settled into our plush seats Ricky said that she'd worked as a dresser the summer before.

"What's a dresser?"

"I helped actors with their costumes."

"Could I? I know some Shakespeare speeches. I could recite something, maybe they'd let me be a dresser, too."

"You'd have to meet the wardrobe mistress. It's her choice, but she likes me, and I could ask her."

"When?" I was impatient. "When could I meet the wardrobe lady?"

"Not till May. The costumes are added just before the play starts."

Listening to Mantovani's violins I started to make movies in my head of working as a dresser at the Shakespeare Festival, even though I wasn't completely sure what a dresser was. "Not till May."

A few months later, when Ricky walked me through the red metal stage door, the blast of air coming from the cement dressing room level carried all those remarkable theater smells. And from the first second it felt like the place the nuns at Holy Rosary said was heaven.

The actors were on a break from *A Midsummer Night's Dream* rehearsal. June Havoc was playing Titania the fairy queen. She was coming down the steps from stage level. With a crown and an enormous gauzy Elizabethan dress, a ruff and gigantic whisk sparkling behind her head, she looked like Billie Burke in *The Wizard of Oz* descending in that big shiny bubble. "Are you a good witch or a bad witch?"

"June, this is my friend Bob. I think he's going to work with us, he's a very nice person." Ricky put my best foot forward.

Lighting a Tareyton, Miss Havoc exhaled a smoky theatrical mezzo. Not like a witch at all. "Hi."

The big wardrobe room was like a kid's idea of a magic factory. Incredible costumes were suspended, gently twirling from ceiling pipes. A glistening universe of ethereal *Midsummer Night's Dream* twisted against the somber sparkle of the costumes for *Hamlet*. Beyond the dazzling forest, past an obstacle course of ironing boards and old ladies sewing, sat the stern wardrobe mistress, and straight from Charles Dickens she was. Lilas Norell looked up over her butterfly-shaped glasses. She didn't smile; she made no pretense at being nice. I never saw her be nice to anyone except once years later, long after I didn't know her, my mother called to say a letter had come from Scotland. Miss Norell's name was on the back of the envelope, no address, just Lilas Norell, a Glasgow postmark, and inside a single wager on the Irish Sweepstakes, no message, just the ticket. It was a silent apology.

The wardrobe lady raised her head to take a whiff in my direction. In a tin ashtray a cigarette sent smoke past her face. She flicked her tongue around in her mouth, taking an uncomfortably long time to evaluate me.

"How old are you?"

"Sixteen."

"Have you done anything like this before?"

"No."

"What makes ya think ya could?"

"I have a sick sister. I change her clothes all the time. I do it fast, she gets nervous. I think I could be a dresser."

She frowned a cranky I'm-gonna-scare-the-bejesus-outta-ya old-lady frown. I stayed calm. I kept my knees apart. "You think you could be Hamlet's dresser?"

Hamlet! "Yes, I could be Hamlet's dresser, Miss Norell, I know all about Hamlet. I know the play. I've read . . ."

She ignored me, and looked at Ricky. "We'll give it a try."

I'm in!

The Festival was in final rehearsals for *Hamlet*. Brilliant John Houseman was the artistic director. He was the topmost person at the theater and as Hamlet's sixteen-year-old dresser I was the ecstatic absolute bottom.

Toward the end of my first week I was in the lower lobby gluing rubber soles to dozens of brand-new boots. Houseman and producer Laurence Langner were in the dark stairway that led to the balcony. They were locking horns over the running time of the play. Every night it was well after midnight when the four captains finally lifted Hamlet's lifeless body and Fortinbras "bid the soldiers shoot." Langner thought the evening too long for the audience, most of whom had an extensive car trip after the show. Before it was seen by the critics he wanted the production to lose an hour.

Houseman was furious. His familiar overarticulated voice echoed into the lobby. "When you erase a word Shakespeare chose," he said, "you've contributed to the process of murdering that word. You want *me* to obliterate *Shakespeare's* course of thinking, to reorganize *his* thoughts."

It was the first time I'd ever heard anyone argue in the defense of a word, and it made me want to cry. Of course the cuts were made. Doing it faster was what our world was about. Just blocks away the construction of the I-95 superhighway was knocking down beautiful old houses so that eighteen-wheelers could careen between Boston and New York. Probably much more to the point, audiences were already a decade into their bleary addiction to word-assassinating television. Houseman himself was producer of highbrow "Playhouse 90." We watched it every Thursday night from our green plastic sofa while my sister beat the refrigerator.

Even a shorter *Hamlet* was too long for some. There were always disturbing evacuees around eleven. Not me. I knelt in the dark catwalk squinting at the stage through an odd angled crack in the teak paneling till the last ordnance was shot. And I loved every minute of it.

The productions were like gigantic operas with thousands of technical bits and pieces coming together. In June of 1958 a hundred people worked on the complicated apparatus of the play. Despite what they might have felt about each other, Houseman and Langner had put together a world-class team of artists. The simple fey dances in *A Midsummer Night's Dream* and the great rural hoedown in *The Winter's Tale* were both choreographed by George Balanchine!

The well-known first scene in Hamlet starts just after midnight, "Tis now struck twelve." And ends with the coming of morning, "Look, the dawn in russet mantle clad walks o'er the dew of yon high eastern hill." As the artificial day came, warmer stage lights were added and the cooler night instruments faded. Finally, bird sounds crept in and just a hint of a musical theme. It was magic.

From the first I loved to stand where all the pieces came together. In the dark near the stage manager's desk I'd listen to him whisper the warnings for upcoming cues. I could just about hear him breathe into the headset, "Warning lights twenty, warning music eleven, warning sound eighteen, warning offstage noises, warning spotlight, warning flies for tapestry." When an actor on stage gave a verbal cue it started a series of reactions. Tiny lights would blink on in concealed places all around the theater. Then, at a word from the stage manager they'd start to pop off. "*Go* lights twenty, *go* music eleven, *go* sound eighteen, *go* offstage noises, *go* spotlight, *go* tapestry!" It was thrilling, and from the first minute it was obvious how easily a play can become your life.

I stole every chance to watch from the blackness of the theater. Houseman was masterful at taking extraordinary care of the play's text. He spent enormous amounts of time on how the production looked and on the flow and smoothness of the scene transitions and the constant balance of stage pictures.

"Move that whole speech fifteen feet down left," he'd enunciate, just like the Wizard of Oz, into a gigantic megaphone. From his seat way at the back of the shadowy theater, he always seemed reluctant to make the long trip to the stage. In the 1950s, those years of the Strasbergs and Actors Studio, Houseman seemed formal and Edwardian. But watching him watch, learning to predict in the dark what his response would be, when he'd stop the whole rehearsal to fix a tiny flaw, became my favorite activity. Leaning against the wall or sitting low with my chin on the back of the seat in front of me I began to learn about Shakespeare on the stage.

On an iron bench all the way down center a tall, thin boy sat bent forward like Rodin's *Thinker*. The murky atmosphere was self-consciously profound as long dust-filled shafts of light crisscrossed the pitch-dark and landed on him. The scene was about as *Hamlet* as a *Hamlet* could get. . . .

> To be, or not to be, that is the question:
> Whether 'tis nobler in the mind . . .
>
> —*Hamlet*, 3.1

In the somberness at the back of the theater the director raised his megaphone. "What the hell is *this*?" No "Excuse me, Hamlet," just a slow, creepy, "What the hell is *this*?"

Hamlet stopped being Hamlet. The actor scrunched his face to see into the pitch-black theater. At a worktable assistants rustled papers and Bernie the stage manager popped his head around the proscenium. "John?"

Again came the famous voice, slower than molasses in an English January. "This is the best-known thirty-three lines that any actor has spoken on any stage in the history of Western civilization, and I can't see a fucking thing! Goddamn it, Jean, turn on the lights!"

Through the reverberating megaphone he was cursing at the most famous lighting designer in the world, Jean Rosenthal. She was sitting in the middle of the theater chewing a yellow pencil, wishing it were a cigarette. Her legs were up, crossed on the makeshift worktable. She didn't respond. There was a whisper of sibilances and more paper shuffling. Before long the lights lightened and Hamlet slowly transmuted from stunning sculpture into a real person with a completely visible young face, a face that wondered if life's worth the pain of living. At the time, a couple of months before my seventeenth birthday, Hamlet's problem was a thing in which I was pathologically interested.

> Whether 'tis nobler in the mind to suffer
> The slings and arrows of outrageous fortune,
> Or to take arms against a sea of troubles
> And by opposing end them.
>
> —*Hamlet*, 3.1

The naive poem for which I'd won the high school scholastic award was about suicide.

The week of technical rehearsals was also the first time I stepped onto the enormous stage. The crew that constructed the costumes had accompanied them from New York. Sewers occupied every available corner, adding finishing touches or making revisions to hundreds of garments. With the eccentric group came milliners, "shoe" people from Capezio, and even a person in charge of helmets and chain mail.

Hamlet's father, the ghost, had a full set of fiberglass armor. To increase the necromantic illusion he was covered head to toe with torn brown gauze that got caught on everything. The ghost was always missing.

"Where's Jack?" an assistant would whisper desperately. "Anybody seen Jack?" A flashlight search through stored scenic elements would find him caught on a jutting corner unable to cry out without being heard by the audience.

Shakespeare was the first person to play the part. Good-natured Jack bragged that "Will" was jealous of *his* terrific performance and was exacting revenge. In the long history of theater tradition and superstition it was a thrill to be the new kid listening to the actor of the ghost accuse the ghost of the actor who first acted the ghost.

Last night I had dinner in New York with a woman who sees herself as a ghost. She's almost immobile. After suffering a couple of strokes, her body is breaking down at an accelerating rate. A restaurant meal was impossible so she asked me to come to her house. The long-kept vain secret of her age not so important anymore, Dina confessed that she was born in Paris eighty-something years ago. She speaks a pocketful of languages and is high minded about her erotic liaisons with an inventory of famous scientists and philosophers. Sitting in the posh library surrounded by a who's who in Renaissance picture making, she murmurs secrets as pretty Irish girls on the payroll pour my favorite Cabernet and discreetly make sure Dina doesn't skip a chance at the toilet.

She leans into my ear. "What's my legacy?" she whispers. Her concerned daughter and gorgeous bouncy show-off seven-year-old granddaughter had just stopped by.

"You have them," I say. "A lot better than me. I've got no one checking in, no one who cares that way. I have work and words I toss, praying somebody will care enough to catch them."

"Exactly!" She clears her wet-dry throat. "That's just what I mean. Memories, ideas, moments of exquisite hedonism or heartbreak—all left unprotected and chewed up by vicious insatiable time. What happened to all that? Where's my life—not my genes, not the color of my eyes—I mean my *life*, my *real actual life*. Where is it? Who's got it? Did it ever happen?"

> Time hath, my lord, a wallet at his back
> Wherein he puts alms for oblivion,
> A great-siz'd monster of ingratitudes.
> Those scraps are good deeds past, which are
>   devour'd
> As fast as they are made, forgot as soon
> As done.
>
> —*Troilus and Cressida*, 3.3

In the speakers I could hear Hamlet fooling around with Ophelia. The sound system let the actors backstage know what was happening so they'd be ready when their cue came. The "tech" rehearsals had gotten to the play within the play, when the troupe of traveling actors facsimilize the poisoning of Hamlet's father. Hamlet was teasing, making sexual jokes. Ophelia was embarrassed and flattered.

> "Lady, shall I lie in your lap?"
> "No, my lord."
> "I mean, my head upon your lap."
> "Ay, my lord."
> "Do you think I meant country matters?"
> "I think nothing, my lord."
>
> —*Hamlet*, 3.2

The playful painful inquisition stopped. The little backstage speakers went still.

"Bob Smith . . . Will Bob Smith please come up to the stage." It was terrifying to hear my name from the same little box that was bringing me *Hamlet*. I didn't think anyone even knew my name. I bolted up the side stairs to the stage manager's desk. Bernie wasn't there.

A couple of deadpan stagehands pointed to the stage. "They wancha out there, must be big trouble."

When I stepped up onto the raked platform the first thing that hit me was the blinding lights and heat. Every actor in the company was out on the stage. They'd been standing for hours in full makeup and costume. From a pair of elaborately carved thrones the King and Queen were staring down at me. Osric was leaning behind Gertrude, Rosencrantz and Guildenstern were mumbling to each other on a landing upstage left. Elegant courtiers and beautiful ladies were arranged aesthetically on various steps and platforms. Polonius, always unpretentious and friendly, smiled a completely out of place greeting and mouthed, "Hi, Bob." Hamlet was sprawled across the stage-right platform with his aquiline head lying gently in Ophelia's lap.

It was like walking straight into one of George Pistey's funeral home religious calendars or being lost in a Caravaggio or Rubens at the Met. I stood breathless in my polo shirt and madras Bermuda shorts, a Connecticut Yankee at King Claudius's court.

This time Mr. Houseman was on the stage talking quietly to the designer and the production stage manager. They were in conference about a cape that was twirled around Hamlet. It was a lot of heliotrope silk that wrapped a couple of times around his chest and twisted up over his right shoulder ending in a long train behind him. The director liked exactly the way it looked. The designer asked if I could get it to look just this way every time? It was fifteen feet of slippery silk, and we had only about two minutes in the dark off-stage stairway.

"I'm not sure," I said. "There's no time, just some trumpets and drums. It's slippery and it's dark. I'm nervous and Hamlet's edgy about tricking everyone. He's jumpy and so much taller than me." It was like Carolyn and all the times when we had to change her with people waiting. "Sew it into a figure eight and I'll stand on the stairs above him and drop it over his head. As long as we get the front on the front we won't have to worry about anything except catching Claudius."

I honestly believed that Hamlet and I were working the play out together. Since my expulsion from the kids' jacket club I'd been alone except for the Canfield girls, and Hamlet was becoming my best friend. I thought of him the way I did the oldest Geese brother, the one who practiced piano and sometimes took us younger kids on dangerous adventures.

My bizarre perception of my job wasn't lost on John Houseman. He was amused. "It will work very well that way." He smiled. "Thank you."

The designer brought one of the neurotic but steady-handed seamstresses onto the stage. Everyone waited while she pinned and folded and folded and pinned the long purple cloth.

By July *Hamlet* and *A Midsummer Night's Dream* were alternating performances. On a *Hamlet* night a series of violent thunderstorms passed through. The deluge was flooding parts of the backstage. About three-quarters of the way into the play, I could hear the crack of lightning and rumble of thunder through the high teak walls of the theater. Fortinbras was taking his huge ragtag army through Denmark, and Houseman had directed the troops to parade across the very back of the stage. In the leaden darkness the specter was a seemingly endless line of weary foot soldiers. In reality the army was made up of anybody available—actors, dressers, stagehands, stage managers, assistants—each threw on an old cape and went round and round.

The line marched across the stage from left to right, and as each soldier got out of sight he'd run like hell down the back stairs and out through the stage-right stage door. Outside, everyone ran to the other side of the building to reenter another door, run up those stairs, and land back on stage left ready to march again. Over and over around and around they went, switching hoods and helmets and capes. Of course, on rainy nights, the army got drenched.

The actor who played Fortinbras also played Oberon in *A Midsummer Night's Dream*. Dicken Waring was a middle-aged Welshman with the expected remarkable voice and leading man looks. He'd been a principal actor the generation before with Ethel Barrymore and he'd played the Mad Hatter in Eva Le Galliene's famous *Alice in Wonderland*. He knew a lot about Shakespeare and English history and was one of the gentlest and kindest people I've ever known.

After the long march and before the final scene Dicken had nothing to do but sit in his sweltering dressing room sipping a whiskey in his suffocating armor. The night of the violent storm he was edgy. With the blinding makeup lights turned off he sat in shadows staring at himself in the smoky mirror.

"Let's visit Titania," he roared in the theatrical voice he'd developed for Oberon. "The capes are wet already, Bobbin." Bobbin is what some older actors called me. I don't remember who started it, but I was thrilled to have an invented, Elizabethan-sounding name—a lot better, I thought, than plain Bob Smith.

"The wig's wet, the plumes are soaked. Let's go wake up June."

June Havoc was staying in an old fisherman's cottage owned by the Festival. It stood on stilts out over the river right next to Bond's Dock. From the stage door you only had to cross the staff parking lot and wind through the wild roses next to the Davenports' higgledy-piggledy saltbox, which sat just next to the theater on that same bluff over the river.

Dicken enlisted a couple of the King's bored Switzers and we headed into the tempest. It was almost 10:30 when we wrestled the wind to cross the parking lot. Fortinbras, now Oberon, hoisted himself onto the old retaining wall in front of the Davenports', just above the swelling river and the little cottage. The lights in the place were out.

"Titania! Titania!" His eerie voice braided into the wind.

As the rain fell in sideways sheets and summer lightning flashed over the river, five of us stood enthralled in our drenched capes and soaked feet. We were Shakespeare's attendants to the Fairy King. We were with a real father.

Water trailed down the furrows in his forehead and saturated plumes stuck to his heavily made up old actor's face.

"Titania!" His voice was darker than a Welsh coal mine. He was drunk and loud enough to wake the dead. He told us to yell and scream while he roared out the text.

> DIAN'S BUD O'ER CUPID'S FLOWER
> HATH SUCH FORCE AND BLESSED POWER.
> NOW, MY TITANIA, *WAKE YOU,* MY SWEET QUEEN.
> —*A Midsummer Night's Dream,* 4.1

In the little house a light snapped on. A window flung open, then a door. Miss Havoc delicately stepped barefoot onto the rain-soaked porch. She was wearing a nightgown. Through the rain she immediately joined the game, "My Oberon, what visions have I seen."

He smiled a big beautiful grin. "Thou and I are new in amity and will tomorrow midnight solemnly dance in Duke Theseus' house triumphantly." He called instructions to us with the glint of a twelve-year-old's madness.

> TRIP AWAY; MAKE NO STAY;
> MEET ME ALL BY BREAK OF DAY.
> —*A Midsummer Night's Dream,* 5.1

The tanked-up old actor leapt off the seawall and ran like a madman, slipping and sliding through the Davenports' muddy side yard with us mesmerized kids tearing after. It was the most exciting thing that had ever happened to me. With the soaked hood dripping rain into my eyes, I'd been let into the magic. I'd been invited to the other side of the words. In the flashes of lightning I'd seen Oberon and Titania and they weren't like any adults I knew. For a kid what's better than a grown-up who treasures imagination? That summer the line began to blur even more between the then and the now, the hard-edged present and the idealized poetic past.

Drenched and filthy I chased after Oberon as he rushed back to be Fortinbras. As I charged down the backstage steps, Queen Gertrude was in the speaker box. Appropriate to the night and perfect for the moment she was telling Laertes that his sister had drowned.

> "... But long it could not be
> Till that her garments, heavy with their drink,
> Pull'd the poor wretch from her melodious lay
> To muddy death."
> "Alas, then she is drown'd?"
> "Drown'd, drown'd."
>
> —*Hamlet,* 4.7

In the entrancement and flashes of lightning I didn't notice Miss Norell at the bottom of the steps.

"What now is *this*?" Her thick Scots accent lent even greater severity to her anger. "Look at the mud on this cape. You're paid to care for them, you're responsible to these costumes." *Don't forget to wipe her good.* "This is your fault, completely your fault."

"The capes were already wet from the march. I didn't think. I was stupid. Please don't be mad at me. I'm sorry."

"You're fired." She said it with no feeling at all. "Just look at the work you've made for me. I've watched you. You love the play, you love the actors, you're swept away. Collect the wet capes, hang them in the wardrobe room, and after you've rinsed out Hamlet's shirts, go home. No need to come back, no need at all. You're a nice polite boy but this is not the job for you."

"Go home." I didn't actually feel like I had a home. I'd been sleeping outside or on a couple of porches. Mrs. Hernon over on West Broad left lemonade and a pillow on her screened-in porch. "Go home." *Kick-chunk, kick-chunk, kick-chunk, kick-chunk, kick-chunk, kick-chunk, kick-chunk.*

"Oh, and I owe you ten dollars for this week so far. Collect the wet things, wash Hamlet's shirts, and before you leave, I'll give you cash."

She was right. I was just some kid from the town who didn't know anything. Anybody could replace me. But she was very wrong that I didn't care about the costumes. I cared very much. I studied them in the library. I found out what things were called or who'd invented them or what monarch made them popular. By the time I was forty I owned scores of books on the history of costume. But when I was a kid that first summer I wanted so badly to be a part of it all that I'd forgotten my job and perilously traded it for ten minutes in the rain as Oberon's henchman.

Hamlet was finished for the night. Almost everybody had gone over to Ryan's Grill for the nightly beers. I was sitting in the green-room holding the ten dollars with my knees knocking together when Bernie sat down.

"She's fit to be tied," he said. "She wants you gone, whatta ya gonna do?"

"She doesn't like me. I told her I'd work for free to make up for it but she just doesn't like me."

In the wardrobe room with Bernie's hand on my shoulder I sniffled and pleaded and begged for another chance. He interjected a hopeful word when he could.

"He's a decent kid, Lilas. He's good at his job and God knows he cares as much as anybody here. Let's give him a second chance?"

Intimidated by the production stage manager, she relented. But she never looked me directly in the face again, not when she had to tell me something, not when she handed me my eighteen dollars every week. She was angry because she thought I'd gone over her head and challenged her authority.

That amazing summer I sometimes missed Carolyn so unbearably that I'd walk the four or five miles up to north Stratford to see her. In a way the obsession with the refrigerator had shut me out. Except for those few times when she'd leave it for a minute, there was nothing else that mattered to her.

Late at night I'd take the long walk and there she'd be. I could see her through the picture window in the kitchen. My parents would have left the night-light on. She'd be leaning exhausted. She could just about lift her foot to kick, her tired hand almost too weak to jerk the handle.

"Hi, sweetheart. I missed you so much that I had to see you. Are you okay? I have to be away for a while. Please don't hate me. Please don't forget me. Do you want me to change you? Do you want me to . . ." I'd fall asleep at the table to the gentle passive rhythm. *Kick-chunk.*

Sometimes I'd call my mother from the backstage pay phone, but after we talked about Carolyn there was nothing to say. "Are you eating?" she'd ask. "These are the best years of your life and you're only young once." She'd never ask anything about the plays or the job. "As long as you're happy," she'd say.

A few times I stopped by to see my father's parents. By the summer of 1958 they'd rented out most of the big old house. It was obvious that they were sinking into a poverty of old age. While my Yankee grandparents and the menagerie tucked themselves into the dining room, kitchen, and one of the living rooms, an unseen couple occupied the rest of the big old place. In the years that those strangers lived in most of Jesse Wells's house, I never met or even once saw them.

Ethel and Earl Smith had no curiosity about what was taking place on the other side of Academy Hill in the big theater by the river. They had their own problems, but I never heard either of them complain. Not even when they'd ended up in a tiny city apartment with no yard and, tragically worse, *no pets allowed.* Every night *Hamlet* made me think of them, every night *Hamlet* made me think of everything.

> for thou hast been
> As one, in suff'ring all, that suffers nothing,
> A man that Fortune's buffets and rewards
> Hast ta'en with equal thanks; and blest are those
> Whose blood and judgment are so well commeddled
> That they are not a pipe for Fortune's finger
> To sound what stop she please. Give me that man
> That is not passion's slave, and I will wear him
> In my heart's core, ay, in my heart of heart,
> As I do thee.
>
> —*Hamlet,* 3.2

CHAPTER 17

The Academy part of the American Shakespeare Festival Theater and Academy was a school held in a tall Greek Revival mansion on the property. Some of the best teachers in the world were on the roster. Voice coaches who'd taught the crème de la crème of the British stage spent the summer struggling with forty young, gifted, American actors. The students played small roles in the productions and understudied. From the day they started, I watched all the understudy rehearsals. The young actors were taken through the play by the stage managers. All of the movements were the same but it was almost unbelievable how a different actor doing exactly identical blocking can make a whole new play.

At the rehearsals actors asked me to "run lines." "How does it sound?" they'd ask. "Is it clear? Does it make sense? Am I getting the points across?" Before long I made suggestions and was thrilled when actors liked what I said. "Show it to Bob, see what he thinks. He's good at spotting things." Students started asking me to watch their monologues or scenes for class. Deep into those torrid summer nights I sat upstairs in the big white building while they went over and over their speeches. I'd never loved anything more than sitting on that sweltering floor at two A.M. watching actors acting, and of course I got to know a lot of text.

"Wanna grab a burger and take a look at my King John?"

One late night in the old academy building a zealous actor vowed a pilgrimage to Canada. Before the highways, the Canadian Shakespeare Festival was a twelve-hour drive.

Canada had a Monday-night performance. That was our "dark" night. We finished the Sunday matinee by six and didn't have a show until Tuesday at eight o'clock. There were forty-eight hours to make the round-trip, twenty-four of which would be in the car. "Wanna come?" one of the guys asked. "Four of us are chipping in for gas and food. We're all broke so we'll split the price of a cheap room up there. There's no time to sleep anyway. We'll get to see Christopher Plummer play Benedict."

I hadn't been very many places before, just those few trips with my grandparents, the Baseball Museum and the Howe Caverns. "I don't drive," I said. "And I'm more broke than any of you. I only get eighteen dollars. But I'll give you most of it. If you want me I'd be wild to go."

Five of us spent a couple of weeks making our crazy plan. Everybody backstage thought we were nuts and every one of them wanted to come. We figured if we ran out the backstage door right after the Sunday matinee and drove all night we could be at the bridge across the Niagara River by dawn. I was useless, but I knew the way as far as Syracuse. An odd thing about not driving is that I can direct people on how to get almost anywhere.

We crossed the Niagara in that russet dawn from the first scene in *Hamlet*. One of the kicks of the trip was jumping a fence on the Canadian side and sneaking down as far as we could in the rocks and water and twisted trees to watch the sunrise from a level spot where we ate stale sandwiches and smoked Tareytons. Polite trespassers, we folded our waxed paper and took it with us. A few years ago when I was teaching at the Actors Center of Los Angeles, an older student asked if I'd ever made an overnight trip to Canada to see *Much Ado About Nothing*? I was startled. "Yes," I said. "How could you know? It was almost forty years ago."

"My husband's name is Elden," she said. "Do you remember him? He did most of the driving. He remembers stale cheese sandwiches at the base of the Canadian Falls."

We arrived at Stratford and slept for a couple of hours in our dreary prebooked room. Sometime in the early afternoon we showered and ran to see the big new theater. We were like kids on a delicious adventure, the Hardy Boys or any of the heroes in the olive-colored cloth books my mother's kid brother kept in his attic room over on Stillman Street. Because we were the crazy guys who'd driven all night from Stratford to Stratford we got special treatment, a tour of the theater and lunch with most of the actors.

Exhausted from the long drive and lack of sleep we settled into our theater seats only to be bounced up again to stand for "God Save the Queen." The evening was wonderful. We'd read the play together out loud in the academy building a week before the trip. As with *The Winter's Tale*, *Much Ado* has a fabricated death, concocted resurrection, and a general forgiveness for terrible past sins. What I remember most was how much I felt a part of things and how excited I was trying to hold my own in the animated discussion on the long car trip back to Connecticut.

It came on so suddenly. Someone mentioned Labor Day and before the thought settled in the summer was gone. People went to what was next for them and I knew I'd never be asked back. Miss Norell couldn't forgive me. At the very end as I hung up the last costume she reminded me of my rain-soaked adventure. I knew that as long as she remained wardrobe mistress I'd never again see the backstage.

The day the season ended I sat cross-legged on a picnic table in front of the theater watching what had come to be my whole world fade with the saffron summer sun. Later in a book John Houseman described that concluding afternoon of the 1958 season:

> At its final matinee with the clowns stretching their scenes and the audience in a sentimental mood, *A Midsummer Night's Dream* ran several minutes longer than usual, and it was after six o'clock when the last fairy train vanished into the stage floor. Almost before the theater was empty, the stage crew took over. By midnight, scenery, costumes, and props for *Dream, Hamlet,* and *The Winter's Tale* had been struck and stored. Another Festival season was over.

Of course it wasn't just another season for me. For me it was birth and death and I was too young to understand the lessons of *Much Ado* and *Winter's Tale*—that like autumn, sometimes death only looks like death. I'd propped myself against a tall actor to watch the plays vanish one costume, one scene, one precious word, one syllable at a time.

> This weak impress of love is as a figure
> Trenched in ice, which with an hour's heat
> Dissolves to water, and doth lose his form.
> —*The Two Gentlemen of Verona,* 3.2

It was time to go back to my mostly isolated high school kid's existence. *Kick-chunk.*

I've been holding Cora's hand for more than an hour. Every couple of minutes she murmurs something and presses her fingers against mine. We've been reading *Winter's Tale,* the copy is twisted in her hospital sheets. Before she fell asleep she had started to confuse me with some person she was telling about me. She smiled the sweetest little kid's smile. "He's so wonderful," she said. "We laugh all the time. He takes us through the Shakespeare plays." Then she made a sour face and other names tangled in, names of people I didn't know, names from long ago, a dead husband, a brother, some deified teacher at Hunter College in the thirties.

"It's the atmosphere." Her eyes open suddenly. "That's what it is . . . atmosphere." She looks angelic. "He makes it safe to be wrong or stupid . . . or . . . just . . . old." She starts to savagely scratch her scalp, like she's trying to free a trapped thought. The doctors are patient. They know she's ninety-four and this time the cancer's got her.

Outside a heavy rain pelts the tinted hospital glass. Cora's busy telling the surgeon, who she now thinks I am, how much the Shakespeare means to her. "I would have died five years ago if it wasn't for the Shakespeare." She suddenly becomes afraid. She's crying and squeezing my hand.

> This world's a city full of straying streets,
> And death's the market-place where each one meets.
> —*The Two Noble Kinsmen*, 1.5

Holding her quivering fingers and locked into her nervous gaze, my mind shifts back forty years and I remember how afraid I used to be.

After the summer at the Shakespeare Festival I read and reread my incomplete *Complete Works*. The worn Shakespeare book was a farewell gift from an actor. It had black-and-white illustrations by Rockwell Kent but almost no notes.

Through the fall I got lots of three-line messages on postcards from actors "on the road," Canada or California. Will Geer, the actor I'd leaned on in the dark backstage, invited me to sit in on drama classes in New York, but with the idyllic summer gone I felt shy. I didn't know how to be with them without the thing we'd had in common, without Shakespeare.

In the mornings my father drove to work and I rode along as far as the high school. We didn't speak. After the summer's absence, we were even more distrustful of each other. I made an excuse to get out of the car a couple of blocks before the school, afraid to let my father see how some boys treated me.

At home my mother carelessly stoked the flames of disaffection. She was years into an awful habit of talking to me about men as if I wasn't one. "You know men." She'd sigh like we were both disappointed outsiders. "Your father's just jealous. You're so smart and good-looking. People are crazy about you. And if he's so smart, what's he got? I'll tell you what he's got . . . Tuesdays! And it's a woman, I know it's a . . . Men," she'd say with a mockingly moronic smile, "can't live with 'em, can't live without 'em."

In my senior year in high school Carolyn was still at the refrigerator. Occasionally we created that circus to get her into the bathroom, but as soon as she realized we'd beguiled her she'd drop to the floor and start the grotesque crawl back to the kitchen. The refrigerator was dead center in the big sterile house so there was no place where you couldn't hear Carolyn's percussion. I sat in the cellar with earmuffs and a scarf wrapped around my head but I could still feel the rhythmic vibrations.

Weekdays after school I taught an art class to little kids at the community center on Main Street. Afterward I'd stop at the Canfields'. Ricky had already gone to Boston for college and I developed a closeness to the silent middle sister.

Charlotte and I took long, mostly mute walks. In the snap and crunch of brilliant autumn leaves, it wasn't the same speechlessness as the frigid mornings in my father's car. Charlotte's stillness was a coffer in which she hid beautiful secret thoughts. At midnight service for Christmas Eve, we were sitting close for candlelight carols when she disappeared down the wooden aisle of the old church. Just when I thought she'd been gone too long, she slid in next to me carrying an enormous old-fashioned cage with two fluttering doves.

"These are for you," she whispered. "Merry Christmas."

I kept the birds for years, till the female got egg bound and died. As doves do, the male pined away.

Mrs. Canfield made lopsided lemon meringue pies and gallons of Earl Grey tea. Charlotte and I spent hours at the big Sheraton table stuffing envelopes to support hopeless causes that her mother had hope for. We encouraged apathetic politicians not to tear down any more old houses and to keep fluoride out of our taps. We tried to discourage DDT and racism. I made colorful posters to help the Shakespeare Guild promote concerts and recitals that occasionally filled the empty wintertime Festival Theater.

In Miss Hogan's art class I started to think if I couldn't quite fit anyplace, I could draw, and maybe somehow that could be my future. If I was a success I could take Carolyn to a house by the sea and lock the refrigerator in the garage so that at last she'd be free. And then, when I was seventeen, I wondered if maybe Charlotte might be just odd enough to come with us. I developed a plan to follow Ricky to Boston. After all, I'd chased her through the red stage door to the wonderland of the Shakespeare Festival.

She'd asked me to visit her over Columbus Day weekend. I got my pay from the Community Center, a handful of five-dollar bills from my mother, and caught the train to New Haven to wait the half hour it took to switch engines from electric to steam for the three-hour trip along the water to Back Bay.

I was very excited when I hauled my grandfather's brown leather luggage through the drafty old train station to meet Ricky at the B.U. freshman girls' dorm. Charlesgate Hall was a Victorian monstrosity that towered over the Fenway like a grand European hotel fallen on desperate times. Waiting in the flaking fakery of the sham Spanish Renaissance lobby, I half expected a parade of giddy nineteenth-century debutantes flanked by finger-waving duennas.

Ricky was late for a meeting at school. I was to sleep in a basement over on seedy Kenmore Square. "If no one answers use this. Walk right in. It's very casual. Half of Boston's got keys. Nobody even remembers whose place it was originally. See ya later," she called over her shoulder as she ran off to rehearsal and I enthusiastically dragged my overpacked luggage along Marlborough Street.

The apartment was down a curved rusted fire stairs. The door was deep in debris from the windy square. A few feet to the left a primitive painted arch of astrological symbols advertised a bleak storefront coffeehouse featuring poetry readings till dawn and a weekly folksinging contest. The Café Yanna seemed like the most sophisticated place on earth. I never noticed that the old iron staircase was just about ground zero for a flourishing market in reefers and God knows what else.

After a timid flurry of polite Connecticut kid knocks I took Ricky's advice and used the key. When the door blew shut I heard voices. It was dark and right away something felt odd. I had the instinct to leave. "Don't be nuts. Say hello."

In a kitchen at the end of a congested hallway I could see two men and a short overweight boy. "Piggy in *Lord of the Flies*" was my first thought. He was drenched. His eyes were wild and saliva trailed in long disgusting ribbons over his chin. He looked like one of the kids in that bus that picked up my sister for a while in Syracuse. He was begging, "Please don't hurt me. I didn't tell anyone anything."

I froze. One guy was holding a knife.

"You're a liar, Billy. Get on the floor and start praying."

The kid dropped to the linoleum. Just behind his head a grungy teakettle started percolating steam. "Please don't hurt me, I swear to Christ, I never told anything."

Violence scared me. The crucifixion terrified me. Carolyn shrieking and throwing herself onto the floor could be stunningly savage. And it always made me feel sick.

The angry man laughed and tossed the knife back into a drawer. "Get up, Billy." As he got off his knees, Billy picked up a knocked-over chair and acted like it was a joke, but the sweat gave him away.

"Wash your face. Have a brew. You'll live to fail your theater history midterm."

From the open fridge beers were pitched. One of the guys looked over and calmly tossed me a bottle. "Bobby? I'm Steve."

He had a Boston accent and apparently a wicked sense of gallows humor.

"Holy shit!" Steve moved toward me. "Who the fuck does he look like?" He squinted his eyes and stuck his chin out. "It's friggin' scary. He looks exactly like Brian! Absolutely no shit, kid, you could be his goddamn brother."

When I was twelve my mother smiled a sad smile. "People say I should have a baby." She'd been sick and was feeling better. She asked me to sit next to her.

"Everyone thinks you need a brother. Whatta you think? Would you like a brother?"

The idea excited me but I knew it wouldn't be long before she'd call sick from her bed, "Don't forget to wipe *them* good."

A few days later we were bathing my sister after an "accident." Carolyn was resisting. The little pink bathroom was sweating bubbles. My sister was screaming and trying to slide away from us, and I was standing in the foul water with her. My mother was crying. "I can't give you a brother." She was sitting on the edge of the tub. "I don't know if he'd be smart like you or 'not right' like her." That's when I gave the blank test back to Miss Hakala and decided not to be smart. But the fantasy of a brother hung on.

*   *   *

Do I stand there? I never had a brother;
Nor can there be that deity in my nature
Of here and everywhere. I had a sister,
Whom the blind waves and surges have devour'd:
Of charity, what kin are you to me?
What countryman? What name? What parentage?
                                    —*Twelfth Night*, 5.1

When I first met Brian he narrowed his eyes the way people do when they're trying to remember. We did look like each other. We both looked just like my grandfather. Brian was in his late thirties, maybe forty, and just as everybody said, we looked like brothers.

"I had a kid brother," he said. "You look exactly like him. He died before you were born." He squinted again. "The only difference is the hair. He had curly hair like you only red, not blond. It was red like mine—no, more, much more red, orange like a pumpkin."

Except for the brief time in the boys' jacket club, no man had ever identified himself with me. Everyone always said that I looked exactly like my mother's father, but he hadn't said very much since I was four and he'd called me "Bucko."

Brian was friendly. "I gotta see some people. Come with me. Wanna come?"

"Sure. Where?"

"To see a guy, don't ask questions. It's better like that."

"Sure. I won't ask questions. I don't have to ask any questions."

"Good. Let's go."

On the way he told me about his brother dying in a car crash and about a girl named Kate. "Wait'll she sees you. She's gonna flip. I hear you're a Shakespeare freak. I played Macbeth once. I was lousy but I had the build and the red hair."

It was starting to snow when we ducked into a crumbling tenement someplace near Scully Square. "This is my kid brother,"

Brian said to the guy and his stoned wife. She reminded me of my mother, except she never stopped smiling.

"I thought he was dead. It's a goddamn miracle." He put his arm around my shoulders. "But here he is. He's a cute kid, don't ya think? Looks just like me, ha, ha. I was good-looking when I was seventeen. You're seventeen, right?"

Just two hours earlier I'd never laid eyes on him. I didn't even know his last name. It was intoxicating to have a new history handed to me. Just like theater, it was a prosthesis for actual intimacy.

"Hey, Brian's brother, cool to meecha."

I played with a large striped cat and struggled to have a conversation with the bleary wife while Brian and the guy did some business at the back of the railroad flat.

It was snowing hard when Brian said, "Let's go visit Kate! She'll be asleep but I want her to see you." He was excited and it was contagious. She lived in one of those beautiful little blind alleys that crosshatch Beacon Hill and I liked her right away.

"He's been through a lot," she said. "He has terrible dreams. Maybe God sent you to give him something back. Now maybe he can straighten out the trouble and get some peace."

I wondered, "Do all women tell on the men they love? What trouble?" I was definitely sensing some kind of danger. But seventeen years of companionlessness let me shove any apprehension aside.

Later, on Charles Street, walking in the eggshell-colored dawn I said, "She's a nice girl. Are you going to marry her?" He laughed. "No, never. She can't have kids. She can't even fuck the usual way. She's got this bone across the inside of her cunt. I'm crazy about her but I have other women, beautiful women."

"Tuesday, his G.D. Tuesdays. . . . It's a woman. . . ."

"She seems like your wife, you act married."

"It's complicated. I'm a complicated guy. In case you haven't noticed, life's a very complicated thing, little brother."

* * *

Back in Stratford the phone would ring. "Robert, it's long distance." My mother would be in a panic.

"Hey, little brother." I'd sit at the table in the dark kitchen on
Oak Ridge. Brian could hear *kick-chunk*. "I can hear her, poor
fucker. You gotta get otta there. Come up on the weekend. I'll
meet ya at Back Bay. I'll bring Kate. You'd like that wouldn't ya? I
gotta do some business over in Cambridge. Wanna see Haavaad
Yaad?"

My life was getting complicated. I was a senior in high school,
running to Boston every chance I got, and it was then that I wrote
that poem about killing myself. One of the lines I remember: "If I
should die tonight, or now?" It won the contest during a week I'd
stayed up in Boston, the same week I went with Brian to some cour-
thouse in Roxbury to watch a guy he knew get ten years. It was
then that I stopped by the Boston Museum School to find out what
it would take for them to accept me. I'd started my own addiction
to the Boston Museum of Fine Arts and, a little bit farther along the
Fenway, the glorious Isabella Stewart Gardner, the Venetian lair of
the muse who, for a while, had caused Sargent to whip all that paint
into a romantic frenzy. It was also that week that my very sweet
high school honors English teacher decided to fail me.

She called me up to her desk. Then, right in front of me, she
picked up her fat fountain pen and put an F on my report card.

"Why?"

"You go to Boston and New York, you stay for weeks at a time.
You're a high school kid. You missed the Chaucer final and you
missed the Chaucer final makeup."

"I won the poetry prize! I'm memorizing *Macbeth*! I know everything up to Banquo's ghost. 'When shall we three meet again . . .'"

"Stop it, Robert."

"I don't care about 'Shoots in April,' Mrs. Schilling, I don't care
about Chaucer!" I was a real jerk. She was a great teacher. And she
pretty much understood me. But despite the obvious content of my
poem, I don't think Mrs. Schilling or anybody else noticed that

after a summer with Hamlet and Ophelia I was taking my first
actual steps to my own breakdown. It took exactly a year before it
hit but when it did . . . *kick-chunk*.

Almost every weekend my last year of high school, I slept on the
filthy sofa in that ice-cold living room next to the Café Yanna. I
went places with Brian and felt closer to him than to anybody I'd
ever known. "You're amazing and charming!" he'd say. "Talk to
those guys in front of the store. Talk to them while I go into the
back with the tall guy. Keep 'em busy. Tell 'em about Shakespeare.
Tell 'em the story of *Winter's Tale*."

Brian was definitely my idea of a brilliant older brother and
everybody treated him with respect.

"Kid, today you even sound like Michael," he'd say. "If it
wasn't for the blond hair, my own mother would think he was
back from the dead."

The last time I saw Brian I was almost asleep on the vomit-
smelling sofa on Kenmore Square. I was listening to the traffic at
the streetlight above me. It was cold and, of course, there were no
blankets, so I had coats and sweaters piled over me.

It was a weekend and there was the usual all-night contest at
the coffeehouse. A blast of freezing air hit me every time the front
door opened so I couldn't actually have been asleep. I was on my
stomach.

Brian came in and wandered around in the dark. He lit a cigarette and fell back into a beat-up plastic chair. Every time he took a
drag I could see his worried wrinkled face. I watched him for a
long time before I let him know I was awake. "What's up?"

"Wanna butt?"

"No, I'm too sleepy."

He crossed the room and jumped on top of me. I remember
that the cigarette was still in his left hand and he'd been drinking.
"Hi, kid! I told Kate I had to come and see you. I gotta go away. I

gotta go out West and I might stay. I just don't know. I gotta go
now. The way things are, I think I'll stay. You okay?" He started
to whisper in my ear, "You know you're my brother. You know I
love you and you're my actual brother, red hair or not. You're *it,*
kid, not just make-believe, not just . . ." He put his mouth on my
ear. "Christ, I wanna fuck you. Jesus, I'm a screwed-up bastard. I
can't friggin' tell if I'm me or you're me or I'm you or you're dead.
Like you fuckin' died a whole life ago," he was yelling at me. He
shoved me over onto my back and put his face as close to mine as
he could. He was incredibly drunk. "I gotta talk to Kate." He
staggered to his feet. "You're the smartest kid on the planet and
don't ever forget it." His eyes were teary. "You make me hard, you
bastard."

He left the door open when he made his way up the noisy cor-
roded stairs. Some would-be folksinger was twanging lamented
love and I never saw Brian again.

My last semester in high school, I decided to put together a cardboard portfolio of my best drawings and take the Museum School
scholarship test. With a lot of help from the dean of admissions, I
was accepted to study painting at the prestigious School of the
Boston Museum of Fine Arts. In those days, it was about the top
place for a serious painter to study. I was far less a serious painter
than a kid searching out a hiding place. I needed to get away from
kick-chunk and Oak Ridge Road to find out if I fit anyplace.

Except for the tacit morning rides and the occasional "Pass
the salt," my father and I had an unspoken pact, as Jacques says
to Orlando, "to meet as little as we can." So the idea of me gone to
Boston pleased him enough to earn the promise of a check. I had to
graduate from high school, make some money over the summer,
and leave.

* * *

In May the Shakespeare Festival came back to town. The advertisements named actors from the previous summer and exactly the same staff. I made a nervous call to the backstage phone and as I expected, an impenetrably polite Miss Norell wanted nothing to do with me. Humiliated not to be asked back, I didn't try to reacquaint myself with the actors, not even the ones who'd written to me. I avoided anyplace I'd gone with them, those midnight swims on Russian Beach or Ryan's Bar after the show.

But every night at eight o'clock I was somewhere in the big theater. The volunteer ladies of the Shakespeare Guild ushered and I'd gotten to know all of them the summer before. So after the last warning bell and a second before Bernie took the house lights out—"Warning house to half . . ."—I'd plop down in any empty seat. On sold-out nights I sprawled on the balcony steps. I saw all three plays every time they were performed, altogether 112 times. I watched them from every possible angle except the place I most wanted to, kneeling at that backstage crack in the teak paneling. All summer I listened to those astonishing words over and over and each time new things popped out. Something I was absolutely sure meant this suddenly meant that. By August I knew all of *Romeo and Juliet, The Merry Wives of Windsor,* and *All's Well That Ends Well.*

But every night as the stage lights faded just before the curtain call, I was on my bike and gone. Sometimes very late I'd wander back to drink beer with the night guard. We'd sit in his torrid pine-scented car in the cement lot with the summer moon casting eerie shadows on the huge odd building. I'd get a little drunk and pretend to myself that I was still a part of it all.

"Ya wanna go in now?" he'd ask sweetly.

"No," I'd say. "I told ya before, that was *last* summer. I have no business in there anymore."

"Ah, ya can go in if ya want, I'll letcha."

"Thanks, I'll just have a beer." What would be the point? *Winter's Tale* was gone with Paulina's cape.

It took a long time for that painful summer of exile to pass. The yearning was excruciating. It was like loving someone you can't speak to or even acknowledge. Shakespeare, the worshiper of heartless beauty, knows all about it.

> I will acquaintance strangle and look strange,
> Be absent from thy walks, and in my tongue
> Thy sweet beloved name no more shall dwell,
> Lest I, too much profane, should do it wrong,
> And haply of our old acquaintance tell.
>
> —Sonnet 89

But finally September came and with it me, the Boston art student.

CHAPTER 18

I WAS GAWKING at a naked lady, not in the ordinary sense a beautiful one. Her skin was thatched with scars and she had extra bits of flesh in the oddest places. Human decay notwithstanding, she was acting like a goddess. Every time she shifted on the platform someone giggled, like a giddy five-year-old who'd been warned that "This was church" and especially "No laughing." Students were perched with drawing boards balanced in their laps, and except for that random titter, the only sound was the dull screech of chalk on newsprint.

"Don't look down," the instructor whispered. "Just let your chalk move across the pad. Find the contours with your eye and translate them through your body down to your hand. Don't look down at what you're drawing, feel it! See how the hip rises, feel it ascend, and then give yourself to how it drops off into the thigh. Don't look at the paper, just keep your eye on the model. Learn to look. If you can't *see* you can't *draw*." It was a freshman art teacher's version of *Hamlet,* holding a mirror up to nature.

The model was a pro, she'd been doing this for decades. For her, freshman life study class was nursery school. The laughing was a relief. We weren't poking fun at the saggy model. The nervous laughter was a studio full of 1950s kids pretending not to be sexually uncomfortable. I realized that I'd come a long way from looking up "naked" and "circumcision" in the little Stratford library.

Whenever I was having any kind of a good time, I'd always think of Carolyn and it always took the good time away. In class or watching punts along the Charles, I'd get whacked with sadness and I could hear the refrigerator. I'd listened to Juliet say it fifty times the summer before. . . .

> Some word there was . . .
> That murder'd me. I would forget it fain,
> But O, it presses to my memory
> Liked damned guilty deeds to sinners' minds.
> . . . .
> There is no end, no limit, measure, bound,
> In that word's death. No words can that woe sound.
>   —*Romeo and Juliet*, 3.2

Kick-chunk.

A couple of weeks after I started at the Museum School, I was feeling morbid and I made the mistake of calling home. As usual my mother wasn't well. She'd developed a habit of losing the inflection from her voice. The sentences were the usual mix of complaints and clichés, but she'd speak like a robot. She sounded exhausted, and no discernible feelings came through. My father never talked on the phone unless he'd had a couple of drinks. "Mil, it's your son. . . . Hurry up, this is costing money."

"Oh Ray, keep your pants on! Learn a little patience. Rome wasn't built in a day."

On the phone she'd tell me sad stories about herself and Carolyn. "Chicken Little," I'd think. My mother's convinced the sky is falling. With me in Boston she'd lost her primary witness. Ever since I was four and my father had gone to the Florida boot camp, she'd shared every detail of her fears. Now there wasn't anyone to give her the sympathy and reassurance she needed.

When my mother could repeat the details of whatever frightened her, she'd lower her anxiety and diffuse her terror. Unfortunately, as one crisis abated the next one always rushed in to replace it. Just like Hamlet's mother says, "One woe doth tread upon another's heel, So fast they follow." I've never had any trouble understanding Queen Gertrude or the panic that prompts her desperation to not be left alone. She always seemed a precise portrait of my own melancholy mother.

On the phone, with the sound of my sister banging away in the background and my mother droning on, I felt hopeless. Carolyn had been at the refrigerator for years.

Other art students seemed to be having a good time. They actually acted like these *were* the "best years of their lives," like they'd "only be young once." I was disconnected and pessimistic.

In Ryan's Bar an actor at the Shakespeare Festival said that if you laid very still in a tub full of extremely hot water you could cut your wrists and not feel it. If you resisted opening your eyes and didn't watch the water turn crimson, you'd start to get very sleepy and before long you'd fade gently away. When I was eighteen I still went to Mass every Sunday and was absolutely sure that if I died in a steaming immersion of my own blood, I'd wake wrapped in the consummate absolution of Leonardo's kind compassionate Christ.

I stopped by the drugstore for razor blades. As I was leaving I passed the boxes of ladies' home permanents and neat colorful rows of hair dyes.

"If it wasn't for the hair." Brian said it over and over. "Curls like yours but orange, like a pumpkin." In the drugstore aisle I thought, "I'll be Brian's dead brother. I'll be somebody that somebody cared about."

In 1959 no boy I knew dyed his hair. When Nana said "bleached blond" she obviously meant cheap and disgusting. "So what," I thought, "I'll be dead anyway. Who'll care?" I compared all the pictures on the boxes and bought the one that was the most like a pumpkin. It was called Helena Rubinstein's Copper Blaze, and that's exactly what it was.

Alone in the bathroom I wanted to erase myself. "Oh that this too too solid flesh would melt . . ." As the eye-burning peroxide seared my real color away, I felt like I was having my fingerprints changed in a B gangster movie.

An hour later I looked more like Brian than ever.

I called a kid from school. His name was Bobby Poole and he was the most talented artist in my class. He lived in a rooming house with dozens of other kids.

"I have red hair," I said.

"What?"

"I didn't feel too good. I thought maybe I'd kill myself, but instead I have extremely red hair."

"Stay where you are," he said. "I'll be right there."

He was shocked. "It's fantastic. I wanna paint you, everybody will. You look like Byron or Shelley or some beautiful consumptive poet. I'll start the picture tonight."

He was right. Everybody in the school did portraits of me! I had an old olive-colored army sweater of my father's. I wore it all the time. In all those pictures I'm sad and skinny and aesthetic in my father's discarded sweater and Brian's dead brother's hair.

I was studying Botticelli in my basement room on Commonwealth Avenue and it was snowing. Above me a drift was closing up the last few inches of window when a hand rapped on the glass. It was

fat Billy who'd almost been knifed in that kitchen on Kenmore
Square. I hadn't seen him for a year. He'd grown a beard and it was
glazed with ice. Through the frozen mask he had the same panicked expression as when I'd first seen him.

"I gotta talk to you. It's important."

"Sure, want tea?"

"No."

I had a sick feeling.

"They're gonna get you."

"Get me? Who?"

Chunks of ice kept hitting the parquet around Billy's dirty
sneakers.

"Get me?"

"You were with them at some very big deals. They think you're
talking about it. Somebody saw Brian. He says they think you
won't keep your mouth shut."

I went cold. I didn't know what he was talking about, but all of
a sudden I couldn't swallow. As an art student I'd been completely
unconnected to that apartment next to the Yanna. I hadn't seen
anyone from Kenmore Square in a year. They'd been tough and I
had liked that. Hanging around drinking and acting like they had
important secrets, they'd seemed like Gratiano and Lorenzo and
Bassanio, just a gang of smart-ass streetwise friends. The worst I'd
thought was that, like Bassanio, they used girls for money.

> In Belmont is a lady richly left,
> And she is fair, and (fairer than that word),
> Of wondrous virtues,—sometimes from her eyes
> I did receive fair speechless messages . . .
> —*The Merchant of Venice*, 1.1

Billy looked at me. For a minute his face wasn't the usual mask
of terror. "They're crazy. Go home!"

Old stuff mixed in. While Billy talked, fears that I'd packed away found me out again. Like Lady Macbeth I had sleepwalked my guilt since I was six. Billy said just what Miss Norell said: "Go home."

I remember climbing over drifts. Under my coat I was soaked with panic perspiration. I knew some students from B.U. who lived on a top floor over on Tremont Street. One of them I knew better than the rest. Phillip was a smart kid; his brilliant father was in the English department at Harvard.

When no one answered the bell I made my way to the B.U. theater. I knew Phillip was rehearsing *Summer and Smoke* in a rehearsal hall called "210."

"I have to stay with you guys awhile. Something awful happened."

I told him about when I'd gone places with Brian and the guys from Kenmore Square. "Ya think I'm nuts? I'm so scared. I'll sleep on the floor. Hide me."

Phillip and four or five other kids occupied the two apartments at the top. He and another boy shared a front bedroom and they piled me in. Phillip brought me art supplies and I set up a place to paint near the front window. Right away it was a place I couldn't leave. *Kick-chunk.* Sissy. I did portraits of everyone who lived there and at night sometimes the actors read Shakespeare and I'd forget that I was hiding. For months the only people I saw came up the five flights and it was exactly like the beginning of *Pericles* when he's sure that what he knows will kill him. And that keeping out of sight's the only answer.

> the passions of the mind,
> That have their first conception by mis-dread,
> Have after-nourishment and life by care;
> And what was first but fear what might be done,
> Grows elder now and cares it be not done.
> And so with me: the great Antiochus,
> 'Gainst whom I am too little to contend,

Since he's so great can make his will his act,
Will think me speaking, though I swear to silence;
Nor boots it me to say I honour him,
If he suspect I may dishonour him;
And what may make him blush in being known,
He'll stop the course by which it might be known.

—*Pericles*, 1.2

The longer I stayed on that top floor on Tremont Street the harder it got to imagine leaving. Alone, with the kids gone to class, I'd get jumpy and think about Kenmore Square and *Pericles*. I'd hide under the bedclothes till someone came home and it felt safe to go back to the easel by the windows in the living room. *Sissy.*

I was painting a kid from the back apartment. He was sweet-tempered and religious. "You're a good Catholic," he said. For the first time in my life I hadn't been to Mass in months. "It's not healthy to be locked in all day and night. Would you talk to a priest? If I can arrange it, would you let me take you to a priest?"

The boy was the nephew of a cardinal. His family lived on the outskirts of Boston. "Would you make the trip with me and talk to a priest?"

Daffodils whipped each other in the March wind as we drove along Route 128. It was so beautiful. I hadn't been out since the blizzard. Eventually there was a long straight driveway, more Iowa than Massachusetts.

The older couple must have been the nice kid's mother and father. And there were some women, busy, scrubbed-looking ugly aunts. We had a big noon meal and in the afternoon the boy drove me to a little stone church. I was disappointed. I'd envisioned a monastic setting worthy of a cardinal, a hermitage with chants in the air. The sweet little church could have been anywhere in Kansas.

At the time I had no doubt about God or any of the saints

whose portraits had been my first Shakespeare. It was myself, not Catholicism, of which I was unsure, and it had become obvious that I wasn't at all like the saint whose protection I'd so carefully picked for confirmation. My apocalypse was terrifying me and I was exhausted from loving people who eventually wanted nothing to do with me. In her way even Carolyn had left, and no matter how many hours I sat with her in the dark in front of the refrigerator, I knew she was never coming back.

The priest was young and that surprised me. I thought I'd be confessing my screwed-up autobiography to a chunky avuncular genius with a perch high enough to see the geography of my life. I was longing for some theological cartographer who'd absolve my past and map me a future. Instead, here's this kid who was insecure enough to be acting priestly.

It was in a small hard room with no rug or curtains, nothing yielding. Except for papers on a desk and a book of Gospels, the place looked unoccupied. The only art was a too colorful crucifix. My eyes kept wandering over to it.

The kid priest affected a frown and pursed his thin lips with concern. He was obviously under orders from the cardinal's family to do his best, and I'm sure he'd been picked just because he was young. I knew right away that he was too narrow to understand the kinds of issues bedeviling me.

From the time I'd gone to Holy Rosary and pleaded to God in Saint Lilac to melt the blood clot, my sister's theological position had plagued me. According to the Church her intellectual disability earned her a privileged category. Purified by Baptism, but incapable of First Communion, my sister was designated a kind of angel. She was a pretty little saint standing there whacking away at the fridge and no goodness I could ever achieve would equal hers. My sister was pure. I was human and a boy and bad.

I thought I needed the goofy young priest to help me straighten out just who I was to God. Was I so bad that my father hated me, that those boys in high school couldn't be my friends, so bad that now some guys thought I oughta be dead?

"Do you want to make your confession?" the priest asked. "How long has it been?"

I was looking over at the crucifix thinking about the one in the room I shared with Carolyn on Tulley Circle.

"Are you thinking about Christ on the cross?"

"Yes."

"You're staring at the crucifix. Is there something particular about it?"

"Yes, as far back as I can think it's been that. It's been my sick sister and the pain of the crucifixion since I was four or five. I've always felt how it felt, the nails, the tiny pieces of ripped skin from the thorns, the gash in his right side, the nauseating taste of blood and the vinegar they offered when he pleaded for a drink, cursing loudmouthed soldiers gambling for the homespun he'd been wearing. Did his mother weave it? I forget."

The young priest slid a metal chair into the corner. "Get down," he said. "Lay on the floor with your arms stretched out. Lay on your stomach facing the cross."

It was the position men took when they were ordained into the priesthood.

I got down facing the cross and lay flat on my stomach with my arms stretched as far as I could.

"Bless me Father for I have sinned. It's been six months since my last confession—"

Sex, he wanted me to tell him everything I remembered about anything sexual. I couldn't see him. He was kneeling behind me and my face was flat against the chilly floor. He asked me to tell him things I'd felt or seen or done. His voice was dull. His questions were flat, almost apathetic, a disembodied voice like John Houseman in the megaphone at the back of the enormous Shakespeare Theater.

The priest asked me to pray. My back hurt and I hate lying on my stomach but I repeated the twenty Hail Mary's and the "good" act of contrition, "Oh my God I am heartily sorry and I detest all my sins because they have offended thee, my God, who art worthy of all my love. . . ."

Later he looked at me in a friendly way, not like a friend, just in a friendly way. I hadn't told him about people wanting to kill me. I'd told him about sex and Carolyn and the high school boys not wanting to know me anymore.

"Your hair is beautiful," he said. "Cut it off. You're just the kind of boy men want. Cut your hair and stay off of Europe." That's exactly what he said, and when he said it I knew I'd never forget it, not "stay away from" or "stay out of" but "stay *off of*" Europe, like the continent was a treacherous iceberg of sin floating by and he was cautioning me never to step out onto it.

On the ride back to Boston the nice boy was curious and courteous. "I hope ya got stuff talked out." He looked at me. "I hope it helped. I hope you feel better."

"Thank you, Frank."

I thought the young priest was a fool and that the afternoon lying in front of the crucifix was stupid. I had the wrong hair and I wasn't supposed to ever see the place where Shakespeare was buried.

A couple of weeks after the pilgrimage to the priest, I'd been up all night working on a painting. I liked working surrounded by all the sleeping students. It felt safe. I was exhausted and I remember burying myself under the dingy college-kid sheets and smelly woolly blankets. I only slept when I had nothing left to resist with. It's still pretty much that way.

When I opened my eyes my father was standing at the foot of the bed. "Time to go home," he said warmly.

I dressed and piled everything into that luggage from my grandfather. His traveling days were done and so, I thought, were mine. There was no talk on the long ride most of the way across Massachusetts and down through Connecticut to the shore. As we turned off the Mass Turnpike I said, "Could I see a doctor? I think I need to talk to a doctor." He didn't answer.

When we got home my mother was tearful and nervous.

"Could I talk to a doctor?"

"Say hello to your sister. She's missed you so much. I'd tell her every day you'd be back. Everything's for the best, into each life a little . . . Every cloud has a . . ."

Kick-chunk. "Hi, baby. Don't be mad at me." My sister frowned past me like I was a distant thunder.

I went upstairs, closed the door, and locked it.

Late at night, after they'd gone to bed, I'd sit on the floor in front of Carolyn. "Some guys wanna kill me. I'm scared." She'd watch the faucet drip. For weeks I lived like a vampire, drawing sustenance from my dazed sister in the dismal light of the late-night kitchen. "Shakespeare's course of thinking," Houseman had said, "his thoughts." Over and over I reiterated Pericles's insanity— "Fear o'ershades me."

Nobody called a doctor and nobody tried to kill me. What I was experiencing wasn't strange in our house. Sometimes my mother made her timid knock. Through the door she'd quietly ask if I could help her. "I can't get her an inch away from the refrigerator," she'd whisper. "I know you don't feel good, but if you could just get her to laugh?"

"Oh no, not again." I'd hear it through the door. "Bobby, do you think you could? I'm just not up to it. My head's killin' me— and don't forget to wipe her good!"

My little room at the back of the upstairs hall had two sliding steel-framed windows, one looking out onto a treeless backyard that bordered the Merritt Parkway, and the other down the hill toward some cottages around a small lake. The lake wasn't visible from the window, just the tiny houses that backed onto it, everything scrubbed and vacant. When I left for Boston, my mother had "cleaned up." All that was left in my room was a large copy of Picasso's Gertrude Stein, no mirror. I think I still had the red hair.

I stuck mostly to the floor under the back window behind the dresser. As weeks went by I moved farther and farther from my mother's whiny requests, first under the bed, then into the shallow closet with the sliding doors slid closed behind me.

"Could I see a doctor? I think I might be dying and I feel really sick."

"You're just upset," she'd say. "You're exactly like me; everybody says so. It's just nerves. When the rain stops and it's warm you'll feel better. I know I will. . . ."

My father'd found me in Phillip's apartment because of a Botticelli book. I'd been studying the techniques of early Italian Renaissance painters, and I was looking at Botticelli. Not a lot of his work survived the purges of Savonarola, but Isabelle Stewart Gardner had a couple in her Venetian palace and I was copying them. For research, I'd taken the little book out of the Museum School library. When it was long overdue the school called my father to say that neither the book nor his son had been around in months. He called my roommates and they got him in touch with Phillip.

Thirty years later my father made his only reference to picking me up in Boston and to the months I'd hid in my room on Oak Ridge. One Thanksgiving, long after I was gray and he was bald, he said, "Ya ever talk to Phillip after Boston? Did you ever respond to any of his letters?"

CHAPTER 19

ONE AFTERNOON a couple of months into my closet exile my mother was at the door. "Ricky Canfield called. She and Charlotte are coming by. Why don't you clean yourself up. It will be good for you to see them."

When the two beautiful sisters walked in I was nervous. When we said hello in the front hall part of me wanted to run back upstairs to hide.

Ricky smiled. "*Winter's Tale*'s coming back," she said. "They're reviving it for the spring season. They're gonna do it for high schools for six weeks and *Lilas Norell is gone*." Hi ho the wicked witch is dead.

"They've replaced her with a jolly fat woman who has a tiny dog that sits in her lap all the time. I think there's a job if you want it. You just have to talk to Peggy, and the dog."

After months of fearful confinement, I jumped into Arthur Canfield's brand-new blue Peugeot and Ricky and Charlotte drove me to the theater.

The good-natured new wardrobe lady squawked Bronx baby talk like a Jazz Age chorus girl. She had an ocean of blue curls, swept into a cheap vivid scarf. She roosted, voluptuous as a Renoir, with the little brown and white terrier sprawled yapping in the hammock of her generous lap. She was married to a retired stagehand who was as diminutive as she was corpulent. "Jack Sprat could eat no fat. . . ."

When Ricky introduced us Peggy Thompson grinned a beautiful welcoming smile, and without so much as a single qualifying question, she squealed, "Ricky's dressing da ka-ween soz youz should take da kink."

Douglass Watson was playing the king and I liked him right away. The actor I'd dressed for Hamlet was always Hamlet. Doug wasn't like that. He was southern and charming. He'd started as lead dancer for Martha Graham and had been Eben for Eugene O'Neill in *Desire Under the Elms*. In the little brick Stratford movie theater, I'd watched him play Octavius to Brando's Marc Antony. Too bright to be too serious, Doug loved practical jokes, and before long everyone was mining the *Winter's Tale* set with goofy booby traps.

We did the play twice a day. The spring season for high schools was more relaxed than the high-profile summer. In April there were no reviews to worry about or superstars to magnetize adoration or scorn.

At nine A.M. the first busloads of bellowing kids rolled into the gigantic parking lots. From my old learning place behind the split in the teak panel, I watched the play win over sixteen hundred raucous teenagers. No matter how bumpy the start, two times every day the troupe of actors took thirty-two hundred kids on a journey they'd never forget. I meet middle-aged people all the time whose first live exposure to acted Shakespeare was one of those wet spring mornings packed into that barn of a theater.

Right away a young actor approached me to share an apartment. "I've got a great place just over the hill. It's an attic in a weird old house. It's sort of in the treetops and a bit magical. Beverly lives downstairs. Charlie has a place at the back. There's a tiny second bedroom if you're interested."

Of course, I wanted out of the little sterile bedroom on Oak Ridge. I'd had it with *kick-chunk* and my mother's lamentations. I was even weary of my print of Gertrude Stein. All of a sudden Picasso's obsession with grotesque sadness was holding me back. I wanted sunlight and treetops and sitting up all night again with young people arguing about art and truth.

"What's the address? Maybe I know the house?"

"840 East Broadway."

By the summer of 1960, Mrs. McGill and her sister, Jenny, were dead. Someone had converted the big old place to furnished apartments. I ended up directly over the room where I'd struggled with fractions with the two old ladies watching my every move.

When I was ten at Center School, the top floor of Mrs. McGill's house had been off limits. Powdery Jenny lived up there and her smoke-filled attic domain seemed spooky. By the time I was eighteen, it wasn't. Every night actors packed into the dinky place to dissect the day's performances. Students sat on the outside steps preparing scenes for class. There was always remarkable language in the warm early summer air as actors argued about the plays, drank beer from our communal fridge, and argued louder.

A couple of weeks after I moved into Jenny's attic, I dreamed that I was inside an ordinary little house like the one we'd lived in on Summer Street. The only sound was a large old clock slowly pulsing time *tick . . . tick . . . tick*. A back door snapped open and I heard just one cheerful warm spring afternoon bird chirp. Outside, the garden was exquisite and not quite real. When I stepped through the door I had a sense of childhood familiarity. I knew each leaf, even the insignificant little buds, two fake-looking willows bending into the placid pond, the Japanese bridge, the picket fence. As I stared at the dozen beige roses winding through the pale blue trellis, I realized that I was standing dead center in the hundred times replicated scene on the wallpaper that lined my grandmother's stairs. How many times I'd stretched my hand over the thick textured paper as I struggled to coax Carolyn up to the bathroom. "Come on, sweetheart. Please don't cry. It's not so bad."

After I stood for a while in my grandmother's pretty wallpaper garden, I woke up gently, and the dread I'd felt lifted like a fog. I was free. In a month I'd be nineteen. In a week the summer company would tumble in from New York and a whole new universe would open, *Twelfth Night* and *The Tempest* and after, toward August, a gigantic *Antony and Cleopatra*.

> There's a divinity that shapes our ends,
> Rough-hew them how we will—
>
> —*Hamlet*, 5.2

Pat Hines had been Rosencrantz that *Hamlet* summer. The day I'd turned seventeen he'd made a present of an origami conifer constructed of twenty elaborately folded brand-new five-dollar bills. In *Winter's Tale* he was Paulina's old husband. Pat was one of those actors whose looks cast them in parts decades beyond their actual age. Pat was thirty, but he looked fifty and twitched.

"Way'ull *she* gits here." When he wasn't a Shakespeare character, he had a thick west Texas accent. "Ay sure hope ya like it cold. She does. You wait an' see, we'll have blue lips and she'll be runnin' around necked."

He was warning me about Katharine Hepburn. She was coming to star in *Twelfth Night* and *Antony and Cleopatra*. She'd already played a season with the Festival and toured *Much Ado* and *Merchant*. She was from Connecticut and had spent her youth between Hartford and Long Island Sound. Miss Hepburn was a genuine Hollywood movie star.

For weeks actors screeched impersonations: "I never thought

that a mere physical experience could be so stimulating," "The calla lilies are in bloom again." Ad nauseam everyone tested their powers of mimicry.

Winter's Tale was still playing to the high schools when the Academy students started to trek into New York to rehearse *Twelfth Night*. Our little attic apartment was abuzz with first reports. According to the very young actors, at fifty-four Miss Hepburn might be a bit long in the tooth for Viola. In her chic pants and aristocratic athleticism, she might be stylishly mannish, but it had been decades since she'd been the pubescent cross-gender nymph the text describes.

> Not yet old enough for a man, nor young
> enough for a boy: as a squash is before 'tis a peascod,
> or a codling when 'tis almost an apple. 'Tis with him
> in standing water, between boy and man. He is very
> well-favoured, and he speaks very shrewishly. One
> would think his mother's milk were scarce out of him.
> —*Twelfth Night*, 1.5

The enormous size of the Stratford stage had always been a problem. Before the technical rehearsals began, a gigantic cave of free-form white plastic chips was suspended as a backdrop to cut down the vacuous space. Inside the "chips" the set for *Twelfth Night* invoked luxurious Brighton by the sea, Jane Austen style. Just behind the proscenium sat two fanciful mansions. The duke's marble rotunda was phallic and classically Georgian male while the Lady Olivia's was a filigree confection of overwrought wrought-iron turrets and curving stairways. Ultimately the lavish production met with harsh criticism. That background of immense plastic shapes sent an undeniable message of modernity and artificiality, and the update of the play was scorned by Shakespearites who wanted their Shakespeare "Shakespearean." It was more than a decade before Peter Brooks's *Midsummer Night's*

Dream would teach audiences that there's more than one way into these texts.

For me the best thing about a modernized *Twelfth Night* was that I had almost nothing to do. Hooking a jabot or cinching a cummerbund was about it. All the rest of the time I could watch. It was fine with the new wardrobe mistress. As long as what needed doing got done, Peggy wasn't about to wander the catwalks to watch a watcher.

The star, however, was dead set against it. Miss Hepburn announced early on that there was to be *no* looking. When they left the stage even principal actors were banished to the greenroom or to their dressing rooms to wait for the little speaker boxes to announce their next cue. Three stage managers and four assistants became unwilling police.

Observing from backstage was never easy. As action shifted I dashed from cubbyhole to crack, from stage left to right, from catwalk to stored scenery.

"Don't let her catch you," stage managers warned. "Wait till she's on the stage before you go into the catwalk."

I was completely star-struck. I watched everything she did. She was bigger than life, more strident than a tree of crows. She smoked like an engine, went braless in Swiss cotton T-shirts, rode a bike, rowed a boat up the river every day, and scolded people for being ordinary. She was impatient, self-absorbed, and the hardest-working person I'd ever seen. She was the only person in an army of fanatically committed people who I thought cared as much as I did. Everyone was afraid of her and she pretended to be afraid of nothing. Other people's expectations greeted her every time she turned a corner. She was the quintessential meaning of glamour and sure she was too old for *Twelfth Night*. But I kept thinking about Richard Burbage. Wasn't he fat and forty when he'd played the first Hamlet? He'd knocked the women dead as bad boy Richard the Third. Couldn't Miss Hepburn knock 'em dead? For that we would have to wait five weeks to take our trip down the Nile.

The Tempest, without a movie star, played back to back with *Twelfth Night.* William Ball was the director and his production was very Shakespearean. The set was a series of unpretentious wooden platforms and steps. Suspended upstage was a massive sepia map of the New World. The costumes were Jacobean in browns and grays with etched details like a pen-and-ink drawing after Inigo Jones. The production was organic and tactile, and this time the background of white chips, so contemporary in the *Twelfth Night,* seemed completely appropriate. As the tale of shipwreck and survival unfolded, the shell of bothersome plastic chips started to take on the look of windblown clouds whistling across the "still vexed Bermoothes." It was a beautiful production.

Morris Carnovsky played Prospero. He'd been Shylock to Miss Hepburn's Portia and was evil King Claudius my first summer. The last day of the *Hamlet* season he had presented me with a spectacular book of Robert Edmond Jones set designs with a loving inscription filled with praise for my budding intellect, and expressing his undying gratitude for helping him make it through a "splendid and arduous summer."

The last time I saw Morris was at Luther Adler's funeral. There were remarkable speeches about the idyllic theater of long ago when honor and purpose clashed with Senator Joe McCarthy.

When the eulogies were done and people milled to share remembrances, I caught sight of Morris. Like an ancient Chekhovian character, he was pink and white and frail as a feather. Bill Hickey was holding him up. It was just before Bill won his Academy Award for *Prizzi's Honor.* When I met him, Bill had been Trinculo and the young shepherd in *Winter's Tale.* He'd been the second gravedigger in Hamlet.

"Do you know who this man is, Morris?" Bill whispered so gently. "Do you recognize Bobby Smith?" I was forty. Morris stared blankly. How many teenaged dressers and assistants, how many young students, must have stood beseechingly before his venerable gaze. But suddenly from the distance of all the years, I saw his memory kick in. His eyes converted to the look I'd known so well. His mouth twitched to a sad reminiscence. "Bobby Smith," he whispered when I bent to kiss him.

He'd gotten almost violent with me that summer when I was Bobby Smith and he was cranky Prospero. On *Tempest* nights, there were no movie stars around to endanger watching so I got to sit barefaced as close to the stage as I needed.

It was during Prospero's speech to Ferdinand when he sums up theater as a metaphor for life and the ephemeral nature of success.

> Our revels now are ended. These are actors,
> As I fortold you, were all spirits, and
> Are melted into air, into thin air:
> And, like the baseless fabric of this vision,
> The cloud-capp'd towers, the gorgeous palaces,
> The solemn temples, the great globe itself,
> Yea, all which it inherit, shall dissolve,
> And, like this insubstantial pageant faded,
> Leave not a rack behind. We are such stuff
> As dreams are made on; and our little life
> Is rounded with a sleep.
>
> —*The Tempest*, 4.1

Morris played the speech distractedly impatient, on a mission to teach Ferdinand about life before time ran out. He'd look around nervously as if his world was dissolving. It was gorgeous. "The baseless fabric of this vision" went to the back of the huge theater, "the cloud-capp'd tow'rs" to the stage-right balcony boxes, "solemn temples" to the catwalk, and landing the final image in my direction. "We are such stuff as dreams are made on." He was like a great athlete on his game and he could take your breath away.

One night the wardrobe mistress needed to talk to me. For the first time since rehearsals, I wasn't sprawled on the offstage step unit getting teary over Morris saying Shakespeare saying good-bye to magic. Later, when I saw him on the stage-left stairway, he looked at me with rage in his eyes. "Come to my dressing room after the performance." I'd never seen him angry offstage.

Sitting in his dressing room with the rows of blinding makeup lights blasting us, he said more calmly, "Sit down." He looked deeply into my face. He was a beautiful old man. "Do you understand . . ." He was almost crying. "Do you understand that when I look over at you it's *you* who are the stuff that dreams are made of. Haven't you always sat on that step since the very first rehearsal? Haven't you had tears in your eyes every time? Haven't you understood that it's a kid watching the magic of a play that's the stuff of dreams?"

I never didn't watch Morris again.

I'd missed Prospero's speech because the wardrobe lady wanted to talk to me about *Antony and Cleopatra*. She'd told me that Miss Hepburn's friend Robert Ryan was coming from Los Angeles to play Antony.

"It's gonna be like a big musical," she said. "There's a ton of costumes. We're hiring extra people. There's *three* armies in the thing."

Fast changes of wardrobe can *make* a moment in a play. They indicate the passage of time or illustrate an important change in the life of the character, whether it's Hamlet's "inky cloak" or Eliza Doolittle's ball gown. But in my experience, dressing isn't only about the wardrobe. It's about helping the inside meet the outside of a part. I've known lots of actors who couldn't make very many acting choices until they'd put the wardrobe on. For others, the costume is a mountain to get over.

In a tunic and sandals Bob Ryan looked like a handsome businessman at a Mardi Gras party. Unlike Morris or Dicken Waring or Miss Hepburn, he sounded recited. His phrasing was stiff and unnatural. He couldn't have been a nicer man. Working with him was a completely happy experience. But Antony's solipsistic tragedy wasn't there.

"Whatta ya think?" he'd ask. "The entrance is too goddamn long." He'd shake his noble head. "By the time I land I feel I should have started talking five minutes ago. Take a look tomorrow and don't spare my feelings." Then he'd whisper, "Is she swallowing me? I know it's in the text, the way Cleopatra goes off on him, but do I come across too passive?"

I think my lowly place made it easy for actors to share their apprehensions. It was Hamlet's mother who'd first spoken to me quietly on a bench in the greenroom. "I look arrogant when I want to seem uncomfortable with Claudius. Can you see my face from the 'A' trap?" When I was a teenager they were demigods in some heavenly synod and watching them from the dark was the privilege I won for being nothing.

During the complicated costume rehearsals for *Antony and Cleopatra,* I got to hang around working out technical problems after important company members were banished to the dressing rooms.

Midway in the play Cleopatra tries to help Antony dress for battle. She has no idea how the armor actually works. It reminded me of my mother around the family car.

CLEOPATRA   Nay, I'll help too.
          [She doesn't know a thing about it.]
     What's this for?
          [He gets impatient.]
ANTONY   Ah, let be, let be! Thou art
          [Her feelings are hurt. He makes good.]
     The armorer of my heart.
          [She tries again and gets it wrong.]

ANTONY   False, false!
    [He teaches her the right way.]
                         This, this!

CLEOPATRA   Sooth, la, I'll help.
    [She almost gets it right.]
                    Thus it must be.

ANTONY   Well, well!
    We shall thrive now.
    [Good job. You'll bring me luck.]

CLEOPATRA   Is not this buckled well?
    [She's proud of helping.]

ANTONY   Rarely, rarely!
    He that unbuckles this, till we do please
    To doff't for our repose, shall hear a storm.

. . . .

    Fare thee well, dame. Whate'er becomes of me,
    This is a soldier's kiss.

                      —*Antony and Cleopatra*, 4.4

Since it was me who usually buckled the armor, I showed Miss Hepburn how it worked and together we decided which she'd get wrong and which he'd rebuckle. It's comedy with a palpable sadness just under the surface. For the last time she's the girl who'd beguiled Caesar in a rug and her coy helplessness helps Antony forget for a moment that he's too old for his life. Age and foolishness will soon dissolve their dissolute glamour and a younger world will say some prayers, build a tomb, and move on. But for the moment it's charming and funny and it could break your heart. It did mine.

I see it in the old people. When couples survive, so often it's she who has more vigor. I watch women protect the fragile ego of their enfeebled love. "Ask what the boss thinks," they say with a wink. "It's him that runs the show."

*   *   *

Just before *Antony and Cleopatra* went into tech rehearsals, there
was a problem with the shoes. The gigantic cast required sixty sets
of sandals and they'd arrived in a sorry state. "They're all going
back to New York," Peggy said. "Everything has to be redone."

One afternoon Miss Hepburn dropped a couple of dozen plastic sandals on the dressing room floor. "I bought everything the
shoe store had." She looked over at me. "I didn't ask about sizes. I
said 'Give me everything you've got,'" she laughed. She knew very
well that she was Katharine Hepburn. "Surely there's something
here we can use till this mess is straightened out."

The company manager handed me a wad of cash, the name of a
hotel, and the address of the Capezio shoe factory. The sandals
were already on their way. On the train I felt like the kid cavalry
coming to the rescue. We couldn't open the play with the legions
marching in full armor, helmets, and sneakers.

The factory was torrid. It was somewhere on Manhattan's
West Side. The guy at Capezio stared into the box. "These Hepburn's? We always lie to Merman." Ethel Merman had just
opened in *Gypsy*. "She's got feet the size of gunboats, but insists
she's a six. We stamp a big gold six into any shoe we make for
her."

For three days we went sandal by sandal, footprint by footprint.
Lists got ripped up and men screamed at each other in Italian and
Spanish. I got a dozen calls from the new stage manager. Along
with Mr. Houseman, Bernie had moved on. Richard was terrific.
"It's getting done, Dick; the place is two hundred degrees, the peo-
ple are nuts, but by Wednesday it will be okay."

"We owe you a big one, kid."

By the opening I was feeling pretty confident. After I helped
with the shoe mess, I got to do more assistant-type tasks. Jobs
doled out to underlings backstage say volumes about trust and
commitment. Anything that came my way I devoured.

Very late in *Antony and Cleopatra* there's a moment in their disintegrating relationship when they encounter each other on a bat-

tlefield. He curses her and runs away. It's horrible given what they've been to each other.

I was asked to hold back a black masking curtain so Miss Hepburn could fly up a set of steps in her wild pursuit of Antony.

We'd stand together in the dark, waiting for the little light to flash indicating my cue to pull back the curtain. As we stood there listening to the action on stage, she'd adjust and readjust her lengthy costume. All her gowns were as much as a foot longer than floor length. Enemies sneered that she used the extra fabric to fuss with on stage, stealing focus as other actors talked. She had remarkable stagecraft. Hepburn would exit an emotional scene with tears streaming down her long thin face. She'd blow her nose into a clutch of tissues and head straight for the stage manager's desk. "Light 22A is dim," she'd say. "And 106 and 203 are *out*."

Standing together in the cool dark we listened to Antony.

All is lost!
This foul Egyptian hath betrayed me.
My fleet hath yielded to the foe, and yonder
They cast their caps up and carouse together
Like friends long lost. Triple-turned whore! 'Tis thou
Hast sold me to this novice, and my heart
Makes only wars on thee.

—*Antony and Cleopatra*, 4.12

I ran my eyes over her. Did his words mean anything? Did she use them to propel her desperation? She was beautiful, but she'd started to be sensitive about showing her neck. People said she'd developed some incurable rash when she'd fallen into the polluted Venetian canal in *Summertime*. Some jealous person said it was only age and vanity. Whatever the reason, as Cleopatra she had a collection of camouflaging necklaces strategically slung from elaborate headdresses. They swooped under her chin concealing her neck under rows of intricate beadwork. She also wore a queen's ransom of rings, earrings, upper and lower bejeweled armbands.

Listening to Antony and looking her over, I realized that her elaborate golden armbands were missing. Actors can attach great significance to the elements that remain constant in a scene, like me on the steps for Morris. The scene Miss Hepburn was about to play was astonishingly painful and terse. All the elements had to be in place.

I ran past the backstage orchestra and tore through the green-room, down the principal dressing room hall. I terrified Phyllis the secretary when I broke past her to the movie star's inner sanctum. No mere mortal had ever violated the muslin hanging for cool privacy on the series of doorways. Just like Pat Hines said, it was amazingly cold in the room. From the vast collection of symmetrically set out jewelry, I grabbed the overlooked armbands. I knew how much time I had because I could hear the onstage action through the little speaker boxes.

Seconds before the cue I snapped the big gold bracelets onto her thin muscular arms. She was looking away. She was Cleopatra. She was hurting. The little cue light flashed and I pulled back the curtain. Lights blasted her and out she ran. An hour later dragging her bike up the back stairs, she called out, "How ja know which ones? I've got twenty."

I acted coy. I pointed to my right eye. "Watch out," I forged a fake threat. "I'm a watcher."

"Thanks for the watching," the movie goddess tossed over her lovely bony shoulder. "Thanks."

Later in the week I was dangerously scrunched in the catwalk to sneak a stare at act one, scene five, *Twelfth Night*. It's the famous "willow cabin" scene. Miss Hepburn entered the stage with a guard of four sailors. Waiting for her cue in the pitch black, she'd pace inches from my hiding place mumbling the lines of the scene. I'd hold my breath every time she passed by.

That night her patent leather shoe landed on my leg. "Who's

that?" she bellowed loud enough to be heard in the balcony. "Who's that? Who's that?" she shrieked like a Katharine Hepburn impersonator. Bending toward me in the dark, ignoring the audience that sat inches away on the other side of the teak wall, she spit, "Get out! Get out! Get out of here!"

We stared nose to nose. I smelled Tareytons and the Kondonwasser's 4711 she splashed on herself between scenes. I took a shot, "I gotta watch. Please let me."

Never a mother, she suddenly acted like one. "Don't make noise and for Christ's sake, don't tell anyone."

> Make me a willow cabin at your gate,
> And call upon my soul within the house;
> Write loyal cantons of condemned love,
> And sing them loud even in the dead of night;
> Halloo your name to the reverberate hills,
> And make the babbling gossip of the air
> Cry out 'Olivia!' O, you should not rest
> Between the elements of air and earth,
> But you should pity me.
>
> —*Twelfth Night,* 1.5

The famous speech is a paradigm of longing infatuation. To Elizabethans, the willow is a symbol of unrequited love. Minutes before Othello strangles Desdemona, she sings a song of willow; and spurned by Hamlet, Ophelia climbs a willow, weaving her way onto the weakest branches, which snap, sending her to a drowning death.

From first to last the plays are invocations of longing. The older Shakespeare got, the more he wrote about ghosts and resurrections and fantasies of reunification, the more he invoked atonement.

CHAPTER 20

IT WAS MY fifty-fifth birthday and I could already feel that the day would be incredibly hot, July in Connecticut. With my feet propped on the blistered porch railing I watched the last of the stars fade and pale watercolors drip into the early morning damp. Familiar, comforting.

I tossed the coffee mug into the deep iron sink and grabbed my bike. On my way down the grassy driveway a flock of noisy geese shrieked not twenty feet over my head. There was no traffic. I could hear my bike wheels on sand and in the distance the echo of the clumsy geese flopping into the river. The muted atmosphere picked up a little more light as I pedaled past a swampy inlet where the first settlers left their boat in 1639, just twenty-three years after William Shakespeare got buried "a full seventeen feet," eleven more than the usual six.

Fearing his famous curse, they'd laid him deep just spitting distance from his river in his Stratford. He, too, had come home in his early fifties when apparently "every second thought" was of that grave.

I circled east to watch the sunrise from a pile of boulders that mark the limit of Long Beach. It's a quiet place at that hour, just birds. A loon was "dive dapping" for breakfast. In the brownish plum dawn, he turned up his tail and disappeared under the easy waves, then popped to the surface like a cork with his bill straight up to swallow and shake.

In the haze I could just make out two fishermen inching along the refuge that continued west of the rocks. The men trudged through the crunch of pebbles and shells at the edge of the water. There's still the odd piece of storybook New England here, Thoreau and Winslow Homer. If you look past fast-food places and drive-through banks, you can find remnants of forthright Yankee oystermen and potato farmers, people hard as the unyielding rocks in the difficult New England soil.

Closer now I could see that the men were old. When they passed my perch they looked up with coriaceous faces and slicked-back, yellow-gray hair and two sets of identical sapphire eyes. Brothers, old brothers. The older one smiled a map of tobacco-brown wrinkles. "Gonna be a hot one."

"Yep," I said, embarrassed to find a country sound not usually in my mouth. "Gonna be a scorcher."

Pedaling back I flicked my Walkman on and circled past the old town dock. Along the dirt road that bumps below the deserted Shakespeare Theater, an annoying contrapuntal percussion braided into the music. At first it seemed to be on the tape, but when I punched off the Walkman the noise was all around me as if the atmosphere was breathing in and out. I pushed the brakes on the ten-speed and twisted into a dusty stop on the sandy road. Over the river the full summer sun cast gorgeous gold through low morning clouds and it reminded me of Antony, or maybe it's Shakespeare himself feeling as broken as Antony. Poor old party boy Antony, just my age, contemplating suicide in the ephemeral movement of clouds.

Sometime we see a cloud that's dragonish,

A vapour sometime like a bear or lion,

A towered citadel, a pendant rock,

A forked mountain, or blue promontory

With trees upon't that nod unto the world

And mock our eyes with air.

—*Antony and Cleopatra,* 4.14

The odd sound was swans. There must have been forty of them flying directly above the old theater building with their long necks stretched tautly forward. *Snap-whoosh, snap-whoosh, snap-whoosh.* I'd never thought of swans flying—gliding over glassy ponds, sure, preening in a pile of down or sometimes walking like Charlie Chaplin, but *flying*? It was absolutely beautiful . . . and prophetic. After Shakespeare was buried that seventeen feet in little Trinity Church, Ben Jonson eulogized his friend by casting him in the image of pure unwavering fidelity gliding on that other river in that other Stratford.

Sweet swan of Avon! What a sight it were

To see thee in our waters yet appear.

—Ben Jonson

I made it to the 8:03. The hot walk to the station is familiar, six minutes of stepping over the same cracks that when I was eight would "break my mother's back." I was already sweaty when I boarded the ice-cold express. Shivering next to a window, I watched smaller commuter towns whiz through my reflection. I hadn't picked up a newspaper. There wasn't a place on the way and I'd gotten to the platform just as the train pulled in, no time to dash into the depot. "I'll just wait," I thought.

There'd been a message on the phone machine. On July 10 an article about me was going to be the lead in the Metro section of the *New York Times.* The writer joked about what a nice birthday present it would be. She said that the editorial staff had liked the interview well enough to run it on the first page of the national edition. Me on the front page of the *New York Times*.

When I was a kid in working-class Stratford, people joked about commuters in their identical clothing. It's mostly still that way, businessmen in duplicate business suits, only now there are women, too. Thousands of people crammed into railroad cars, facing the same direction screaming frustration into bad connections on cell phones. Most people read the paper, first page first, then Metro section. People who work in New York want to know what's happening in New York.

I felt like the king of the mountain and a damn fool. In the paper, there was a full-length picture of me right next to Shakespeare. I looked silly, like a show-off. From the back of the train I watched my foolish picture appear dozens of times. As people read the long article they lifted the paper higher and higher. I was *dancing* everywhere in the frigid railroad car, and suddenly it reminded me of my little retarded sister, twisted like a pretzel on her beloved three-wheeler. Peopled used to gawk, that's what my mother called it, "gawking."

"People are so mean," she'd say. "Look how they gawk. You'd think there was something wrong with them, ignoramuses!"

A couple of minutes before eleven I leap the outside steps to a basement door on Washington Square. From the other side of a card table an old woman feigns annoyance.

"Hello, 'Mr. Shakespeare.'" In a gruff New York accent, she's flirting with me. "They're all up there waiting. Those people wouldn't miss a Friday if the bomb dropped." She's getting a kick out of acting tough. "Ya got 'em bewitched, that's what it is. One of these days I'll check up on you myself. I wanna see what kind of shenanigans goes on up there. You just wait, 'Mr. Shakespeare,' and see if I don't."

She's threatened me at 10:50 every Friday for years. "How's your shoulder, Ada?"

She wrinkles a prune face and flips a pencil at me, "Don't ask!"

I add my name to a list of old people but I don't stay for the dollar lunch. By one o'clock I'll be in another crowded senior center on the other side of town.

I stop by the office. Gladys runs the place. She's not so young herself. A worrier, she mumbles her fears. When I turn the corner she looks up from her monologue and smiles a flickering jumpy smile. "You got enough copies? The machine's broke again. I had to use the place across the park for . . . What play is it?" Disappointed, her voice drops to a conspiratorial sibilance. "See, I forget. Why shouldn't I? Just look around. Some days they drive me batty." She doesn't mean it.

"Come on, Gladys. We're starting *King Lear* today."

She squints and points at me. "Right. I had a hundred copies of *King Lear* made over on LaGuardia Place. The Pakistani kid gave me a good deal, thirty-five bucks, musta felt sorry for me."

"So how ya doin', Gladys?"

"I'm okay." She burlesques pathetic then acts perky. "I'm fine. Don't I look fine?" She wiggles and straightens her spine like a caught kid hiding a cigarette from a nun.

The beautiful old building was a convent. Retired nuns still occupy the top of the place. Because I'm a man I've never been allowed past the first floor.

> When you have vow'd, you must not speak with men
> But in the presence of the prioress;
> Then, if you speak, you must not show your face;
> Or if you show your face, you must not speak.
> —*Measure for Measure*, 1.4

The hushed halls still echo the tangled rules of the religious life. Just past the temperamental copy machine there's a small dark chapel.

In the big double parlor at the front is a stage. It looms behind me like a potent metaphor. I keep the cherry red velvet curtain drawn tight. I like floor level, closer to the people. I'm nervous on a stage.

I read the Shakespeare plays hemmed in by wheelchairs and grocery bags. I'm the only one younger than sixty-five, most are in their seventies and eighties. Not cowed by time, word by word we thumb our noses at the inevitable strokes and heart attacks, navigating the English Renaissance with amazing athleticism.

Shakespeare's an armature on which to build a document of long life remembrances. It's a way for the old to look back, take stock, and confirm what matters most. For an hour the future's not so important. We're together right now sharing astonishing poetry and brilliant ideas. I listen closely to the Shakespeare . . . and to the old people. They are, in just a wink, who I'll be.

> Look for thy reward
> Among the nettles at the elder tree . . .
> —*Titus Andronicus*, 2.2

I pass around the Pakistani copy shop copies. "Today it's *King Lear*, Act One, Scene One." The beautiful old people interrupt with a big ugly cake and sing "Happy Birthday."

CHAPTER 21

Bᴜ 1960, Jack Landau had replaced John House-
man as artistic director of the Shakespeare Festival, and the morning after the opening of *Antony and Cleopatra* he called me into his
office. He was slouched over a pile of papers. "There's going to be
a tour," he said. "Th-th-thirteen cities coast to c-coast, *Dream* and
Winter's T-tale." Jack was a stutterer with the thickest eyeglasses
I'd ever seen outside of a joke store. As he stammered his tiny eyes
darted behind dizzying magnification. "B-Bert Lahr's been hired to
play Nick Bottom and Autolycus. He's never done any Shakespeare
and you'd be a tremendous help. We'd give you billing as production assistant. It would be like a paid va-vacation."

I'd seen Bert's photograph in theater books at the little granite
library, and like everyone I'd adored him as the Cowardly Lion in
The Wizard of Oz.

The next week, when Jack introduced us, Bert shot a challenge
in my direction. "So, kid, how do you store neckties?" I'd never
thought about storing a necktie. "Roll 'em!" he barked. "If ya

want a tie to stay smooth roll it against itself." He frowned his disapproval. Maybe a year on the road wouldn't be much of a "paid vacation."

As he took Bert's arm, Jack winked an amplified eye in my direction. "We start rehearsals M-Monday up over Lovell's."

I'd just turned nineteen and didn't know a thing about being a dresser to a person who thought a dresser was a servant. Robert Ryan was a movie star. I ate with his family all the time. I didn't know if he ever rolled his ties.

The day after the Stratford season closed, the tour rehearsals moved into the Lyceum Theater on Broadway and I stayed at a crummy hotel down the street.

On a break in the dingy sublobby at the front of the old theater, Bert blew Tareyton smoke at me. "Come to my house tonight," he said. "I'll show you the trunk." Apparently part of my "paid vacation" was going to be helping Bert to look posh.

He lived on Fifth Avenue across from the Met. I'd passed the building hundreds of times on my visits to the Renaissance. It had a long canopy structure jutting toward the street and the fifties-looking lobby was a sharp right at the end of the awning.

Bert frowned when he opened the door. "Henry's here." I think his name was Henry. He was an old black man who usually "helped" Bert to look like Bert. Henry'd apparently gotten too frail to handle the rigors of a cross-country tour. When I walked in he was standing in a hallway on the other side of the kitchen bending over an enormous steamer trunk.

"Henry's packing. He's very organized. He knows exactly how I like things. Don't ya, Henry?"

The two old men argued over which rolled-up, wide Italian ties went next to which other rolled-up, wide Italian ties. They quibbled over collar stays and missing cuff links. Bert occasionally flashed me a look of disgust. Here was perfect, familiar Henry, and they had so much history together. *Who the hell was this kid and would he get the starch in Bert's beautiful shirts right?*

For a couple of hours I listened as the two men re-fought ancient, piddling gaffes. "No, Henry, it should have been the dark green, *not* the brown one. It's always the green hat with the camel coat. It's always been the green, it always will be the green, I like the green. . . . You getting this, Bill?"

"Bob, Mr. Lahr."

"Henry, get Bill a glass of water. I'll have one, too. No ice."

I remember that I wondered what it must be like to be Bert's son. It was an inevitable question since John was exactly my age. He'd just left to start Yale, and I was about to spend a year hand-washing his dad's underpants.

All across America I starched Bert's beautiful imported shirts and periodically dyed what was left of his hair to match an odd little oval toupee that he wore on stage. I polished his shoes and saw to the laundry, packed and unpacked his trunk at theaters and his suitcases in hotels, and all to the relentless staccato whine of his dissatisfaction. As it had been with my own father, nothing I did was good enough and I'm sure that it probably wasn't.

Nervous about a major critic in Chicago, on opening night Bert got careless and mishandled a bottle of champagne; bubbles spewed in every direction. "Get down and wipe everyone's shoes," he bellowed. I felt mortified crawling around on the dressing room floor between tuxedo legs and gowns.

On a street in Detroit he'd insisted that I'd given him mismatched socks. He wore lisle stockings with a minute escutcheon called a clock woven into the side. Two pairs of the brown ones were indistinguishable. Late at night, sure that I'd get them wrong, I did.

"Twice!" he bellowed on the street corner. "Twice! This is the second time you've mismatched these socks." Sure that funnyman Bert was setting up some brilliant knee-slapper, a small crowd gathered to gleefully witness my belittling.

What I couldn't see when I first looked into Bert's sour puss was his genius. In life he was crusty and short-tempered. But on stage it was completely different. In front of an audience, he was disarmingly funny, with impeccable timing. More often than I could count I'd watch him improve a fledgling actor's connection to the audience by making a few offhanded crabby suggestions.

Over the next months I learned a lot about aging and frustration. I also got valuable lessons in play structure and stagecraft.

When I returned to the seedy New York hotel, after my first trunk-packing lesson, the stage manager called. Would I like to see Ethel Merman in *Gypsy?* It was the hit of the season. "Jack got you tickets, house seats. Take your family."

I called home. "How ja like to see a big hit Broadway show?" Nana offered to watch Carolyn and my parents came into the city.

During the overture I thought about Miss Merman's size-"six" feet. She entered from the back of the theater, "Sing out, Louise!" The audience went nuts. "Smile, baby!" The show was a huge hit but the star didn't act like it. Her famous voice was subdued. She jumped her cues, cutting other actors off. "Maybe she's sick," I thought.

I'd never seen any actor at Stratford not give their all. Maybe it's Shakespeare and the energy it takes to do those layered texts with all that glorious language. Then halfway into the first act, something caught her interest and everything in the place got a hundred times brighter, the packed-in audience started to have the wonderful time they'd expected. Miss Merman was truly incredible, and I realized that a star might react strangely, even to great success.

After the show my parents had to rush back to relieve Nana. My mother cried. I wouldn't see my family again until the tour finished in California and headed back east. "I can go just so long without seeing you," my mother whispered. She still says it.

* * *

In Boston we were set to open at the Colonial. The theater had just undergone a year's restoration and they'd picked our pretty play for the grand reopening. It was obvious from the first that *A Midsummer Night's Dream* would be wonderful. Bert as Nick Bottom the weaver and Margaret Phillips as Titania were terrific together. Bert acted the blue-collar braggart showing off for a classy dame. Maggie was the smitten aristocrat trying to tactfully dodge his faux pas. The production was beautiful. The magic Athenian forest was a glistening midsummer pool of dappled moonlight blues and dark purples. The fairy queen dozed in a dazzling golden cobweb guarded by iridescent fairies and elves.

Before the opening Bert started to worry that the critics might ridicule him for taking on Shakespeare. He was afraid and it made him defensive.

During the photo call, Jack was hiding in the dark at the back of the theater. "Tell B-Bert we need him in the donkey's head."

Bert was exhausted. It was a long photo call, he'd been rehearsing two plays at the same time, and the person who usually interpreted the world for him was still in New York. (Bert's beautiful wife, Mildred, showed up on the tour periodically. She held the key to his heart and without her he'd mostly close it up.)

"Bert, they're ready for you on stage again. They want to photograph you and Maggie and the donkey's head."

He smashed his cigarette into a pile of butts. "Don't these people know anything?" I watched him through the wall of makeup mirrors. "It's the number one rule in comedy, you never give the gag away." He stood up. He looked silly being angry in his Elizabethan weaver's costume with his orange Pan-Cake and basset hound eyes outlined in umber. He looked funny, but he was hurt.

"Over my dead body. They'll plaster pictures of the donkey's head everywhere and tip the main bit."

I thought he was kidding. Sometimes he'd impersonate himself to make a joke. "Bert, the gag's three hundred and fifty years old. There're movies, a ballet, and a couple of operas. It's a safe bet that most people buying tickets to *A Midsummer Night's Dream* have some idea that Bottom gets turned into a donkey. There's the Mendelssohn."

"Tell Jack I'll stay exactly where I am."

I went upstairs to Maggie.

"Poor Bert," she said. "He's frazzled. We all are." All summer Maggie had been Olivia to Hepburn's shakily received Viola. She knew exactly how to make it across the frayed rope bridge of a frail ego.

In the dressing room she pulled over a chair and sat next to Bert. She looked remarkable in her elaborate Elizabethan costume. Her face and wig were covered in sparkle dust. Her crystal crown shivered with glass droplets. She stared at Bert in the mirror and lit a Tareyton. "Cagney has the donkey's head. In the poster for the Reinhardt film, Jimmy Cagney's holding the donkey's head. I think it's quite traditional with the role, almost expected. Besides, Bert, you're wonderful in the part, so darling, so funny. I wouldn't worry about anything except getting some rest."

They were Titania and Bottom. They were from different worlds and for just now he was in hers. He trusted her and she always wanted to make life easier for him. In our inept way, I think we all did.

He reached for the donkey's head. "You're right," he said. "I'm worn out." He scowled in my direction. "And I'm getting your goddamn cold."

The play opened to wonderful reviews and all the papers carried pictures of Bert holding the donkey's head. Opening night after he came offstage from the first scene, he was the happiest I'd ever seen him. "There's *nuns* out there," he whispered. He told me there'd been a time in his life when he was sure no nun would ever come to see him in anything. "They're having a very good time, all those nuns in the fourth row."

Winter's Tale was another story. Bert was miserable. Part of the problem was that his character didn't make his first entrance until after the intermission, by which time the audience had bathed for an hour and ten minutes in exquisite Jacobean tragedy. Bert felt that he had to turn the audience a one-eighty through slapstick.

"It's really two plays," he was complaining in his dressing room in Baltimore. "It's a tragedy, then all of a sudden it's a comedy. It's everything everyone hates about Shakespeare. The jokes aren't funny, and the language is obscure and hard to play. What the hell do you do with 'a codpiece of a purse' or a goddamn 'placket.'"

A few times I've been lucky enough to see an actor bring a Shakespeare part completely to life, and Bert's oily portrait of the charismatic rogue Autolycus left no doubt that this role was penned by the genius who'd given breath to Sir John Falstaff.

But what I thought didn't matter. I was a nineteen-year-old dresser who never got the starch in Bert's shirts quite right. In Baltimore I knew that Bert would close the play. He was mad at it. He had nothing good to say and he didn't want to have anything good to say. Like a snotty kid, he kept looking for proof that it was an obscure, unplayable text. Outside the dressing room he'd sneer at the speaker box. Doug Watson was on stage working his way through one of the mad king's jealous rages. "There may be in the cup a spider steeped . . ." "What the hell's he talking about?"

In Cleveland the shows ran into a couple of tough audiences. It happens to the best performers in the most successful productions. It's chemistry, and one of the things that makes live theater dangerous and thrilling, but it was hard on Bert and it closed the coffin lid on *Winter's Tale*.

The months with Bert were difficult but his contributions to my growing collection of Shakespeare insights were invaluable. Bert's battles with *Winter's Tale* exposed me to information I'd never gotten in a schoolroom.

"These sons of bitches are killing me." Bert was a worrier and a perfectionist. "Ya think I'm nuts? They hate everything. *You* look. You'll see I'm right. They eat their young!" Detroit was our fourth stop and in Detroit *Winter's Tale* stopped, too.

When he felt lonely Bert would find some job for me. On the day off I'd be reluctant company in his hotel room. He'd sit in his navy blue Brooks Brothers bathrobe, send down for food, and recount a litany of disappointments and resentments. Straddling Bert with my fingers covered in dripping hair dye was like being with a more sophisticated version of my own mother.

Backstage, the Actors' Equity deputy pulled me aside. Everyone knew I stayed late to hand wash Bert's underwear and socks. By then, I did his shirts, too, and most people heard him criticize me in the offstage dark.

Upset over the loss of *Winter's Tale* and blaming Bert, the deputy thought our star might deserve a rebuke. The union rep talked to me while Bert was onstage with Maggie. The conversation made me feel disloyal. "No," I said, "it'll be over in a couple of months and he *is* Nick Bottom the weaver. He can be selfish and insensitive, but he has more talent in his finger than I'll ever have in my whole body."

Around that time the company manager was itching for a fight. Bert got a percentage of the ticket sales. Usually the money would have been paid by check after a tally of the week's grosses, but Bert had played some sleazy places in his early years and never lost his mistrust of theater management. He was convinced that unless you watched carefully, "they'd cheat the pants off you."

In Detroit Bert went into a drugstore and bought a little handheld counter. It was bright pink. Every night he got ready early so that he could position himself on the set before the audience came in.

Click, click, click . . . click, click . . . click. For one half hour Bert stood in full makeup and costume narrowing his eyes under his little felt weaver's cap. *Click, click, click, click.* His thumb pounded the little plastic knob—*click, click, click*—"That son of a bitch isn't gonna cheat me."

The company manager was a bitter bully who was nasty to all the lesser actors and he couldn't stand Bert. Because of Bert's contract, Milton had to appear at intermission with all the figures from the night's take *and* an envelope containing Bert's cut. The implication was that if the money wasn't there, there'd be no second act.

Every night while Milton sat at the dressing table with the donkey's head leaning against the mirror, Bert questioned everything. He'd even started to carry a little pad so he could note how many people sat in which sections. He'd go through the night's sheet meticulously comparing his own notes to the company manager's. The ritual drove Milton wild. He was irate that Bert counted the house, but at last he'd found a way to injure him.

"I hear you're going to complain to the union about Bert?" Milton was mean to me and I was afraid of him.

"I think you heard it wrong. I'd never complain about Bert." And I meant it. Bert was difficult. We all got that right away, but Bert was a star and he put himself out there every time. Bert never did what Miss Merman had done. Bert never let anger or exhaustion or boredom pull him back from playing the part full out.

But Milton had had it and apparently decided to stab Bert with me. Intermission was over. Bert had his envelope of cash. We were ready for the second act. I was holding the donkey's head.

"Your dresser's making trouble. It's my duty to tell you that he has a plan to submit a formal complaint to the union about your treatment of him."

I looked at Bert in the makeup mirror. I could see myself holding the donkey's head. I looked like a guilty four-year-old. Milton was smiling. Bert looked up and over at me. Then he did something that changed our relationship forever.

"Milton, get the fuck out of my dressing room. I know this kid, this kid knows me. I can be a pain in the ass. But Bob's a smart kid. He's a big part of the success of this show. He defended *Winter's*

Tale until I wanted to shoot him. From now on you go over the figures with Bob and give *him* the envelope, and unless I call for you, stay the fuck outta my way."

A couple of minutes later Bert made his lyrical entrance with Maggie from stage left.

> Come sit thee down upon this flowery bed,
> While I thy amiable cheeks do coy,
> And stick musk-roses in thy sleek smooth head,
> And kiss thy fair large ears, my gentle joy.
>   —*A Midsummer Night's Dream*, 4.1

After that, every night at intermission, I went around to the front of the house and Milton took me through Bert's sheet. When I understood, he handed me the envelope.

Bert showed me a part of theater the Shakespeare summers had never even hinted at. At the Festival the business of show business rarely made its way backstage. The regular actors probably didn't make huge salaries and the only time I'd heard a star's salary mentioned was when Donald Davis, who'd played Orsino opposite Hepburn, told me that she'd turned her salary back into the productions and that all those lavish outfits she wore in *Antony and Cleopatra* she'd written a check for.

After *Winter's Tale* was dropped we made our way west, city by city, to L.A. One of my favorite memories of that winter of 1960 is chain smoking at midnight alone with the lights out in the Super Chief dome car, chug-chugging through starry skies in the snow-covered Rockies with "Moon River" playing over and over on Pat Hines's big heavy tape player.

I love train travel, even these days on the crowded 8:03 going in to do Shakespeare with the old people. On tour most actors and stage crew got a bunk in the Pullman car. They had a great time stacked together playing games or testing each other on obscure Shakespeare phrases. I paid extra to get a room. It must have looked odd for the kid dresser to book equal accommodations to the star, but despite how much I loved the actors, between cities I liked hiding out to stare at the scenery with the text of the play in my head. Well taught by Nana and the moss rose dishes, I'm a sucker for what's beautiful. Watching mountain passes from my mahogany stateroom was one of the most pleasurable experiences of my life. I've flown across the country hundreds of times, but four times I've sat in a small quiet room with America running by a big clean window, and it's wonderful.

After Salt Lake, Bert was staring at the scenery. "Come in, kid. I'll tell ya about L.A. and the movie business." We were hours away but he already had his polo coat over his shoulders. As he talked the view was shifting from the rugged terrain of Bierstadt landscapes. Palm trees started flying by and everything was suddenly pink and azure-laced southern California.

The adobe-colored L.A. Union Station was saturated with morning sun as our sleek silver train pulled into the railroad yard. In 1960 there was still the specter of movie stars stepping from railroad cars to the pop of flashbulbs and the press of press pizzazz. It was December and it was hot. "Unusually warm for Christmas." The nice-looking black porter seemed to think it was a good thing. "You might even get in a swim."

Bert was staying downtown next to the theater. I'd taken a place far away in Hollywood. I'd been in a lot of downtowns, and I wanted movieland. Bert promised me that Hollywood was still recognizable as the place I'd seen in the little brick movie house across from Lovell's Hardware, the Hollywood of myth, of Gloria Swanson and Sunset Boulevard. We weren't booked into the theater for a few days and I felt pretty happy, L.A. for the first time, money in my pocket, and time to kill.

In the hotel lobby coffee shop I bought a newspaper and saw an
ad for the new Bergman film. I was wild for Ingmar Bergman. *The
Seventh Seal* and *Wild Strawberries* didn't play at the little Stratford
movie theater. Subtitles were too much for Stratford. There were
"art" houses in New Haven and Fairfield for Bergman and Fellini.

When I asked the cashier if *The Virgin Spring* was a walkable
distance I didn't know how big L.A. is, how flat. And I didn't know
that no one in L.A. walked. I asked her to draw a little map on the
corner of the ad.

That first afternoon, walking in the bright heat, I heard saxophone music. I hate saxophone music. I can't stand the way it gets
under my skin and feels tawdry and lonesome. I love Los Angeles,
but when the sun's so insistent that it doesn't make shadows, I feel
there's no place to hide, and I absolutely always hear saxophone
music. It's a soundtrack to destroyed dreams. It's about a run-
down, rented little Spanish-style house and a job that doesn't hurt
too much. It's about being hot and running an ice cube up and
down the back of your neck and not quite noticing how the luster's
off your life. The glamour is up in the hills; it's the flat Hollywood
that hurts.

If I'd looked at the stills from *The Virgin Spring*, I would never
have bought my ticket. The little girl in the grotesque allegory of
rape and murder and resurrection looked alarmingly like the one
I'd left banging on the fridge a continent away. I didn't want to see
her or be hurt by her. I wanted to be three thousand miles away in
a kidney-shaped pool forgetting she existed.

Maybe it was the medieval movie or being in the west, but I had a
longing to go fast on a big horse. California, for the first time,
made me wish I'd brought my bike. The constant exposure to the
play, listening from the wings or through the speaker boxes, left it
like a disc going round and round, over and over in my head. A
horse was just right. I looked up stables and asked which was

closest. The next morning one of the actors with a car dropped me off.

The place was set far from the road. After a long walk it was just a few broken barns and a couple of corrals. I'd only been riding a few times but I figured I'd learn as I went along. It was treeless and hot when the man who owned the stables gave me a simple test on a docile Morgan. I was a "decent" rider he said, so he'd get me a "decent" horse.

I started to take the bus there. The owner got to expect me and let me in earlier and earlier. By six o'clock every morning I was up on a large palomino. I rode until it was so hot that the back of my neck burned. Just beyond a mountain trail there was a couple of miles of flat land. When I got up there I'd bust loose. I'd yell and scream.

There's a moment on a horse when you start to go very fast, and the movement smooths out, the sound changes, it gets very quiet, and it feels like Pegasus.

> I will not change my
> horse with any that treads but on four pasterns. Ch'ha!
> He bounds from the earth as if his entrails were hairs
> —*le cheval volant,* the Pegasus, *qui a les narines de feu!*
> When I bestride him, I soar, I am a hawk. He trots the
> air. The earth sings when he touches it; the basest
> horn of his hoof is more musical than the pipe of
> Hermes.
>
> —*King Henry V,* 3.7

Just like the kid I'd been on the fat red Schwinn, I raced along the winter-wet canyons and up to the Griffith Observatory. Some days a few people joined me, but I liked it best by myself. Maybe as my mother's Summer Street friend said, I spent too much time alone.

We were in L.A. a month and I rode every morning except Christmas, when I went up to Topanga Canyon to have chili with

Will Geer's friends, who seemed to be what was left of Beat poets. Wild-haired, middle-aged men and anorexic women in Mexican clothes read poetry and sang folksy political songs. Afterward we went down the mountain and along the ocean to burst in on the Housemans at Malibu. There were movie stars, and famous designers. I sat on the floor and talked to Dorothy Jeakins. She'd designed the costumes for *Winter's Tale*. I told her how I'd slept in Paulina's cape.

In L.A. that Christmastime, forty years ago, there were late-night parties up in the hills, and up in the hills was different from the mostly depressing flat part. In the hills people dressed up and chatted about the play with what John Houseman called "mid-Atlantic" accents. Bert and Mildred came along and actors sang near a piano.

It was exciting, but I wasn't completely a part of it. My participation in the play was so slight. I was a nervous kid and Bert's bouts of crankiness were shoving me down exactly as my father's had. I felt so nonessential. These days it's different.

A few months ago, when I started *Hamlet* with the seniors, a woman reappeared. She'd been gone for years. I was startled.

"I wondered where you went," I said. "You always seemed so devoted to the plays that I thought maybe I'd said something to push you away."

She got teary and smiled. "I've been sick," she whispered. "It started the last day I was here. I had an annoying earache. We were doing *Coriolanus*. I was fascinated but I had this damn pain in my head. It was a tumor. For the last two years I've been through the struggle of my life. I'll tell you something . . ." She looked deeply into my eyes. "I thought about this class. I kept picturing you reading the Shakespeare and wondering if I'd ever get back here. If I did would I understand what you say?"

She's a gorgeous, tall woman with intense eyes. I have no idea how old she is; it's hard to tell.

"Today's the test," she said. "I'm nervous. When your brain's been carved up, it leaves you scared that it won't come back. All along I told myself that the day I could read Shakespeare again I'd know I'd gotten myself back. It's been so terrifying and I feel like I'm coming home."

"What would you like for Christmas?" my mother yelled into the phone after she'd told what little news there was. Of course I could hear Carolyn. "She's been at the refrigerator for more than two years now, or is it three? Well, at least she's healthy, but dear God almighty, will it ever stop?"

"I'd like a portable radio."

It was time for the long ride back east. The company was due in Philadelphia, Wilmington, and finally Washington, finishing a few weeks before the spring season started again in Stratford.

We'd make the trip to New York and have a week off before the opening. Back east there were an impending rail strike and record snowfalls.

In the mountains west of Harrisburg, I sat against the icy window, fanning my spread hand across the cold wet to clear the glass and see carriages, black and skeletal in the snow. Horses stood silhouetted next to lean nineteenth-century men in flat hats and long black coats. Women sat under bonnets and shawls, no color, Amish, poised in the huge snowfall. Through the dripping train window I watched a time from before, like staring down a Shakespeare passage.

My radio was pressed to the glass. "It's from my father," I liked to say. "He sent it to me." People were piled in so close, everyone listening to the fuzzy sound. I was gently turning the tiny dial back and forth when a remote radio voice crackled, "Ask not

what your country can do for you . . ." Actors got emotional at
new beginnings, and in the snowy Pennsylvania mountain pass I
felt so safe to be a part of Shakespeare. Inauguration Day, January 20, 1961. We were the last train in before the strike. Someone
met us and I got a ride home.

It was almost dawn when I took the key from the mailbox. I could
see the night-light in the kitchen. No sound. No *kick-chunk*. When
I turned from the little hallway, there she was leaning like Michelangelo's dying slave collapsed against the fridge. She was asleep.

It was still snowing. I didn't take my coat off. I just sat watching as I had a thousand times before. I could hear my father snoring upstairs. I felt so guilty for how much I hated being there. I
didn't want to wake Carolyn. I knew she'd just start pounding
away. "Let her rest," I thought. "Let everyone rest. It will all be
back to hurt us in the morning."

CHAPTER 22

O VER COFFEE the next day my mother said,
"We're moving. I can't take this godforsaken place anymore. I need
to be back in civilization."

"Where?"

"South Main Street, a couple of blocks from Shakespeare. It's a
sweet old place with a little barn way out in the back."

"What's the kitchen like?" I asked. "Where's the refrigerator?"

Being away from the tour for a week was strange. I felt removed
from my family in a way I'd never been before. For years with my
parents I'd had a sense of longing. They'd never asked me about
school or work. If I started to talk about the plays, my father would
act distracted. He'd rattle the change in his pocket or start to fiddle
with anything within his reach. "How stupid I am," I'd think. As I
searched for anything that might engage his interest. "I had dinner
with James Cagney. In L.A. Bert took me . . ."

"Mil, did you turn the heat down to sixty-eight?" he'd call
past me.

"Yes, Ray, I told you I did."

My sister was changing, too. She was bigger and starting to look like an adult. And always that sound, that awful *kick-chunk*. By then nobody heard it anymore. "If you need anything from the fridge," my mother would say, "try to get it all at once so she won't have 'ten fits.' "

The day I rejoined the tour, my father drove me down Main Street past the little granite library to see the new house.

"There's no garage," he said, "just that barn and it's too far back to use in winter."

At the end of the long yard was a beautiful little carriage house wrapped in cedar shakes. The place was surrounded by gnarled trees and overgrown vines. In the deep snow it looked like a magic cottage, a perfect place to draw and read Shakespeare.

"I'd love to live in it," I said.

"Just a barn," my father wrinkled his face, "no plumbing or electricity."

After the Philadelphia opening, Bert looked forward to the end of the tour, but stressful as it was, he held on, still tracking missing laughs and policing scene-stealing movement till the last performance.

In the dressing rooms everyone was focused on the spring. Jack had decided to revive *Twelfth Night*. The high school audiences didn't require a celebrity so anything was possible. Actors dreamed of being hired for the spring, then sliding right into the summer season. Maybe there'd be another tour. With luck it was possible to have another full year of employment, such a painless transition in such a catch-as-catch-can profession.

I didn't know what I was going to do. Dressing Bert had stolen the innocence from the job. I wasn't sure that watching from behind that teak panel would be the same after the tour.

Peggy said, "Whacha gonna do? Wanna come work wit me on *Twelfth Night*?"

Jack said, "I hope you'll stay with us."

I told him I wanted to but I didn't know as what.

"When this is over," he said, "let's sit d-down in New York."

Philadelphia was beautiful in the snow. I went to the museums and walked along Pine Street staring into all the antique shop windows. I bought a brass bed for the little barn up in Connecticut. I was determined to live in there.

By the end of February I'd finally gotten the starch in Bert's shirts completely right and it was over, time to talk to Jack about what was next.

Many years later I was in Omaha, Nebraska, when I heard that Bert had died. The first thing I thought of was him eating pistachio nuts after the final performance in Washington.

"It's always the same," he said. "It doesn't matter what you've done, or who you are, you think no one will ever ask you to do it again." His fingers were brilliant red, so was his mouth. In the dressing room mirror, he was watching himself reach into the bag of pistachios. The floor was a mass of discarded shells, the counter of the dressing table was, too. He was in his superwhite underwear. His tan skin hung in wrinkles on the frame of his body. His bare feet were half shoved into his worn leather slippers. He was looking directly into his own sad eyes. He'd do that all the time, just stare at Bert staring back at him.

Once I said, "You look like you're trying to find something, Bert. What are you looking for?"

"These people don't know a goddamn thing about comedy."

The New York offices of the Festival were on Forty-fourth Street in an eccentric Beaux Arts building that looked like the back of a Spanish galleon. Jack sat with one of the elaborately carved windows filling a whole wall behind him.

"You survived B-Bert Lahr and America." His eyes darted behind his Coke-bottle glasses. "What's next? I think you should

be part of the stage m-m-management. We'd start you off as assistant and after you learn the ropes there'd b-b-be no reason you
couldn't move up." He smiled and I remember thinking that I'd
never seen Jack smile. "We're grateful for how you handled things
on the road and most especially that m-mess with M-M-Milton
and Bert's 'cut.' "

"I want to be a student at the academy." I figured Jack would be
disappointed. Everyone wants to be Hamlet down center in a spotlight, spilling his guts to a sympathetic crowd. "For a couple of
years I've watched everyone leave me in the wings to cross into the
play. I don't want any lines. Once I'd just like to be inside what I'm
outside of."

Jacked looked sour. "How old are you?"

"Nineteen."

"Oh my God," he said. "You're a kid." He called Pat Hines in
from another office. "Did you know how *young* Bob is?"

He was smiling again. "Come back in two weeks with the
p-prologue to *Henry the Fifth*."

> O for a muse of fire, that would ascend
> The brightest heaven of invention,
> A kingdom for a stage, princes to act,
> And monarchs to behold the swelling scene!
>
> —*King Henry V*, 1.1

After a knee-knocking audition, I was accepted into the academy. "We'll pay you a stipend. You'll understudy and take classes;
at the end of the season, we'll sit d-down again." Jack was
indulging me.

In Stratford, my parents weren't having any luck selling their
glamorous split-level. I wondered what real estate brokers said to
potential buyers when they saw the big modern kitchen with the
beautiful dazed girl pounding the refrigerator? The house on Main
Street was sitting empty.

"Why not let me live there," I said. "It's only two streets from the theater, and I could do some work on the place instead of paying rent."

In early March, *Twelfth Night* started rehearsals up over a deli on Second Avenue. Doug Watson was Orsino. "If music be the food of love . . ." The year before I'd knelt in the dark to watch his tortured Leontes; now I'd get to stand right next to him. Mariette Hartley was Olivia. Bill Hickey was Sir Andrew, and Pat was Toby Belch.

I was excited to meet other students. The group of twelve young actors had been together at the New York Academy all winter. At the dressing table next to mine was one older than the rest, a formal, melancholic guy who'd decided he'd put off his dream of being an actor almost too long. Douglas Sherman had deep doleful eyes and sparse stringy dark hair. He knew a lot about theater history but didn't say much about his own. Once I mentioned Syracuse and he said he'd grown up "near there." Douglas took his spear-carrying duties as seriously as any of us. When actors complained backstage he was always a gentleman. "If you don't care for the acting," he'd grin a sort of mortician's condolement, "just listen to the wonderful words."

It was Douglas who most influenced my decision to leave home permanently. Ultimately there'd be an inescapable lesson in his lonely loveless life. But the beginning, that spring when *Twelfth Night* started, was a joyful time for me. After the constant worry of failing Bert, it was great to think only about my little part in the play. And the high school kids loved the production.

The "cutest" actors got to be Orsino's sailors. They had to look sweet enough to match Viola when she concealed herself as one of them. In our long hair, Billy Budd white canvas sailor suits, and patent leather shoes, the five of us did all kinds of fancy military marching maneuvers and the school kids loved it. They called out when we entered, and threw impromptu gifts and their phone numbers onto the stage. Girls hung around the stage door to coo over us. For a rainy six weeks we were a boy band forty years before boy bands. I lived in the big empty house with my brass bed from Philadelphia. And took my first tentative breaths in a speech class.

I'm definitely *not* an actor, but a couple of weeks ago at the Stein Center a senior walked up to me. We'd been chipping away at the text of *Troilus and Cressida* for three months. "It's amazing," the old man said. "You're *there,* you're actually standing on the Phrygian plain in front of Troy, and because you're there, all of us old people are there with you." It might be the most wonderful thing anyone's ever said to me. I love the image of me and a hundred old men and women standing in the dust and blood of the flats below Ilium.

While we were having our springtime fun with *Twelfth Night* for the schoolkids, Jack picked *Macbeth, As You Like It,* and *Troilus and Cressida* for the summer. Undaunted by criticism, he'd decided to set *Troilus* in the American Civil War. Rumor had it that he'd invited the black actress Ruby Dee for Cressida. *As You Like It* went to a guest director, Word Baker, who'd just made a huge hit with a tiny musical, *The Fantasticks.* The Shakespeare comedy was to be completely modern, set in Central Park.

Jack was careful with the tragedy. *Macbeth* would kick off the season with all the bagpipes and brutality expected from the "Scottish" play. Jessica Tandy was set opposite Pat Hingle. Kim Hunter was the first witch, and would be Rosalind in *As You Like It.* The two leading ladies had made a smash on Broadway as the DuBois sisters in *A Streetcar Named Desire.*

It was a Sunday in April when we all got trucked in to New York for the first time. At the Macbeth rehearsal in the hall on Second Avenue, two things struck me right away. In a hat and gloves Miss Tandy seemed a bit refined to be sharing such barbarous thoughts . . .

I have given suck, and know
How tender 'tis to love the babe that milks me:

I would, while it was smiling in my face,
Have pluck'd my nipple from his boneless gums,
And dash'd the brains out, had I so sworn
As you have done to this.

—*Macbeth*, 1.7

The second thing I noticed was the brutish crowd seated around watching. One of the *Twelfth Night* kids whispered, "It looks like Jack pulled people in off the street." Something very rough was in the atmosphere, too rough. Sure it was the text, but more than that it was something I'd never felt at any rehearsal. And I remember thinking that something was wrong with Jack. He didn't act like the person who'd directed *A Midsummer Night's Dream*. I thought about the movie of *Suddenly Last Summer*. Maggie had starred in the original play in New York, and of course Hepburn did the film. There's a part at the very end when the protagonist baits a group of dangerous and desperate boys. It's a dark, homoerotic allegory of self-hatred and cannibalism, and I couldn't quite get it out of my head. When I watched Jack in his wrinkled seersucker suit awkwardly trying to kid around, he looked unhappy. He looked self-conscious. He looked like fat Billy in Boston begging the guy not to hurt him with the knife.

Macbeth and *Troilus* sicken the spirit, and living inside of them all summer shoved my face into the dis-ease of art. Jack hired non-actors to add an edge of genuine danger to the plays. For that 1961 season, the safest place I'd ever been became an environment not so different from my high school halls.

I decided to embrace what was coming, even be excited by it. After all, I'd spent some teenage time smoking on street corners. I could act the wise guy. And in Boston I'd learned the language of tough. I asked Jack if I could be excused from the comedy. He had so many young men coming up for the summer why not one of them instead of me?

"I'll trade with you," he said and there was a hint that he might be expecting trouble. "You learn every part in *As You Like It* and sign in at every performance ready to do anything in the whole play and I'll excuse you from being in it." "Sure. Can I be an apparition?" While Jack was in a trading mood, I wanted most to be one of the future kings the witches show Macbeth.

During the week of *Macbeth* techs, there was a lot of debate about fog. How much? Which flavor? The manufacturer offered various scents and Jack tried them all. As the lights in the theater dimmed—"House to half"—the sound of distant bagpipes droned from the bluff over the river. Eerie light slowly drifted in. As the pipers made their way through the lobby and down the aisles of the theater, the stage filled with gourmet fog. The bagpipers disappeared into the catwalks and the witches were suddenly caught center in a sharp unforgiving down light. "When shall we three meet again?"

There was thunder, rain, and, from offstage, the clash of steel and the bloodthirsty screams of battle. As a nineteen-year-old extra, I adored how scary the artificial atmosphere felt.

My first swirling, fog-filled entrance was seconds before Lady Macbeth's. My strength was levelheadedness, not acting, so I carried her chair. I hauled a lot of furniture that summer. Jack knew I'd always hit the almost invisible "spike" marks taped to the encrusted stage floor.

I'm not sure that anybody actually saw very much of the *Macbeth*. By the time the fog lifted, allowing the actors to see each other, the mist had settled into a solid block in the orchestra section of the theater. For the first few scenes, the audience couldn't see much of us, then for the rest of the act we couldn't see them. At every performance actors injured themselves tripping over step units and each other, confirming the famous curse connected to the "Scottish" play. I listened to the words.

It's odd, considering its relentless brutality, that *Macbeth* has such elegant language. Little, unremarkable scenes glisten. King Duncan's ill-fated visit to Inverness uses the nest-building martin to lift the audience to the rarefied air of Macbeth's Highland home.

> DUNCAN   This castle has a pleasant seat; the air
>   Nimbly and sweetly recommends itself
>   Unto our gentle senses.
> BANQUO   This guest of summer,
>   The temple-haunting martlet, does approve,
>   By his loved mansionry, that the heaven's breath
>   Smells wooingly here: no jutty, frieze,
>   Buttress, nor coign of vantage, but this bird
>   Hath made his pendant bed, and procreant cradle:
>   Where they most breed and haunt, I have observ'd
>   The air is delicate.
>
> —*Macbeth*, 1.6

Shakespeare the country boy pictures bucolic, idyllic summer as the little bird constructs his swinging cradle of a nest. Delicately suspended, it is like the lives of the two speakers, perilously set on the very edge of disaster.

Once night comes, stealth steals sweetness and Macbeth, like Brutus, convinces himself to destroy a monarch.

> Now o'er the one half-world
> Nature seems dead, and wicked dreams abuse
> The curtain'd sleep: Witchcraft celebrates
> Pale Hecate's off'rings; and wither'd Murther,
> Alarum'd by his sentinel, the wolf,
> Whose howl's his watch, thus with his stealthy pace,
> With Tarquin's ravishing strides, towards his design
> Moves like a ghost.
>
> —*Macbeth*, 2.1

Moments later the bustling martlet is replaced by the bird of death. A rookie soldier is first to observe it.

> LENOX   The night has been unruly; where we lay,
> Our chimneys were blown down; and, as they say,
> Lamentings heard i'th' air; strange screams of death,
> And, prophesying with accents terrible
> Of dire combustion, and confus'd events,
> New hatch'd to th' woeful time, the obscure bird
> Clamour'd the livelong night: some say, the earth
> Was feverous and did shake.
> MACBETH   'Twas a rough night.
> —*Macbeth*, 2.3

In its way the Shakespeare summer was like that. Fights broke out. Drunken students made lunatic late-night scenes on the otherwise quiet Stratford streets. All of a sudden it wasn't unusual to see police cars in the Festival parking lots. Backstage robberies started, at first just a few bucks lifted from a dressing table, but before long jewelry, watches, paychecks. It went on for the whole season. On the last day an arrest was made. No one was shocked that the thief was one of the brutish guys hired for type and not for the remotest interest in Shakespeare. Jack had seen him shirtless, a member of the grounds crew, and invited him into the plays.

In the meantime I was gratefully sopping up the thickness of the fermenting summer. In my rough, glue-on beard and scratchy kilt, I growled primeval grunts along with everyone else. As we slid around on the slick left by interludes of drizzling, odoriferous fog, some of us took our job and most especially ourselves very seriously.

CHAPTER 23

By THE TIME *Troilus and Cressida* started rehearsals, serious-minded students had segregated themselves into one dressing room while Jack's gang of street thugs hung out looking for trouble in the halls. It was difficult for fervent Shakespeare disciples to watch nonactors kid around in the wings and play vicious jokes on each other out on the sacred stage.

> In Troy, there lies the scene. From Isles of Greece
> The princes orgulous, their high blood chaf'd
> Have to the port of Athens sent their ships
> Fraught with the ministers and instruments
> Of cruel war: sixty and nine that wore
> Their crownets regal, from th' Athenian bay
> Put forth toward Phrygia, and their vow is made
> To ransack Troy, within whose strong immures
> The ravish'd Helen, Menelaus' queen,
> With wanton Paris sleeps—and that's the quarrel.
> —*Troilus and Cressida*, Prologue

In our callous backstage, no more appropriate voice could have issued warnings from the little speaker boxes. *Troilus* arrived as a perfect metaphor for the spoiled summer. Seven frustrating years have taken the luster from the struggle to bring Helen home. Morals are debated, not lived, as the crowd of legendary heroes crumble on their own turf feet, and in the end love isn't much more than the sexual addiction Shakespeare disembowels in the less pretty sonnets.

It was the beginning of the end of the Festival as I'd known it, and despite some beautiful work by later directors, I always think of that *Macbeth* summer as the poison let in for which no antidote was ever found. Something had changed. After the season, Jack would be gone and, in not too many years, dead. Killed, I was told, not unlike Sebastian in *Suddenly Last Summer,* hacked at by ruffians in a hotel room.

Over on Main Street, my father, grateful for work I'd done on the new old house and wanting the third bedroom for TV, in the end put plumbing and electricity into the barn that everyone called the "studio." I lived in it from the opening of *Troilus and Cressida* until the day after my sister took the ride for ice cream and never came home.

It was left for the moving men to tear the refrigerator from Carolyn's grasp. By midsummer of 1961 it had been three years since she'd first paused to grab the handle. We were all terrified about how she'd react.

The day of the move my father half carried her to the studio and went back to the empty house to wait with my mother for the moving truck. Carolyn sat in an old rocker. In three years I hadn't seen my sister sit anywhere except for those frustrating moments on the toilet. She sat as if she actually enjoyed sitting. She was docile, relieved to be freed from the nightmare. For the next year she spent most of her time with me in the studio. I traded some books to Mrs. Canfield for furniture.

* * *

At the academy we'd gotten a terrifying acting teacher. She'd once been a great actress who'd starred for Eugene O'Neill at the Provincetown Playhouse. It was also rumored among the students that she'd had his child. When I was nineteen she seemed too old to have had such spice in her life.

Mary Morris could be brutal when she ripped through students' work. Mercifully, she mostly ignored me, choosing to shed light where light would nurture growth. She'd sit dead center in the room. She was overweight and wore the same heavy shoes and old lady dresses as my high school teachers. Mary was brilliant. She'd have sudden fits of insight and, electrified by her own inspiration, she'd shake and tremble. Her voice would go low and gravelly. She'd vibrate like a Holy Roller and launch into a dramatic discourse on "truth in acting." She was spectacular to watch but scary as hell.

In the big theater Jack was putting together a wonderful *Troilus,* though maybe that's an oxymoron. He'd stuck to his Civil War concept. Troy was the Confederacy. I was a Trojan. Jack cast me as the servant to *Troilus* fleetingly referred to in his first line: "Call here my varlet, I'll unarm again." I think it was Jack's idea of a joke. A varlet's a gentleman's son in service to a knight. I'd been Bert's valet. As Troilus's varlet I wore a beautiful gray Confederate uniform with elaborate gold trim. On a rehearsal break Jack said I looked like Leslie Howard in *Gone with the Wind.* I'd never seen *Gone with the Wind,* and for a while I didn't know it was a compliment.

I got to spend most of the play hanging around Ilium, which was represented by a stage-wide, antebellum mansion. Ted Van Griethuysen was Troilus. He'd been Florizel in the *Winter's Tale* for the kids. Carrie Nye was a heartbreakingly theatrical Cressida. Will Geer was Priam, Pat Hingle was Hector, Jessica Tandy was the mad sister Cassandra, and Kim Hunter was Helen. I experienced some breathtaking nights in Priam's royal palace with that collection of very good actors.

* * *

The morning after the final dress rehearsal I was helping Will Geer in his brand-new Shakespeare garden when the scary Miss Morris waved and plodded into the muck. She grabbed the front of my hair and pulled very hard. She bent in close and put her nose on mine. From some demonic depth she growled, "I saw *Troilus* last night and I couldn't take my eyes off you." She was ripping my hair and I could definitely smell bourbon. "You're the best thing up there. I could track the whole story through your face and you're so goddamned beautiful, you look like Leslie Howard."

She released my scalp and stepped back. She was so theatrical in her chiffon dress, picture hat, and thick-heeled lace-up shoes. She frowned toward Will. "I've had Leslie Howard in front of me all summer and didn't notice." She forgave herself. "But like all real actors Robert lives truly only on the stage, the rest of the time he's protected by . . . invisibility."

Miss Morris leaned exhausted against the garden fence. "I've decided to do *Romeo and Juliet* for the student production. The speech people will help, the movement teacher will choreograph. It will be very hard work. Imagine Leslie Howard." A minute later she was gone, stumbling down the road to pick up her mail backstage.

"Will, is Leslie Howard good-looking?"

"Yup, but not like Monty Clift."

> Call here my varlet, I'll unarm again.
> Why should I war without the walls of Troy,
> That find such cruel battle here within?
> Each Trojan that is master of his heart
> Let him to field: Troilus, alas, hath none.
> . . . .
> The Greeks are strong, and skilful to their strength,
> Fierce to their skill, and to their fierceness valiant;
> But I am weaker than a woman's tear,

Tamer than sleep, fonder than ignorance,
Less valiant than the virgin in the night,
And skilless as unpractis'd infancy.

—*Troilus and Cressida*, 1.1

Under Miss Morris's penetrating, paralyzing gaze, my fledgling Romeo was for sure as "skilless as unpractis'd infancy." I remember how nervous I felt and how talented everyone else was. She broke the play down to a kind of Las Vegas version focusing on the gang of boys and Romeo. Passionate, middle-aged Miss Morris was less interested in nubile Juliet. We did the balcony scene, the nurse in the square, the Queen Mab, and the sad good-byes of the second balcony. We wore tuxedos and did the cut-up play twice in the double living room of the academy building.

At the first performance I gulped, perspired, and was spastic with terror. It was humiliating. But the next day, the second time we did it, something odd happened. Suddenly I had nerves of steel and remembered every word of counsel mad Miss Morris had vibrated in my direction. I was completely in control. Later Will and Pat and everyone else acted shocked at how well I'd done. No one was more surprised than I. Romeo's world is sick and violent. Maybe I was in love with the pain of that summer as much as I'd been wooed by the pleasure of the first one.

In August it was announced that the Festival would present a limited fall season of *Macbeth* for the high schools. Everyone was invited to stay on for an additional six weeks. Not everybody could. Miss Tandy was committed to other work and she was having health problems. Waiting for an entrance in *Troilus*, she'd gotten caught up in some horseplay and slipped, injuring her back. When we had stage business together, she'd wince and admit to having spasms. Unlike Miss Hepburn, Jessica was an available person. Sundays after the matinee she'd sit in the parking lot waiting while students finished understudy rehearsals. Then she'd load up her car with broke kids to save them the train fare home.

I was never quite sure what I thought of her Lady Macbeth. Somehow her portrait of clout-craving sovereignty seemed from another production, maybe a better one than the fogbound epic we were skidding around in. Her Cassandra was gorgeous. Her hallucinatory insertions into family debates were ferine, and she had one of the most beautiful faces you could imagine. When she entered with her wild hair flying and hot tears tracing her face— "Cry Trojans cry. . . ."—she wasn't just Troilus's mad sister, she was mine.

A couple of days before the season ended a few students rented a boat to row up the river for a picnic. Not everyone was staying for the fall *Macbeth* and it was a way to close the months we'd been together. Douglas Sherman came along. I remember that he was nervous about the sun. He seemed fey, almost ill, sitting in the back of the boat under a hat and layers of flimsy summer clothing. In early September 1961 on a blazing day on a river in Connecticut, most people couldn't get enough sun. In the Shakespeare plays, smart, educated, upper-class people avoid it, but in the Kennedy years brown skin and sun-blasted hair was shorthand for a new American aristocracy.

I was shirtless and oiled up as we rowed under the Devon Bridge. An hour later we pulled the boat onto a small island just past the Merritt Parkway. We went for a swim and sat swigging a couple of bottles of Chablis. With our feet in icy river water, we reminded each other of the amiability of the *Twelfth Night* weeks. The more bitter kids documented the sour adventures of the curdled summer.

Douglas seemed tired. I hadn't spent a lot of time with him since the spring. He'd stop by when I lived alone in the big old house, and he helped me paint the ceiling of the studio, but the summer was different. Miss Morris hadn't reacted much to his work so he'd fared poorly in the *Romeo and Juliet*. Of course, he'd wanted Mercutio. She naturally gave those fireworks to a kid who could explode. Dour Douglas wasn't the type.

We took a walk along the rocky shore. He seemed distracted. "You okay?" I asked.

He smiled. He was such a sweet man. "Sure, just contemplating the fog of my future." He wasn't staying on for the fall *Macbeth*. For him the long season would be over in a couple of days. That was the first time he let all his feelings out. In the spring he'd dreamed that he'd be discovered, plucked from the rest of us ordinary students. He was angry at the way things had gone. He said that what mattered to Jack was "pornographic brutishness." It had left poor soft Douglas and his Edwardian aesthetic wheezing into a lace hankie.

"I can't imagine why anyone would want to stay on." He made a mock sad face. "Of course Jack likes *you*. You don't even want to be an actor and you have all those scene-stealing bits in *Troilus*. Jack likes you the same way Mary does, because you're good-looking."

"I get a lot out of the plays," I said. "I'm not here for the acting. I don't expect anyone to 'pluck' me out. I don't want them to. It's no secret that I mostly couldn't handle it when Mary pushed me into *Romeo*."

Douglas was staring at the water. With his large dark eyes and scraggly hair, he looked like engravings I'd seen of Edgar Allan Poe. "Ever think of doing a one-man Poe? You'd be incredible."

"Poe's *not* Shakespeare!"

The final weekend of the summer it was *Troilus and Cressida* for the Saturday matinee, then *As You Like It* for the evening. That way everything could be packed away, leaving *Macbeth* for Sunday afternoon and all set to start up a week later for the kids. There'd be five days' rehearsal. Some actors were moving into larger parts. Maggie Phillips was coming back to replace Miss Tandy and, hungry for her flamboyant charm, I was delighted. We were sort of friends. For those few years, all the actors that came in and out of my life seemed like members of a club, and for a while, unlike poor Douglas, I definitely felt a part of it.

Just before the final Saturday *Troilus* the assistant stage manager popped his head into the dressing room. "Where's Doug Sherman? He forgot to sign in."

In *Troilus* Douglas was a Union soldier. With his pathetic eyes and faded blue uniform, he looked like an emaciated prisoner at Andersonville or a pathetic Mathew Brady daguerreotype. Just before curtain at the five-minute call the production stage manager looked in. "Seen Douglas? He hasn't shown up."

"Did you call his landlady?"

"First thing we did." David sat down for a minute. "Think there's any chance he's left? He's not staying on for the student *Macbeth,* so as of tomorrow he's through. Maybe he's pissed off and cut out early."

"Not like him," I said. "He's a T-crosser, an I-dotter; not come to a performance? It's not in his character."

"The afternoon's covered," David whispered. "It's tonight that's a problem. You've been signing in at every *As You Like It* all summer. I've never had to put you to the test. If he doesn't show can you be Douglas tonight?"

"Sure," I said, "but unless he was abducted by Martians he'll be here."

All through the *Troilus* matinee I kept thinking he'd come running in with some amazing excuse. On the dinner break I rode over to his furnished room. "Is Douglas around?"

"No," his landlady said. "I heard him in the kitchen early this morning. Is anything wrong?"

"Do you think he could have left?"

"Maybe," she said. "He's paid up. Should we look in his room?"

Everything was pristine. His bed was made. On the dresser his towels and washcloth were neatly folded. Completely centered on the bed, as if it were measured, his suitcase was snapped shut. The closet door was open. The empty hangers hung neatly spaced an inch apart. A summer blanket was folded perfectly on the shelf above. He was obviously ready to go, but not gone.

"When you see him will you ask him to call me?"

At check-in time for *As You Like It* David said, "Looks like you're it for this performance."

Douglas played a very old man. As I got into the makeup to do his part, I wondered if it reminded him every time of how much older he was than the rest of us?

Outside the dressing rooms, in front of the gigantic mirror, Kim Hunter playfully teased: "Why . . . Douglas Sherman," she said to my reflection, "and how are we this evening?" For some reason right then I knew he hadn't gone back to New York; he hadn't been abducted on a spaceship. The thought didn't cross my mind until I looked at myself looking like him that maybe something much worse had happened.

After the show, like a crazy person, I rode all over town on my bike. Every half hour I looked in at Ryan's Bar, I went by his room hoping to see a light, I pedaled back and forth on the road in front of the theater. I called his name in the woods. Up the river I'd seen how much being invisible had hurt him, and I felt awful. I kept picturing our talk and his bony feet flexing back and forth under the icy river water. I left notes everyplace. Douglas had a close friend for a while. I pedaled over to his place. Not in the plays, just there to study for the summer, Alan was already gone. I went by the *As You Like It* closing party. I could see the lights and hear the band from the river road. The kid that was Benvolio in the *Romeo and Juliet* said, "Have a beer. If he's hiding there's nothing we can do." He laughed. "It's just what Benvolio says about Romeo, " 'tis in vain to seek him that means not to be found.' "

* * *

And it is great
To do that thing that ends all other deeds,
Which shackles accidents and bolts up change,
Which sleeps and never palates more the dung . . .
                                        —*Antony and Cleopatra*, 5.2

The final matinee of the 1961 summer season was over. The audience was still applauding when the voice of the stage manager demanded the company congregate in the greenroom. "Do not go to your dressing rooms. Go immediately to the greenroom."

Running down the cement stairs one of the principal actors was angry. "You put in a season of hard work and not even a *please* go to the greenroom."

The assembled crowd looked like they'd died in a horrible bus crash. We were a brutal-looking bunch in our scary makeup and stage blood from the final battle at Dunsinane. The witches were huddled to say good-bye when Jack slid a bentwood chair to the center of the room. I could see the back of his wrinkled seersucker jacket reflected in the big mirror. There was so much noise, everyone shrieking good-byes, laughing. One of the stage managers helped Jack up onto the chair. "Quiet! Quiet, please! Will you *please be quiet!*"

Jack was shaking. Over the last three and a half years I'd seen him in a lot of uncomfortable situations. But this was the worst I'd seen him look.

"I-I am ext-tremely sorry to inform you . . ." Some idiot yelled out a one-liner about the end of the season. "At two o'clock today, just before the matinee, the body of Douglas Sherman was found at the edge of the river road. Two boys going fishing at B-Bond's Dock found him in the h-high g-grass. H-he'd obviously taken his own life. The police are here. They need to ask some questions of people who might have known him best." Jack looked at me. "Bob, they want to see you first."

On TV these days and in the movies violent death doesn't seem to mean very much. Everybody's gotten used to it. In Shakespeare there's an enormous amount of brutality but it doesn't go unnoted, even the hardest isn't hardened to it. There are consequences just as the Macbeths find out. The summer I turned twenty, after spending so much of my childhood nervous, Douglas's suicide was like a mirror.

The Stratford detectives were gentle. I was still in my Macbeth paraphernalia. In the dressing room mirrors, I watched my burly bloody self answer their questions. At one point I asked if I could pull off my beard and mustache.

They'd found him on a mound where all those daylilies grow. He was surrounded by a pack and a half of smoked butts. He'd borrowed a knife from Mrs. O'Boyle's kitchen and driven it straight into himself. "Hara-kiri style," David said later, when he asked me to go with him to pick up Douglas's suitcase from the middle of the bed. The hysterical landlady was convinced that she'd been in peril. Missing the issue completely she thanked God out loud for "sparing her from a madman!"

The big white funeral home on Main Street got the job of sending Douglas to his old parents.

"Where?" I asked. "Once he alluded to some place near Syracuse."

"Yes," David said. "The Red Cross had to drive out to tell his family. They're mud farmers. They don't even have a phone."

When I got home my mother and Carolyn were on the screened-in front porch. "Douglas Sherman killed himself."

"You mean the nice quiet man with the sad eyes? I could just tell that he was 'not right.' I knew there was something wrong with him."

I sat in the studio with Carolyn. After a while the stage manager dropped by. David Bishop was a young guy and he didn't know quite where to put what he was feeling.

"I don't want to be in the *Macbeth* for the kids," I said. "I can't go back into that fog and violence. I'm nothing in the play. I mostly move furniture in the dark. As long as I live I'll never forget Jack on that chair and all of us in our *Macbeth* gear. Tell him I need to hide."

I didn't go back. I didn't even stop by to see Maggie. Twice a day for almost two months the play was three minutes away and I blotted it from my mind. How do you grieve a failed life? I was twenty and it was like the death I'd expected for so long had finally happened, but it wasn't me who'd died.

> To-morrow, and to-morrow, and to-morrow,
> Creeps in this petty pace from day to day,
> To the last syllable of recorded time;
> And all our yesterdays have lighted fools
> The way to dusty death. Out, out, brief candle!
> Life's but a walking shadow; a poor player,
> That struts and frets his hour upon the stage,
> And then is heard no more: it is a tale
> Told by an idiot, full of sound and fury,
> Signifying nothing.
>
> —*Macbeth*, 5.5

CHAPTER 24

THIS MORNING I mowed the lawn. A couple of
years ago my father loaned me an old-fashioned hand-pushed
mower. He keeps trying to get me to take a gas or electric one. He's
got quite a collection down in his clean cement basement. Neighbors near the old red house offer noisy super-wide, three-speed cutting contraptions. "No thanks," I say. They think I'm nuts. "This
one's just fine." I like to hear the mower cut the grass. I like the
hoarse blades going round and round and round.

While I was cutting the wet summer grass I thought about Charlotte Canfield and how she was just down the street when I was trying to figure out suicide. After Douglas died I decided to read all the
plays and underline any reference to killing oneself. I thought that
someplace in there would be the answer to what he'd decided on
the bee-buzzing bluff between the river road and the theater.

That September when I hid from *Macbeth* I got a little addicted
to Prokofiev. In the studio at the back of the garden behind the old
apple trees and a row of lilacs where no one could see or hear, I

found it a very consoling thing. And Carolyn seemed to, too, sitting on the floor tapping a stick.

I'd stretch out on a plum-colored horsehair sofa with a glass of Venus pencils on a table next to me. I underlined what Shakespeare had to say about self-slaughter and I listened to the Lieutenant Kijé Suite a couple of thousand times. I clicked the replay button in September and didn't flick it back until after Christmas.

When I was twenty Charlotte Canfield was a senior in high school. In the late autumn afternoons we resumed our long, speechless walks by the river and eventually, before the first snow, we sat for a while on the little tuft where Douglas died. I did a painting of her in my mother's decaying wedding dress. For a couple of hours before dinner she'd pose perched in a delicate wicker chair with Carolyn near on the floor. Charlotte didn't mind the Prokofiev. She said she liked it. "It's like perfume," she said. "It's always in the air." Listening to the music while I painted, the three of us seemed happy together, each of us isolated in our own way. After all the confusion of the summer I was so grateful for the quiet and to have my sister back. That last winter Carolyn seemed happy. She'd scoot over on the sofa to sit so close that our bodies touched from shoulder to ankle. She'd stare at me as if I were a hero. "Bobby, Bobby, Bobby," she'd sing out under the trees. But as she more fully rejoined our lives, other problems increased. Frustrated at not always being able to come along she'd grab a doorknob and start to kick. It was impossible for my parents to coax her away. We lived in terror that her mind would get stuck and the whole thing would start again. Sneaking out became the only way to leave. I started to hide my coat on the back porch.

And all of a sudden the seizures were happening more often. A couple of times a week she'd keel over and start that awful shaking. One afternoon, first at the top of the stairs and then again on the landing, she had back-to-back fits. My mother and I held her and used a big wooden salad spoon to depress her tongue. When the second seizure was over and Carolyn had wet herself and fallen into a deep sleep I remember looking over and thinking for the first time that my mother wasn't young. Sitting with my sister's head in her lap, Mildred Mary Elizabeth McKeon looked spent.

Later, while we bathed Carolyn, my mother slowly shook her head. "How long . . ." She was starting the question I'd heard at least a couple of times a day since I was three. "How long can I keep this up? How much longer will you be around to help? When you're not here it's almost impossible to get her to cooperate." She'd gotten too big to carry. "If you're not here to talk her into it, there's no way. Your father works hard all day and it won't be long before we're both too old to do all this."

My mother wasn't angry or self-pitying. This time it wasn't her usual device to diffuse frustration. It was a statement of the simple truth and I could see it in her pained, pretty, unsmiling Irish eyes. It had always been inconceivable that my parents could actually take my sister someplace and leave her, but right after they'd moved to Main Street my mother started to be in bed a lot again. "I'm beat." She'd exhale a loud quivering sigh. "My nerves are just shot." She had bouts of bursitis and pernicious anemia and one week between B_{12} shots the "Tuesday woman" terrors came back full force.

For years my parents had adjusted to my sister standing in one place. *Kick-chunk* always told everyone exactly where she was. Now that was all changed. Finally liberated from her compulsion, Carolyn had to be dealt with.

"Where's her highness?" my mother would call out. "See if she's okay" began to rival "Don't forget to wipe her good."

My sister made her way up and down the stairs. She wandered the big yard and sat for hours on the floor of the studio, but if she decided to stay anyplace, nothing could induce her to move. If she was content under a tree at bedtime it took hours to motivate her into the house. It was like having a two-year-old who'd gotten bigger but never older. By the spring of 1962 my parents were forty-five, and for eighteen years they'd tended to Carolyn twenty-four hours a day.

"Let's give her back to the Indians," my grandfather had teased when we were little, hiding under the table on my grandmother's perfectly polished floor. Now, all these years later, I could feel the idea growing week by week. My father and I had still made no peace with each other. No discussion lasted more than two minutes without erupting into an argument. It was time for me to leave, and maybe that was a part of it, too.

I was suspended. I had no idea what I should do with my life. The painting of Charlotte was good, but looking as honestly as I could between the brush strokes, there was no camouflaged genius. My summertime Romeo for Miss Morris had confirmed that I was no actor. I read Shakespeare every day, pausing for a short side trip that winter into Theodore Dreiser, but in all the years with the Festival I'd never seen a job that I felt capable of fulfilling. Jack had probably been right. Like John Houseman, he was a talented caster. I might have made a good stage manager, and his prophecy of my directing was accurate, but not for decades to come and almost never at the level he'd casually hinted at. But Jack was gone. After *Macbeth* I dropped him an obsequious note, and a year before he died I ran into him in New York. He stammered and shook as we stood in the rain on a corner across from Bloomingdale's.

The last spring I spent at home I did odd jobs. I lived in the studio and worked part-time in a box office over in Bridgeport. Traveling plays came to the Klein Auditorium and I picked up a few bucks as a dresser. I did posters for Mrs. Canfield's causes and after a while I collected unemployment from the *Midsummer Night's Dream* tour. When the first couple of checks came I made a weekend trip to visit Douglas's friend Alan in Philadelphia. He'd written me a couple of times and I was anxious to see the Thomas Eakins at the museum again.

When I got back on Sunday night my father hid upstairs in front of the TV, my mother was tearful. "We drove up to Southbury yesterday. Nana watched Carolyn while we took a look around. I'm all mixed up," she sobbed. "I know it's for the best but to just leave her like that . . . and we wouldn't be able to see her for a while. They said she'd have to take time to adjust to life without us. How do you just leave your child?" She cried silently for a long time. I'd painted some blue ribbons across the valance over the sink. My eyes went back and forth over the swirling strips. Back and forth as I tried to take the hit. My mother did what she always did at the end of a painful thought, she blew her nose into one of the pretty hankies she always had in a pocket. "Oh well," she half-smiled, "we don't have to decide tonight, it doesn't need to be tonight . . . or tomorrow."

It was exactly then that the company manager of the Festival called and Ricky Canfield and I got asked to pose for a spread in *Seventeen* magazine. "Show-stopping fashions" was an editorial about plaid. What better place to hawk tartan than the set of *Macbeth*, sitting, compounding dust, over on the huge stage. On a windy March day Ricky and I paraded around in costumes from past seasons. I got to be Hamlet while Ricky's Ophelia cast a concerned glance in my direction. As usual my printed persona is an embarrassment. I'm made up like a transvestite. Evidently the magazine didn't think so. It's a full-color, double-page humiliation.

I hadn't been backstage since the last day of the summer. Right after I'd talked to the police I packed up my stuff and fled. I felt alienated at my old dressing table while the magazine people lit the stage and tended the perky models. I'd read in the *Bridgeport Post* that after a troubled summer, the Festival was making major changes. The old guard was gone. There'd be no spring season for the high schools. The official summer season would present two histories, *Richard the Second* and *Henry the Fourth, Part I*. The two texts run sequentially and the third slot was a glamorously "Shakespearean" evening of selections with Helen Hayes and Maurice Evans. It was quite a departure from the smelly fog and backstage dissipation of the previous year. The plays were to be completely traditional, no clever anachronistic concepts, thank you very much. The cast was announced. Dicken Waring had survived the transition, so had Pat Hines. None of the rough people were coming back, and I noticed that the academy was limited to students who'd participate in the plays and none of them were to be under twenty-one.

Just like when we were kids, I sprawled with Carolyn on an old oriental in the studio. I liked to hear the wind and the rotten apples dropping on the old roof. There was also the squeal of a weather vane—an iron squirrel. Years later, when my parents left Main Street, I took it down from the roof of the studio. It's still squeaking in the middle of their little garden up on Woodcrest. I sat on the rug and read the two plays but stayed away from the theater. I didn't want to torture myself staring over the fence. When summer came, the only actors I saw were strangers.

Just past our house, down on the corner of South Avenue, was a great little family grocery with fabulous produce and a terrific butcher. My mother and her friends shopped there, so did some actors. Actors with kitchens walked by and returned forty minutes later weighed down with grocery bags.

One of them, a very old man, would smile a hello. Another actor who walked by almost every day stared as if we knew each other. I felt like a counterintelligence spy. In my summer tan and crewcut, I looked for all the world like a "townie." Mowing my father's grass or hammering a screen door, who'd ever be able to tell that I'd toured with *Dream,* or gotten "smashed" in the Rockies above Denver with Maggie, or had dinner in L.A. with Bert and James Cagney. It was impossible to know I'd slept on the dressing room floor in Paulina's cape and taught Kate Hepburn how to buckle Antony's armor. I'd been a shaky Romeo for Miss Morris and Troilus's varlet, but noticing a guy stare at me was the closest I was to the Festival that May and most of June.

"Your birthday's almost here." My mother was pretending to feel better. "What would you like to do? Nana can watch Carolyn if you'd like us to take you to dinner." She smiled. "But *I* think it should be a party, a big party in the yard with strung-up lights and tables loaded with food. After all, a person's only twenty-one once in his life." She started to cry. "And it's the last time we'll all be together. After the summer it won't ever be the same. I know it's for the best but I'm not going to fool myself into thinking it will ever be the same . . . and balloons," she said, "dozens of balloons. If it rains we can do it all in the studio."

If Carolyn was going, and I was having a very hard time convincing myself that it would happen, there'd be no reason for me to stick around. My mother's nerves made me very nervous. My father was uneasy and competitive in my company. With my sister gone there'd be no place I'd think of as home. The word had actually never meant much unless maybe it was that big odd teak building over on Elm Street.

I had started to think more often about moving the sixty miles into New York. I still went into the Met most Saturdays. I'd carry a sandwich and suicide wrapped in my bag: *Romeo and Juliet, Antony and Cleopatra,* or *Othello.* After Douglas died my focus had shifted for a while to David's *Marat* grotesquely stabbed in his tub.

I was sticking it out helping my father fix up the old place. He wanted a pool halfway between the house and studio. It meant taking out some densely rooted forsythias. I thought my willingness would deflect the tension around Carolyn and that the "institution" idea would fade again as it had so many times over the years. I wanted to leave but I couldn't because I knew that it would be a confirmation that we should stop fooling ourselves about how hard the care for my sister was becoming. With me out of the daily equation, it was obvious my mother would fold.

Two weeks before my birthday the stage manager called. "You've got an important birthday coming," he said, "and I've got a gift for you." An actor was leaving. Did I want to join the company, "to be a part of things for the rest of the season?" There'd be no brilliant poetic lines to speak but I'd get to carry the Crown of England in what had been a very important time in British history.

No lines? I didn't want lines. I wanted to hear them, not say them, and I was completely grateful to be let into that world again, where all the moments made four hundred years ago came alive all around me. I'd left the Festival so hurt and it was a real gift to be given the chance to feel good about it again. David said I'd rehearse alone with the stage managers and then on the day I'd start, I'd get to run through it with the actors.

My mother was in Carolyn's room. Like the denominated "studio," Carolyn's room wasn't actually Carolyn's room. She'd never slept in it. I don't have any recollection of her ever even being in there. It was just another girlish bedroom my parents had done up in saccharine prettiness, more a facsimile than a fact. Over the pink bed was a tiny picture I'd bought on a trip to Cooperstown with my grandparents. It was a minute portrait of a blue-eyed, blond girl saying her prayers. When I was ten, in the gift shop of the Howe Caverns, it had looked to me exactly like Carolyn. "Wouldn't you rather have a tomahawk?" my grandfather asked. "Or a feathered headdress?" Nana offered. "No," I said, "I want Carolyn to know I never forget her."

On the very pretty bed in Carolyn's room, my mother was making her way through a pile of shorts and blouses. "No time like the present," she sighed. "She's not going to need all these, and besides, she won't need any till spring. I thought I'd get rid of most of them now while she's still here." My mother's eyes glistened. "I'm thinking of using this closet for towels and stuff."

Years after Carolyn was gone to live in Southbury, decades after I'd watched her limp excitedly to the car, my mother would say, "If you need a washcloth, there's some in the closet in Carolyn's room." Until they moved again many years later, the room stayed exactly as it was that summer when it had been newly decorated to perpetuate the dream of Carolyn Wells.

"The Festival called," I said. "They want me to replace a student. I'd start on my birthday. Could the party be the following Sunday night?"

I grabbed my torn paperback of *Richard the Second* from a glass-front secretary my parents had contributed to the studio. Carolyn was under the apple trees. "Better come inside," I told her, "don't want to get beaned with an apple and it looks like rain." Curled up on the old purple sofa near my sister, I imagined the horns and drums that signal King Richard's first entrance. I read again about all his terrible mistakes and how he learns too late what counts.

> For you have but mistook me all this while.
> I live with bread like you, feel want,
> Taste grief, need friends—subjected thus,
> How can you say to me, I am a king?
>
> —*King Richard II, 3.2*

When I finished the play it was raining and my mother had come to take Carolyn into the house. I closed my eyes and my whole body vibrated with what I was about to do. By the end of the summer I would have participated in fifteen Shakespeare productions. I never had anything important to do, anyone could have made my contribution, but those fifteen productions changed my whole life.

My job was to carry the crown in both hands, to kneel until someone took it from me, and to remain kneeling until the end of the scene. That was the simple task. I carried the crown into the famous deposition scene, where the new king forces Richard to publicly give up the symbol of his reign. I was the person who'd hold that symbol and carry it onto the stage.

On my birthday, late in the afternoon, I met Richard Basehart, who was playing the king. We shook hands and briefly walked through what we'd do together on stage; he shook my hand a second time and disappeared. We never spoke again as ourselves but over the next two months we shared an intimacy in the pitch black of offstage right that I've rarely known in my personal life.

In the dark before the guards came to bring us out onto the stage he'd reach for me and eventually hold me and cry. This was the king's most anguished moment, and he let me agonize with him. Years before, I'd been a witness to Hamlet's pain, now I was actually a part of it. As we stood there and cried, Richard's awful sadness reached right down inside of me. I was crying for losing Carolyn and for my fear of the future, my morbid mother and Douglas's suicide, Nana's terrible accusation and my father's disdain. Richard's heartrending sobs brought me back to every pain I'd ever known. I whispered to him all the words of tenderness I knew. As the weeks went by, I said all I longed for someone to say to me.

In the dark the prop man's hand gently touched my shoulder and I'd reach for the crown. Moments later we'd hear the raucous soldiers who'd bring us out onto the stage. They marched into the catwalk to escort Richard to humiliation and deposition. Emerging from the pitch black teakwood catwalk, where I'd learned so much, onto the brilliantly lit stage was chilling, three hundred lights directed at the king, sixteen hundred people watching him, watching the crown. Actors said it was heartbreaking. We brought out onto the giant stage all that we'd prepared in the dark. He'd look at me and I'd kneel.

I kept my eyes on the crown glistening in my hands as Richard defended himself with gruesome self-awareness. Kneeling there listening, I'd gently move out of my own life and into that place and time in Westminster Hall. All I cared about was the king, *my king,* picked by God and destroyed by Bolingbroke. Like when I was a kid kneeling next to my crying mother in Saint Charles, I could see my tears hit the floor. Years of watching my sister laughed at flooded in as Bolingbroke taunted Richard. My own loneliness melted with poor, sad Richard Bordeaux. Pat and Will stared at me and, just behind them, Dicken Waring as the sympathetic Bishop of Carlisle. Pat said that everything that was love and loyalty to a broken person was there, and each time it hurt and healed me.

Two blocks away, my parents sat watching a big new color television in a small hot room with a floor fan clicking, and my sister waiting for me downstairs, leaning again against the door, compulsively rubbing her thumb over her forefinger.

"Bobby birthday, birthday Bobby, Bobby, Bobby, birthday Bobby." She'd found the word *birthday* a few weeks before and everyone repeated it hoping she'd get to hold on to it for a while. She did and it was her present to me. Like the gift Houseman gave me when, resisting the *Hamlet* cuts, he shouted, "Words matter."

A woman who had a shop near the theater supplied ropes of pretty paper lanterns, and picnic tables were lined up at a safe distance from the plummeting apples. The Canfields came, and all four of my grandparents, and my aunt Claire. Will Geer and Pat Hines were there and Dicken Waring stopped by with Marlene, "his lady friend," my mother called her. King Richard made a toast, and so did the man who murders him.

My sister looked beautiful in a perfect white dress. Bedazzled by the crowd she sat trembling in a kitchen chair with her hands twisting round and round.

David the stage manager said, "She's so lovely," and as everyone always did, he whispered, "Isn't it sad?"

CHAPTER 25

ULTIMATELY THERE'S no place to hide from such things. From the minute I decided to write about what Shakespeare meant to my young life it was obvious that the moment I most feared and hungered for was pressing closer. While I re-collected the shards of my childhood, my sister became as present as if she were sitting right next to me. In the middle of the night in London or Venice, she'd bang away at the fridge, forcing me to search the four A.M. pavement to solace my panic. Even when the little kids next door squeal at some delight an old alarm goes off. Is she okay? Is she having a seizure? Is she afraid or as deeply lonely as I am? On the 8:03, or at midnight in a blowing blizzard on Academy Hill, there she is riding her tricycle back and forth on the fifty-foot Summer Street sidewalk.

My father forces himself to ask a question to which he can bear only a limited answer, "How's the book coming?" While I've been a kid again my handsome young soldier father and curly-haired mother have started to slip away, and the truth is that I miss them already.

"How did I get here?" my mother asks. "I know where I am, but just how did I get here? Is this *my* house?"

My parents have moved a final time. One afternoon, quietly staring at Stillman Street, Claire died, and despite a lifetime's rivalry, she left her tiny yellow house to my mother.

"I keep thinking about Claire."

"Well, after all, she was your sister."

"Yes," my mother looks at me wide-eyed as a kid, "she used to visit all the neighbors and drink beer."

"I know," I say. "She was unhappy; she was always so unhappy. But she was lovely, so beautiful to look at."

"Yes." My mother smiles a faraway smile and then all of a sudden tears. "I have a daughter. Did you know that? Maybe you didn't. I think of her and it makes me cry. She looks like Claire. If you saw her you'd think she was a very pretty girl. The school called last week. The lady told me that I was a very good mother. She said that Carolyn is such a well-behaved child that I must be an excellent mother."

"That's very nice. Doesn't it make you proud?"

"Oh yes," she says, "proud, very proud. But did I tell you that I don't know how I got here?"

Where's the awful bell coming from? Why won't it stop? Can't the person ringing it see that I need help? My sister's tearing at me. Her eyes are wild. She's begging me not to let go. I've got hold of her wrist but my hand's so slippery. I'm getting weaker and my arm's too small. It's a kid's arm, a ten-year-old's arm. If she'd just stop screaming that terrified little kid's howl. . . .

Silence . . . dark . . . me breathing . . . all of a sudden, just above me, the noisy geese on the way to the river, then crows in the big pine down the block . . . *caw, caw.* I'm wet, cold, and shaking with the unfathomable dread left by a nightmare. The phone starts again. . . . "Hello."

*   *   *

Everyone who knew offered to take me. In the end I decided that it should be the woman who does my typing. She'd been there line by line for the exhumation of all the buried memories.

"Name the day," she said. "Joe can take the kids."

"I don't want to tell my parents. I won't even call Southbury, that way if something happens I won't ruin other people's expectations."

"Name the day."

"How about next Thursday?"

"Good morning, it's Karen. It's raining. Is it still on?"

"Yes, ten o'clock. I'll take the bike out for an hour. See you at ten. Oh . . . and thank you."

"Of course, Bob. This is a wonderful thing. I'll be in the driveway at ten."

While coffee gurgles through a filter, I remember that I'd forgotten to put the bike away. It's out in the back leaning against a dripping laurel. I tie a plastic bag over the soaked seat and snap Miles Davis into the Walkman. On the way to Bond's Dock I torpedo through umber puddles and by the time I reach the river the rain has stopped. The dung gray dawn is suddenly midsummer pink.

The road between the dock and Elm Street has been closed for months while the EPA digs for toxic waste. Stratford's playing ecological catch-up and while they're at it the "powers that be" have decided to pave the old road. It makes me sad. Since I was a kid, that quarter mile of dirt has been a spectacular obstacle course of driftwood and fascinating junk deposited by storms and tides. Overnight it's become a palette of tar and it changes everything. The new road is set higher. That bank of bee-buzzing daylilies is altered. The elevated road diminishes the bluff. The little mound where Douglas gave up so many years ago is gone, buried like his memory. The old theater is changing, too.

Every so often someone tries to get the Festival back on its feet. The latest attempt has gone far enough to initiate some basic repairs. The cracked and overgrown parking lots have been repaved. Those wooden stairs from the river road to the theater have been put back together and even the doors on the big odd building have been changed from their original red to a tasteful forest green.

I hope they get the old theater running, but they've renamed it. It's now the Stratford Festival Theater. I guess someone decided to blame Shakespeare for the empty barn on the bluff so they've made him invisible. "What's in a name?" Take it from Juliet and me, it's not so easy to abandon a ghost.

By the time Karen honked from her brand-new adorable car the day had turned gorgeous. The rainy summer has left things astonishing shades of green. We turned onto Route 8 to make our way upstate.

"Take this left." I hadn't been on the road for forty years, but I remembered a redbrick church on the right. "It should be up this way a couple of miles."

All of a sudden there it was, exactly as it had remained in my memory. There's a great sweep of bright green hillside scooping down to the main road. An old billboard stands in a dimple just below the large colonial-style administration building. Jet-black roads crisscross, zigzagging up the hill and disappearing back into the woods to the "cottages." I'd forgotten that they're called cottages. The cottages are where the children live. I somehow still thought of them as children, that the enormous place was a hospital for unwell children.

"Let's pull up to the back," Karen said pointing to an open door.

It was noon and the day was hot. The two-story central hall in the south-facing building felt sticky. The bold lettering on the door made me jumpy, THE SOUTHBURY TRAINING SCHOOL. "Can I actually do this?" I wondered.

"Hello, I'm the brother. Perhaps you've heard of me. I'm the coward brother who took one look forty years ago and fled right back down that hill and all of the way down the state to New York City. No, I've never been back, not even when Christmas came thirty-eight times. I sent a painting once for the annual auction sale. I got a very nice thank-you. But no, I myself have never been back. You people must see this all the time—you know, midlife crisis, time to reevaluate, check in with the past, swallow your terror, make good on your first promise."

I was halfway through my mental flagellation when the nicely dressed woman behind the desk leaned forward. "Isn't this wonderful," she said. "You are the brother. Here it is right in her file. This is quite an event, this is very exciting, you are the brother."

I hadn't heard those words since I was twenty-one. Of course all my life when I met people they'd ask the normal stuff. Where are you from? Are your parents still living? Do you have brothers or sisters?

"A sister," I'd say, "in Connecticut." If they pushed it and I was in the mood, I'd let more out. "Retarded, injured at birth, institutionalized."

The woman was pressing phone buttons. It was out of my hands. She was tracking down Carolyn.

"Hi, Marianne. Carolyn Smith's brother is here . . . yes . . . right here in my office. Oh . . . can you have her brought back? Is she on the property?"

That's okay. I'll be going now. You seem so nice, so kind. Sorry to have put you to all this trouble, but I think I left the stove on.

"Carolyn's on a day trip but it's just a picnic. She can be back in fifteen or twenty minutes."

"I should have called," I say. "Maybe it should be another time."

"It's absolutely no problem to bring her back." She looked at me deeply, sincerely. "This is *important*. Her *brother* has come to see her."

It took just about everything I had not to cry. The woman was acting as if I was a swell guy. She wasn't letting anything get in the way. She didn't ask why I hadn't called before I'd stopped by. She didn't ask why I hadn't bothered to come back when I was twenty-one . . . or thirty-one . . . or forty-one . . . or fifty-one?

While I was busy beating myself up she handed Karen a little map to Cottage Eighteen.

"Oh," I said. "Cottage Eighteen, that's the number I remember. Is it possible she's never moved from the very first place?"

"Let me see . . . yes, it's right here in her file, Cottage Eighteen, September 1962. Marianne's expecting you. Everyone's very excited."

On the way up the winding hill just before the last turn in the road there's a pile of boulders.

"What is it?" Karen asked.

"Something odd," I said. "Forty years ago there was an old woman sitting on those rocks. She was propped up surveying the road. See the way it drops back into the valley? She was sitting right there. She was stout and worried-looking. I remember asking the nurse from Cottage Eighteen what the woman was doing way up there."

"Helen's waiting for her mother and father," the nurse had said. "She's climbed that rock every Sunday for years. Of course they're dead now. But when they left her here, they said 'We'll be right back.' They never once made it."

"Bobby will be right back." For years my mother said it to my sister. "He has to go to school. Your brother's only going upstairs to the bathroom. He'll be right back."

I'd hear my sister on the other side of the bathroom door. "I'll be right out," I'd say. Right down . . . right in . . . right up . . . right over . . . I'll be right back.

Cottage Eighteen is nestled into the top of the hillside. Once it was probably sweet-looking, but years of wear and odd bits and pieces of long-ago playthings make it look junky. Up on this particular Connecticut hill nobody much steps back to evaluate the aesthetic. It's lunchtime. Some aides are sitting in a fenced-in area smoking. They're masculine-looking and laughing at a story one of them is illustrating. The small group of women makes me nervous. I'm spectacularly disguised as a gray-haired New York professional. WASPy looking in a suit and fresh haircut, I can incite what a friend termed "immigrant paranoia."

Marianne greets us at the door. She's pretty with lots of sable curls like Hamlet's father. She's nervous and full of talk. She launches into an instant tour of my sister's world. It is completely goodwilled but a bit much for me. I nod and act fascinated while I fret about which door my sister will come through. Will she be in a wheelchair? Will she be old?

My mind was wildly searching for emergency instructions. Wasn't Carolyn supposed to be only half-conscious, drugged in a hospital bed? Wouldn't there be hushed halls and drowsy nurses' aides? Wasn't I going to quietly enter a room and work my way stealthily to the bed before she'd turn and see me? Wouldn't our first greeting be sacrosanct as a memory? For almost forty years that's the world my mother had poured into my ear.

Marianne was enthusiastically showing me a bulletin board covered in Velcroed objects. "These symbols are ways for them to tell us what they want, a hairbrush, a VCR tape, a toilet paper roll."

"Does Carolyn actually use the toilet? Does she understand that touching this cardboard roll will signal her desire to use the bathroom? You see, in all the years we could never . . ."

"Caroline? Oh yes, absolutely. Well, most of the time. Not to say there hasn't been the occasional accident, but it's more and more rare. Maybe it's happened once in the last six months." She smiled. "I could have picked you out anyplace. You look exactly like Caroline. There's no doubt but that you are Caroline's brother."

"Caro*line*?"

My mother always hated it. All through my childhood. Every day some schlump would get it wrong. "Caro*lyn*," my mother would insist, "her name is Caro*lyn*, not Caro*line*. Bobby, don't you hate the name Caro*line*? It's so ugly. Not at all pretty like Carolyn Wells?"

"While we're waiting would you like to see Caroline's room?"

"If you need a towel," my mother would say, "look in the closet in Carolyn's room."

At the Southbury Training School my sister's room is cinder block, like a lot of the senior centers. In fact, it's yellow cinder block, like that big cafeteria where we first did the Shakespeare for the old people. My sister's room in Cottage Eighteen is a happy place. It doesn't contain any of the bathos I'd gotten used to in the powder pink reliquaries of the eight houses of my childhood. Up on the hill at the Southbury Training School I was starting to notice nothing is dramatic or overwrought, nothing's sad.

Marianne continued to bring me up to speed. "It's all being phased out. This is no longer the way. These days it's small groups in home settings. It's less hidden, not so removed from the real actual world."

"The real actual world," I repeated.

"The population here has decreased. We stopped accepting new people more than ten years ago. Many of the older people have died, but these women will remain in Cottage Eighteen for the rest of their lives. After all, these ten ladies have been together for almost half a century." Marianne was proud of maintaining this made-up family. "They don't talk politics or browse through fashion magazines together. They sit across from each other at meals or side by side when we show a movie. We're glad to try to teach them new things every day. This is the world they know and for the most part I think they're happy and safe. Our staff is wonderful. Caroline has had the same caregiver since the early eighties. Your sister's devoted to Kim."

When the door at the end of the hall opened I felt more than I thought I had room to hold. The way the light was behind her I couldn't see her face. There was a woman following a few steps in back. I'd forgotten the exact rhythm of my sister's gait. I hadn't remembered until the second I saw her making her way toward me. I'd forgotten how her right foot twisted in so far that she needs to work the other one around it to move forward.

Karen stepped aside to open the space between Carolyn and me. Kim the care provider was coaxing her forward. Marianne cooed in a loud clear voice, "Caroline, guess who's here? Guess who's come to see his sister?" You could have ripped my heart right out of my body as I listened to the pleasant voice lilt baby talk at the gray-haired ghost advancing toward me in the shadowy hallway. "You'll never guess who's come to see you. It's your big brother Bobby."

"She used to say that," Kim said. "Marianne, do you remember how she'd sing that all the time? Bobby, Bobby."

Kim paused; Marianne backed away behind me; Karen sat at a table in the corner. Carolyn hadn't noticed me yet. I didn't want to scare her. I didn't want to advance on her or make her afraid. Marianne kept documenting the moment. "It's Bobby, it's your big brother Bobby. Remember when you used to say it all the time, Bobby, Bobby."

Finally my sister darted a look straight at me. I was shocked. She looked exactly like Nana. Of course she's as old as Nana was when we'd stood in Howlands dish department. My sister looked right into my eye. She looked stern, judgmental.

"Uh!" she shrieked. "Uh!"

Who I'd been to her all those years ago came back automatically. "It's okay," I whispered. "I'm so glad to see you." I wanted so much not to cry; well, I wanted very much to cry but not in front of strangers who thought my sister's name was Caroline. Close, but not her name exactly, not Carolyn Wells Smith, not the name my mother picked from a children's book seventy-five years ago under a cherry tree in the Simons' backyard over on Stillman Street.

Of course Carolyn didn't know who I was. And that's what Nana would have called "a mercy." Every time Kim moved, Carolyn adjusted. If she backed off a bit, Carolyn got vigilant. I was compelled to keep talking, to weave through my feelings in front of people I didn't know. I also had an unexpected need to prove that I'm not the crazy brother showing up late in the game to make some kind of trouble. My father has never put my name on anything at the Southbury Training School other than that check mark in the file to indicate that my sister has a brother.

At one point Kim turned toward the window and Carolyn pivoted to be sure she wasn't being abandoned. It was a movement I'd seen thousands of times. Something in the way Carolyn turned took me back to when we were little kids. "I used to be you," I sobbed toward Kim. "For many years I was to her who you are now." I turned to Marianne. "This is very hard for me."

"Of course it is," she said. "We should leave the two of you together. You need to spend some time without all of us staring at you."

Kim helped Carolyn into a chair at the head of the big table. I sat to my sister's right. She'd had eye surgery and was still favoring her right eye. The three women went into a waiting room midway down the hall.

Carolyn was gently stroking her fingers on the edge of her shirt collar. Her hands were wrapped in each other like always, but they were calmer, not twisting and winding like they used to. "Medication," I thought. "She's eased," that's just what I thought: *eased.* She wasn't looking at me. She wasn't searching for Kim. She trusted that this was where she should sit just now. I kept talking, "Do you know who I am? I'm Bobby. Do you remember Bobby? Does Carolyn remember Bobby?"

"Uh!" She flashed a look. "Uh!"

I remembered being in that high, windy cornfield the last time I saw her. I remembered looking down at my parents standing by our car, and I remembered that I didn't know who I was and that I didn't know how to be with my sister or my parents.

Sitting at the table with Carolyn, it was so completely clear that she is her own person. She's no longer who we needed her to be. I could see it in her face, in her body, in the people around her, my sister has a life, an actual life and it's a good full life. "We do enough to fill in the blanks," Marianne said. "We teach them what they can learn. If they can get the shoe on we work on the tying. We don't force it but we want her to have some independence, some freedom."

"I love you, Carolyn Wells Smith," I said. I felt that she wanted to look at me but she was shy, *not* terrified, *not* even nervous, *shy.* "Bobby has a pretty watch on," I said. "Can Carolyn see Bobby's pretty watch?" As I lifted my sleeve she snuck a look at the watch. Her eyes lingered. "If you can't look at Bobby maybe you could look at Bobby's watch instead?" For the rest of the time she looked only at the watch and slowly her body started to turn to welcome me.

"One step at a time," I said to Marianne and Kim.

"I know you don't drive but you don't have to come here all the time to be right at the center of things. Of course it's great to visit, it's good for everyone, but we'll keep you as included as you'd like to be."

In the car Karen said it was the most beautiful thing she'd ever seen, "like the years hadn't existed."

It's time to leave, time to give up the little red house near the river, time to go back to the other end of the 8:03. My parents for the moment have each other, and my role as listener to my mother is diminishing as she has less to say. My dad has promised to amend the documents at the Southbury Training School to include me. "Oh, by the way," he whispered, not quite looking at me, "thanks for going to see your sister."

Marianne said something tiny that was huge. When Kim was trying to help Carolyn into the chair Marianne said, "Your sister's in a bad mood today. She's cranky." I'd absolutely never thought about that, the fact that, like any "normal" person, sometimes Carolyn might just be in a lousy mood. The casual comment made my sister less deified for her disability, more real and human and less fantasy.

Preparing to move, I stopped by the big antiques mall a short bike ride from where I live. Over the few years I've filled the old red house with objects from the Stratford Antique Center. Not sure where I'll be next and suddenly interested in things less attached to the past, I stopped to talk to Steve about selling the contents of the house.

While we were joking around a woman came up to the counter with a pile of books. The place has several stalls of antiquarian books. As the woman plopped them on the counter I noticed a small, faded, beige *Marjorie in Command* by Carolyn Wells. "Oh!" I said, "may I look at that?"

"Sure," she said. "Are you a collector?"

"No, when she was a kid my mother loved this writer. She named my sister after Carolyn Wells."

The woman smiled that "gotcha" kid's smile. "There was no such person," she said. "There wasn't any Carolyn Wells. It was a made-up name to sell books. They used to do that all the time."

My name is Bob—Bob Smith—Robert William John Smith, a plain American name. Almost every day for as long as I can remember, someone has jokingly asked, "Is that your real name? Come on, what is it really?" It's been a steady, good-natured, lifelong tease and in its small way has helped me to feel invisible. I've seen my ordinary name as a promise to be unseen, unheard, unnoticed. And for most of my life I've honored the contract.

ACKNOWLEDGMENTS

My thanks to Chris Rennolds for telling Janny Scott about my reading Shakespeare to the elderly. And thanks to Janny for her beautiful *New York Times* piece, without it much that's wonderful in my life might never have happened. I'm also incredibly grateful to Cis Corman at Barwood for urging me forward.

At Scribner, Susan Moldow has kept me amazingly safe while she and Nan Graham set the bar higher than I could have dreamed. Thanks also to Molly Friedrich for straight talk and speaking from the heart. Without the miracle of these women I couldn't have made the journey.

In New York, I read my pages to Ann Ettinger and Helen Tonken. In Connecticut, Chris Wright braced my courage and Karen Obuchowski transformed scribbles on legal pads to gorgeously typed pages. To maintain the necessary silence at my desk, Mary Elwood kept roofers and painters and barking dogs at bay, while Kate the neighborhood cat snoozed in the lamplight at my elbow. When at last there was a manuscript, Sarah McGrath winnowed what's purest with astonishing perceptiveness.

Impatient for me to finish, hundreds of sage old men and women coaxed me on. A few left early, and it may be to them I owe most. I tuck them here to be a part of what they didn't live to see. Thank you Zoe and Joe, Arthur, Hiam, Charlotte, Dina, Lillian, Mary Elizabeth, Paula, Sonia, Arnold, and not least, my mother.

I should also point out that, since my use here of Shakespeare is primarily self-revelatory, and as no definitive text authority exists, I've depended on various editions, mostly Arden and Riverside.

About the Author

BOB SMITH has directed Shakespeare for the Temple University graduate program, the State University of New York, Kent State, the University of Bridgeport, the National Shakespeare Conservatory, Musical Theater Works, the Hartman Theater Company, the Williamstown Theater Festival, Boston's North Shore Music Fair, the Nantucket Arts Festival, St. Clement's, Theater at Trinity, and the Arden Players, among many others. He has taught at the Actor's Center of Los Angeles, the T. Schrieber Studio, the Charles Simon Center for Adult Life and Learning at 92nd St. Y, the Stein Center, Educational Alliance, and the Hudson Guild.